Good Knight

THE GOOD SIDE OF BOBBY KNIGHT FROM THOSE WHO KNOW HIM BEST

© 2001 Rich Wolfe. All rights reserved.
Printed in the United States.
No part of this book may be reproduced, stored in a retrieval system, or transmitted, in any form or by any means, electronic, mechanical, photocopying, recording, or otherwise, without the prior permission of Rich Wolfe.

Cover photo courtesy of Joe Don Buckner/Allsport

Knightmares

THE DARK SIDE OF BOBBY KNIGHT FROM THOSE WHO KNOW HIM BEST

© 2001 Rich Wolfe. All rights reserved.
Printed in the United States.
No part of this book may be reproduced, stored in a retrieval system, or transmitted, in any form or by any means, electronic, mechanical, photocopying, recording, or otherwise, without the prior permission of Rich Wolfe.

Cover photo courtesy of AP/Wide World Photos (AP Photo/Tom Russo)

Contents

Chat Rooms

Preface

Sports in America, in general, have run amok. Just a few years ago, Barry Alvarez led the University of Wisconsin's football team to victory in the Rose Bowl and was voted the National Coach of the Year. Meanwhile in Columbus, Ohio, the fans were ready to run Ohio State Coach John Cooper out of town—again. Ohio State and Wisconsin had exactly the same record that year: 10–1–1. One guy was the National Coach of the year; the other guy—the fans wanted to tar and feather. In the United States, there are far more sports writers than religious reporters. Put that in the "Go Figure" file . . . under the category "Basketball is Almost a Religion in Indiana."

This is my sixth book in the last four years. In none of the previous books has there ever been anything really negative about any of the subjects. However, when it comes to Bob Knight, a book would have no credibility if it did not deal with the controversial aspects of his career.

Thus, the conundrum was, "How do you do a fair book on Bob Knight and cover all his scrapes with the players, administrators, fellow coaches, and even the law?" It also became evident early on that a book on Bob Knight would be aimed mainly at the people who reside outside the state of Indiana. In the summer of 2000, the Hatfields and McCoys were transformed into Knight and anti-Knight camps in the Hoosier state giving new meaning to Indiana's state slogan: The Crossroads of America.

I had never seen such a controversy since the O. J. Simpson murder trial. Who can forget that? I remember the day back in the summer of 1994 when a friend said a famous ex-football player had murdered his wife. (Immediately, I prayed that it was Frank Gifford.) Shortly after that trial got underway, and long before a verdict was reached, a very interesting book was written by Sheila Weller, called *Raging Heart.* In this book she examined controversial episodes of O. J. and Nicole Simpson's life together and merely quoted both sides as their friends saw it. She drew no conclusions whatsoever.

Thus while comparing the controversy and divisiveness of the Simpson trial to the Bob Knight ongoing and simmering debate in Indiana the past summer, the thought came: Why not do the Knight book the same way? Just talk to the friends and enemies, and let the chips fall where they may.

I have no reason to believe that any of the people in Knightmares lied. With the exception of one person, most of them were calm as they discussed their problems with Coach Knight. I'm certainly not here to vouch for them. It's just that I have no reason to disbelieve them.

In an effort to get more material into the book, the editor decided to merge certain paragraphs and omit some commas which will allow for the reader to receive an additional 30,000 words, the equivalent of 80 pages. More bang for your buck, more fodder for English teachers, less dead trees.

When all is said and done, remember this is just a book. It's a book to entertain you. It's not a treatise. It's not a bible. It's not a declaration of absolute facts. It's just Bob Knight as seen through the eyes of other people. I have no dog in this hunt. So don't get any ideas about shooting the messenger. On the other hand, if you have some good constructive criticism, feel free to jot it on the back of a twenty-dollar bill and send it along to the publisher.

Go now.

Rich Wolfe
Scottsdale, Arizona

Bibliography

Albom, Mitch. *The Fab Five:* Warner Books, 1993
Alford, Steve and John Garrity. *Playing for Knight:* Simon and Shuster, 1989.
Feinstein, John. *A Season on the Brink:* Macmillan, 1986.
Hammel, Bob. *Beyond the Brink:* Indiana University Press, 1987.
Jamison, Steve. *Wooden:* Contemporary Press, 1997.
Keteyian, Armen and Alexander Wolff. *Raw Recruits:* Pocket Books, 1990.
Meyer, Ray and Ray Sons. *Coach:* Contemorary, 1987.
Mylenski, Skip. *Winning at Illinois:* Sagamore, 1987.
Odom, David. *The End is Not the Trophy:* Carolina Academic Press, 1998.
Pluto, Terry. *Tark:* McGraw-Hill, 1988.
Scanion, Pat. *Digger Phelps and Notre Dame Basketball:* Prentice-Hall, 1981.
Wartenberg, Steve. *Winning is an Attitude:* St. Martins, 1991.
Weiss, Dick. *Campus Chaos:* Time Out Press, 2000.
Weiss, Dick. *Full Court Pressure:* Hyperion, 1992.
Weiss, Dick. *Refuse to Lose:* Ballantine, 1996.

The author would like to sincerely thank the following authors, subjects and/or publishers for their kind permission to cite, reprint or quote from their works:

Carter, Cris and Butch. *Born to Believe:* Full Wits Publishing, Inc., Upper Tantallon, Nova Scotia.
Douchant, Michael. *Tourney Time:* Masters Press, 1993.
Feinstein, John. *A March to Madness:* Little Brown & Co., 1998.
Gildea, William. *Where the Matters Most:* Little Brown & Co., 1997.
Golenbock, Peter. *Personal Fouls:* Carroll & Graf, 1990.
Guest, Larry. *Confessions of a Coach:* Rutledge Hill, 1991.
Johnson, Roy S. *Outrageous:* Simon & Shuster, 1992.
Kirkpatrick, Curry. *Just Your Average, Bald, One-Eyed, Basketball Wacko:* Simon & Shuster, 1998.
Monteith, Mark. *Passion Play:* Bonus Books, 1988.
Mortimer, Jeff. *Basket Case:* Doubleday, 1988.
Phelps, Teresa Godwin. *Coach's Wife:* W.W. Norton, 1994.
Ryan, Bob. *Drive:* Doubleday, 1989.
Savage, Jim. *The Encyclopedia of the NCAA Basketball Tournament:* Dell, 1990.
Sperber, Murray. *The Chronicle of Higher Education:* May, 2000.
Weiss, Dick. *Holding Court:* Masters Press, 1995.
Weiss, Dick. *Time Out:* Berkley Books, 1992.
Wojciechowski, Gene. *Pond Scum and Vutures:* Macmillan, 1990.
Yaeger, Don. *Tiger in a Lion's Den:* Hyperion, 1994.

These Guys Are Declarin' Shenanigans

Russ Brown
Gene Wojciechowski
John Feinstein
Terry Reed
Murray Sperber
Pat Williams
Clair Recker

Calling Bob Knight "Bobby" is like calling Attila the Hun "Tilly"

Russ Brown

Russ Brown of the Louisville Sports Report *was born, raised and still resides in Indiana. He covered Indiana basektball for 14 years for* The Louisville Courier Journal *and makes no secret of his disdain for Coach Knight.*

Russ Brown

I can remember the very first time I ever talked with Knight in my life and it went downhill from there. He got the job at Indiana and a friend of mine, a mutual friend who is now dead, John Flynn, knew Knight when he was assistant high school coach in Ohio. John had the best line about Knight I've heard so far. He wrote a story for the Courier-Journal Sunday Magazine, which is no longer published, and in it he said, "Calling Bob Knight 'Bobby' is like calling Attila the Hun 'Tilly'."

Some do call him Bobby; I never called him that—always Bob. Flynn was a Knight defender and, I think, liked him—realized what he was, yet liked him. It was kinda funny, because for all my bad relations with Knight, we had two really good mutual friends. I used to always debate with them—Billy Reed, a sportswriter for Sports Illustrated in Lexington, was a good friend and also a friend of Knight's. And John was a friend of Knight's and, also, a real good friend of mine. We didn't see eye-to-eye on Knight at all.

When Knight was hired at IU, John Flynn and I both worked at the Louisville Courier-Journal. John said, "I'll get Bob on the phone for you." This was the day after he got the job—that night. So John got him on the phone, and I got on. Of course, he didn't any more want to talk to me than the man in the moon, but I got on and asked him a legitimate question. George McGinnis, IU's sensational sophomore, was thinking about going pro and there was a lot of talk that spring that he would go pro. I had probably asked Knight a couple of innocuous questions. I can't remember how I phrased the question. But I asked Knight what were his thoughts about the possibility that George McGinnis would go pro. He said, "That's a dumb fuckin' question." And it went downhill from there. It was the first time any source had talked to me like that. I thought maybe this guy was—John had told me that he was volatile. I hadn't heard all that much about him, and I just couldn't believe the guy had done that. What's the point here? Why would you talk to somebody like that? Why wouldn't you just say, "I can't answer that." Or something like that. I tell people all the time, "I never have in my life, either personal or professional life, dealt with anybody who even remotely approached Knight for mean-spiritedness, for purposely putting people in uncomfortable positions, relishing confrontation. Most people avoid confrontation; he seeks it out."

That's been so long ago—1971. I think when I got off the phone and said something to John, he just laughed. You have to know John, but he just laughed about it. But it really wasn't a laughing matter to me. I just couldn't believe the guy would talk that way to somebody he had never met. That was not a stupid question. It was a legitimate question that you would ask the coach who was taking over any program. I don't know this for sure, but I'm sure he got asked about it when he finally did a formal press conference.

I can't remember the first time I met Knight, which is kinda strange. I can say I didn't like him. John and I had these conversations all the time. Knight is a very difficult person to like. Unless he's turned on the charm with recruiting, and I've seen him when he is trying to be charming, he's very hard to like. I supposed the first time I ever saw him personally was during his first formal press conference at IU and I don't remember anything about it except here was this guy that I thought was very sullen, very boorish, sarcastic, smart ass—even during his first press conference. That's the way I came away.

I tell people that nobody is all good and all bad—I'm willing to admit that. I just have a hard time, because I've been around him so much, and seen how he has treated people and seen how he manipulates—that alleged apology and the whole latest situation at the University is just typical of him. I can't find a lot of good to say about him. In defending him, people say, "Oh, but he does a lot of good for people and blah, blah, blah." Well, Maybe. But so what!

To me, you judge people on how they treat people on a daily basis and not just by a few good deeds they do here and there that he probably thinks cancels out the bad stuff. It's like people who go to church on Sunday, and feel like that absolves them of all the sins of the first six days. You'll never hear anything sincere come out of Knight's mouth—any kind of an apology. He's already started now; he's already mounted his offensive now against this new ruling by the University. He said he was not going to teach that class in basketball anymore because he's under this "zero tolerance". I haven't figured out what that has to do with it. I guarantee you—mark my word—he will not have press conferences this year. He will not have post-game press conferences. I'll bet you he won't. That will be one of his ways of "I'll show you!"

You couldn't be a "beat" writer and do your job and have any kind of relationship with him because he wouldn't allow it. He sees things in black and white, you're either for him or against him. If you're for him, you'll cover up anything or not write certain things. If you're against him, you couldn't be objective in his eyes. Again it would be either for or against him.

I covered him from his very first year until after they lost to Virginia in the NCAA so about fourteen LONG years! He would call the house, and it would be funny if it weren't so. . . . My wife would answer and he'd be real nice, "Oh, Hi Mrs. Brown, how are you? Could I speak to Russ?" Then I'd get on the phone. "You little son of a bitch! You fucker! Don't you ever come up here anymore! I'll ram your fuckin' head through the locker room wall." Oh, he threatened me on a number of occasions.

The Courier-Journal was always there for me. Did I want to sue him for wanton endangerment? No, I didn't want to do that. Now if he had ever laid a hand on me, I would have.

It was an Illinois game, probably '77–'78; Illinois had a good team that year, and it was a good game, and Indiana won. *60 Minutes* was there doing a profile of him. Dan Rather was on the program at that time. Knight was kinda flying high—they had won. So he walks into the interview room, and this was on *60 Minutes;* I always sit in the front row—always ask the first question. I wasn't about to let him intimidate me. So Knight came up to me and said, "I really feel good. I feel so good, Russ, that I'm even gonna shake your hand and ask you how your family is and how you're doing." I said, "Well you must feel pretty damn good then." So that was the end of that part of it. I think that part was on *60 Minutes.* He did that because it was a "show" plus he had won a pretty big game. So he gets up and he does his press conference. He goes out and stands outside the interview room.

Lou Henson, the Illinois Coach, comes in and I listen a little to Henson, then I get up to go to the locker room. I walk past Knight; he doesn't say a word. I get maybe fifteen yards down the hall, maybe; this is in Assembly Hall, and he says, "Hey Russ." So I turn around and he's got this pistol pointed at me, and he fires it. There is concrete on both walls and the sound is—just whap, whap, whap, whap—just reverberates—loud as hell. I said, "You missed." He said, "Wait till you shake your head." I had a job to do so I just turned around and kept going to the locker room. I know this sounds weird, and people always say, "Weren't you scared?" This is why I don't think it was done maliciously. He didn't give me time to really think "Uh-oh, that son of a bitch is going to kill me." It was like, I turned around, as I recall, and almost immediately he fired. Bob Pille from the Chicago Sun Times was standing next to Knight, and said, "Bob, you're crazy." Knight said, "I've got to be crazy to keep from going insane." I think that's an old Willie Nelson line or something. It's funny, because he's never mentioned it to me; I've never mentioned it to him. I think it was his way of apologizing or sort trying to mend fences or whatever and that was just sort of his way—his sense of humor.

As I recall, it wasn't like he pointed at me—like I've got you now—I'm gonna kill you or whatever. He's crazy enough that I probably would have thought—course he would have gotten off Scot-free. I mean, he kills a reporter—BIG DEAL! I mean, at Bloomington, he's winning—didn't matter. Shooting a reporter— he *might* get charged; he'd probably get off.

There was another time—this is kinda funny, too. I had written some stories that he didn't like and he called me and said, "If I ever see you around here, I'm gonna run your fuckin' head through the locker room wall. I don't ever want to see you again. And blah, blah, blah." So the next game was away—Notre Dame at South Bend. I can't remember who won. I was there in my usual spot—front row at the press conference. Well he comes in and says, "Has anybody got a question?" I asked the first question, Knight doesn't even look at me—says, "Does anybody else have a question?" So I ask the question again. And again, "Does anybody else have a question?" I said, "Does that mean you're not going to answer my question? He said, "That's right." At that point then, you either back down or 'cause a scene so I didn't say anything else.

So that was sort of our relationship.

He doesn't talk to anybody really. I mean he doesn't give you access. I've been in this business thirty five years. Covering the Indiana basketball team is the worst job in America. You have no access. You've got to put up with his bullshit all the time. If he would at least talk about or discuss with people some of the things he does, or answer questions about them, it would at least make the job maybe a little more bearable.

For instance, the time he went to Illinois and benched all his starters. I think Alford was one of them. Then afterward he never would talk about it. He wouldn't answer questions. He didn't come to the press conference. That's so typical.

Then there's the Puerto Rican incident. I wasn't there, but I will guarantee you that it happened just like the policeman said it happened. He tried to pull his power play on the guy, and the guy wouldn't have any of it. You know, Knight wants to say that he was the victim. Bull. Anybody that knows him and knows how he. . . . I mean you can just see how that all played out. He comes in. The women are still in there practicing. He throws one of his childish temper tantrums and they arrest him.

John Flynn told me this story: He had talked to the grandmother who virtually raised Knight. He said the grandmother told him that anytime they played a game when Knight was a child, the grandmother would let him win because if he didn't win, he'd throw a temper tantrum and throw the board, and destroy the game and all that. My theory in part is—I think the guy's got a screw loose—but on top of that, he found out at a very early age that if he talked dirtier and yelled louder than anybody else he could pretty much get his own way.

Lou Henson called him a "classic bully." And that's basically what he is. He's found out that if he employed all those tactics he used as a child in adulthood, it would get him what he wanted. On top of that, he did win early. Indiana is just a "rabid" basketball state, a lot of people who don't see beyond the wins. We, the writers who cover him, have always said "As long as he is winning, we were joking during his prime, he could have shot a player on the basketball floor. And fans would have said "That's okay, the player deserved it, he traveled or whatever." "Coach was right." It's just that simple-minded attitude and the University has gotten themselves into a position where there's either nobody willing or considered powerful enough to stand up to him—from Presidents on down. And he just found out he could do virtually anything he wanted. And did, and then would make excuses for his behavior, and his followers AND the University would make excuses for it.

Looking at the whole list of what he has done, can you imagine any other University in the country tolerating that? Or can you imagine anybody holding a job who behaved like that?

How could you walk in and throw something at a secretary and keep your job? And talk to people the way he talks to them—the foul language and everything—you couldn't; there's no way. He's got the only job in America he could keep and act the way he does.

Early on when I would go back to Louisville and explain what was going on, my bosses believed me. The publisher at the time, Barry Bingham, wrote a letter to Knight one time about his threats toward me. Bingham got back this bizarre letter—just a childish and bizarre letter—that Knight had signed it "Mickey Mouse," with copies to Donald Duck, Pluto—just some weird stuff. This is just an example.

Here's another story. My sister, a student at Purdue at the time, was 32 or 33 and was killed in an auto accident. My mother and dad were on an airplane; they live in Indianapolis. Knight got on the plane, and he was talking to people and came to our parents. They told him they were my parents, "We're Russ Brown's parents." He said, "Oh, I'm so sorry to hear about your daughter." I saw him several days later—walked into the rest room; we were peeing in adjoining urinals and he not only did not say a word to me about "sorry to hear about your sister" or "I gave your Mom and Dad my condolences", he jumped on me about something I had written, "How can you write such stupid fuckin' stuff?" It's mind-boggling. Why would the guy be nice enough to my parents to say something like that? Then see me, and know that I'd just lost a sister, and treat me like that. He's so mean spirited.

I got to the point where I hated going up to Bloomington. I grew up in Indiana; I've been an IU basketball fan all my life. But I just got to the point where I just despised doing it. I finally went to my sports editor and said, or I think they even asked me, "Would you consider another assignment?" But people always thought that I got off the Indiana beat because of my conflicts with Knight and that was not the case. The real reason I wanted off was I could no longer stand being around the guy and seeing how he treated people. I'm a big boy. I can deal with whatever he can dish out, even though it made my job miserable. But just seeing how he treated people on a day-to-day basis and being around his arrogance and his bulliness and his mean-spiritedness—I just didn't want to do it anymore. Why do I need this? I don't need to be around somebody like this.

I don't know his current wife. It was kinda funny, because even during the periods when Knight wouldn't talk to me or when he was calling me and threatening me, his first wife was always real nice to me. She would come down to the press box and talk to me, and I wanted to say to her, "Nancy, do you realize your husband won't have anything to do with me?" She would tell me that she would hide newspapers from him so he wouldn't see some stories and get upset.

Nancy still lives in Bloomington, as far as I know. I don't think she ever remarried. Bill Benner, of the Indianapolis Star, and I have always thought—if anybody could ever talk her into writing a book—you talk about a best seller! My God. It would be. . . . But I don't think she'd ever do it.

She was not an unattractive lady, not beautiful, but I always liked her. I felt she was a little bit crazy, too, but she'd have to be after living with him. I never heard any stories about him screwing around; I will say that. I never got the impression from him or friends or anybody that he even talked about women. I think he, basically, hates women.

One time he took a dump in the middle of the floor (this came from a player) and said to his players, "You guys are playing like shit and now you're gonna have to play in it." Those were his words. I know it's accurate—real accurate, came from a player.

Then there's the tampon story with Landon Turner. He put a tampon in Landon Turner's locker because he had told him he was playing like a pussy. There's probably more to it than that. A lot of people would be tickled to death if he got his comeuppance, so to speak. I think there are a lot of people who dislike him, who don't respect him and a lot of other things but are too nice, too intimidated or whatever to say anything derogatory about him.

Even when I was covering him, I was honest about him if somebody asked me. I probably wasn't as outspoken as I am now, but I wasn't gonna sit there and tell people he's a nice guy. And people knew, it was common knowledge, that we didn't get along. Of course, he didn't get along with anybody that tried to do a good job. After the gun incident, I think he was civil to me for a while, but his idea of being civil and anybody else's are two different things really.

This is interesting—a friend of mine has told me that Knight's secretary (this is all second-hand information) told a mutual friend that Knight was more uptight and angry than ever this summer of 2000, and "he'll never make it." Knight is so jealous of Alford. He can't stand the fact that Alford is so well liked in this state, so personable. And the fact that when Alford was coming into Assembly Hall and overshadowing Knight. The way he treated Steve Alford was just typical—that's about all you can say about that.

You know why Luke Recker did what he did in waiting 'til Knight was out of the country before faxing his transfer? He tried to quit after his freshman year, and Knight told him—now this is just childish, and I can't believe Recker would fall for it—"If you quit, I'm gonna resign, and I'm gonna tell everybody that you're the reason I'm resigning and your name will be mud in this state." So Luke starts feeling guilty about it, doesn't quit and then the next year when he wants to quit, waits 'til Knight's out of the country and faxed his transfer. That's why Recker did it then.

Luke Recker was almost killed in an automobile accident. His girlfriend is paralyzed; her brother's in a coma. Knight has never ever once called Recker, called Recker's family, offered any kind of sympathy or anything. Wouldn't play in the golf tournament that Recker had to benefit them.

These things I'm telling you are not from rumors; they came from really good sources. I also have it from a good source, and anybody with brains could figure it out. The only reason Indiana didn't finally stand up and say to him, "You're fired." The attorneys, in fact I was told Knight didn't go to the President's home to apologize at all; he went to threaten a lawsuit. Because the whole deal was, not in these words, "you've let me get by with this kind of behavior, you've tacitly approved it. If you fire me, I'm gonna file a two hundred and fifty million dollar lawsuit against you," or whatever it was.

I don't know what will happen with Coach Felling—I would guess they'll pay him to go away or settle out of court, I think that's what they'll do.

One time Knight didn't like something Kit Klingelhoffer, the IU Sports Information Director, had put on a quote sheet or in a release, came storming into Kit's office, started berating him and screaming at him, knocked him down and out cold. Then the next day, Kit comes in, and there's about half a dozen new dress shirts on his desk from Knight. That's the way he is.

Clarence Doninger, the current Athletic Director, was his personal attorney; he's the one who helped him out of the Puerto Rican mess and with his divorce. Now they don't even talk. Not all these people could be wrong. Give me a break. Then with the Neil Reed situation—he would have gotten off on that. They were all ready to sweep that under the rug, but then Felling had the tape. Felling had saved the tape and gave it to ESPN or CNN or whoever it was. If not for that tape, Knight would be walking Scot-free on that. This type thing happened over and over with other kids. These kids come in, they leave. All of a sudden, the machinery kicks into full gear. All of a sudden the kid's a bad kid, or he's a troublemaker, or he couldn't play—one thing after another—character assassination is what it is. Too bad that some of the players who have credibility won't speak out. Most of the guys who speak out are guys who have left for one reason or another. I know for a fact __________ can't stand him but would __________ ever say anything bad about him—no.

There's something mentally wrong with Knight. People don't act like that who are sane and have any sense. I don't think anything could have happened to him to mess him up as badly as he's messed up.

You know I just never—I'm 55 years old—I've never felt about anybody the way I feel about that guy. I think he's an evil person—I really do. I wouldn't put anything past him if he thought it was going to further his agenda, or make him look better, or feed his ego, or whatever. I'll admit it.

I don't have a whole lot good to say about the guy. Hammel wrote that pseudo-apology back in May after the first flap—Knight didn't write that. Hammel wrote it. If you ever get hold of Hammel, ask him point blank; make him lie to you, 'cause Knight didn't write it. It was the "apology that wasn't an apology." How could any reasonable person read this and think that it's a sincere apology?

Mike Ditka had to apologize last year. He grabbed his crotch or something. But it wasn't written or anything else. You knew that he meant it—knew he was sincere about it.

Knight won't see anything in your book that is negative as the truth. I don't think he'll read it in the first place, but people will tell him about it.

In my opinion, his arrogance, and ego and pride are keeping him from mending his fences with Steve Alford, Krzyzewski and others. If they came to him, and begged his "forgiveness" and got down on their knees to the great "God of Basketball" then maybe he would do it. But he's not gonna do it.

Take the way he insulted John Wooden. John Wooden is one of the best, most kind, most anything you can say good about a person. During that interview last May, Roy Firestone asked him what he thought about John Wooden saying he didn't approve of Knight's message and wouldn't let a son of his play for him or words to that effect. And Knight said, "If Pete Newell said that, I'd be concerned about it, but Wooden's never been to one of my practices, never seen many of my games, etc." Well, here's a guy who's a fine human being, a fine example for everybody and has won more championships than Knight can ever hope to—and that's part of the problem right there. He knows he can never equate with Wooden and for him to make some asinine. . . . I read a column that referred to it as a "jaw-dropping insult" to John Wooden, and that's basically what it was.

There was a short-lived Conference Commissioner's Association tournament and Indiana played in it one year in St. Louis. They played Southern California when USC was coached by Bob Boyd. Knight gets up at the press conference. Course this is typical, too. He always praises coaches he can beat. You never heard him praise anybody that beat his ass. Well, Bill Frieder did that. He told me one time that he got along fine with Knight—until Frieder's team started beating his. By that time Wooden had already five or six or maybe even seven NCAA titles. Knight gets up at the press conference and talked about the game, and—this is true—he called Bob Boyd the best damn basketball coach on the West Coast. Now Bob "Fuckin'" Boyd! Who is that? He's some crony of Knight's that Knight knows he can beat; he's insanely jealous of John Wooden so he gets up and insults Wooden. I couldn't believe it. Then he makes those remarks about Wooden—Pete Newell—who's Pete Newell?—Yeah, he's a good basketball coach but nothing compared to John Wooden. It's just typical. Back in the days when John Powell was at Wisconsin, Harv Schmidt was at Illinois and some of those stiffs who couldn't coach anything, and he would get up after he had beaten them by 40 or 50 points and talk about what great coaches they were and how people in Madison, Wisconsin or Champaign, Illinois or wherever ought to get off their ass. (Insinuating they were so good!) Well, yeah, he was beating the shit out of them. You won't ever hear him defending Gene Keady or Steve Fisher or Bill Frieder or Lou Henson or any of the people who could beat him with some regularity.

One of the untold stories about the Fred Taylor (Knight's college coach at Ohio State) situation was Knight could not stand—and this came via John Flynn directly from Knight—Fred Taylor. These days you would think Taylor was Knight's best friend, until Taylor died recently. Knight couldn't stand him until another coach Knight respected told Knight before he ever got to Army, "If you ever want to get anywhere in the coaching business, you better make peace with Fred Taylor." So that's how that all came about.

I know a former associate athletic director at Army, who lives in Louisville now, and I was talking to him just last year. After the Neil Reed reprimand deal, I said. "You know J. C."—a retired general or something—"a lot of people say that Knight just brought that military mentality to Indiana, and he could get by with anything. That all kind of sprouted at Army." But my friend said Knight was in trouble at Army; he had been called in and told "any more incidents and you're history" because of some of the things that he had pulled at West Point. So it started long before he came to Indiana.

To let somebody treat people like that, what kind of a person are you? What kind of a school or anything else? It's stuff you can't get by with in real life. You couldn't do any of what Knight did if you worked for a company or a corporation and get by with it. The first thing they'll tell you is "he runs an honest program and he graduates the players." Well that shouldn't be an excuse or justification, it should be expected.

(Brown was re-interviewed after the firing.)

I think it should have happened a long, long time ago. I can't believe that they let it go on as long as they did. I watched the ESPN thing, and I can sum it up in about two or three sentences. According to Knight, everybody else lies. It's everybody else's fault. He took no responsibility. No accountability. I don't know; it's just weird. He and some of his friends want to portray him as this innocent victim who was targeted by this bad administration. When he grabbed the kid, I told *everybody* that they had two choices. They either gotta ignore it, or they gotta fire him. Because if they admit it happened with the kid, obviously it violates zero tolerance. Now they could have done what they've done with him so many times—ignore it. But they only had these two choices. They had to ignore it or fire him. They couldn't admit that it happened and then say, "Well, we're gonna give him another chance."

I think a lot of people, even IU fans, are glad they finally got rid of him. He was losing a lot of support. In the last few years, in fact, I rarely, and this is a real change, talked to an Indiana fan who didn't want him out of there. They said, "We're tired of his bull shit, and he's not winning." Not winning was probably the bottom line. I think IU would be better off getting rid of him.

I think, and I haven't really polled anybody, if you're not an Indiana fan, you got to feel like it's a good thing. He doesn't have a lot of followers outside of the Hoosier faithful. I think he is evil and extremely mean spirited and yeah, evil's a good way to describe him—very evil. He's still got his defenders, and I still don't know how anybody could justify or rationalize that kind of behavior. I was glad to see it happen. I guarantee you though that somebody will hire him.

The Write Stuff

Gene Wojciechowski

Gene Wojciechowski is currently the top basketball writer for ESPN the Magazine. Prior to that he was a Sports Illustrated writer.

Let me begin by saying that Bobby Knight is one of the finest coaches ever to wear an ill-fitting sweater that emphasizes a prodigious beer gut—bar none. And while I've never chosen an Indiana University team to win our office NCAA basketball pool, I can admit a certain fondness for the Hoosiers' man-to-man defense and Knight's insistence on running a pristine program.

As for the numbskull things Knight has had to say about sportswriters, well . . .

Fact is fact: With the exception of Puerto Rican police officers, I can think of nobody whom Knight despises more than someone carrying a press pass and an independent thought.

It was Knight who once said of sports reporters: "All of us learn to write in the second grade. Most of us then go on to greater things."

Like basketball, which we learned to play in third-grade gym class?

And it is Knight who mostly treats sportswriters as if they were dirty jockstraps. To Knight's way of thinking, you are either for him or against him. And if you choose the latter, God help you.

Is Knight a great coach? Undoubtedly, A humanitarian? Often. A writer's best friends? Are you kidding?

If I had a son who wanted to play college basketball, I'd want him to play for Knight. However, if he wanted to be a sportswriter *and* cover Knight's Indiana team, I'd tell him to consider the wonderful world of aluminum siding.

This is the problem with covering college hoops: The coaches become the stars, not the players. Players come and go. Coaches stay, as do their sometimes-dictatorial ways when dealing with the Fourth Estate. Knight is merely president of the club.

Knight's most publicized tirades involved sportswriter John Feinstein, who wrote *A Season on the Brink.* Knight hated the book and hated Feinstein for writing it. At one point Knight accused Feinstein of being a pimp. Later, Knight accused him of being a whore.

"Well," said Feinstein, "I wish he'd make up his mind so I'd know how to dress."

It wasn't always that way. There was a time when Knight and Feinstein almost were pals.

Back before the book was published, Knight and Feinstein were leaving the University of Illinois basketball arena after an important Hoosiers victory when they were stopped by autograph seekers. Under normal circumstances, Knight might have signed a few scraps of paper and moved on.

But this was different. His Indiana team had won a big game and by doing so had beaten Illinois coach Lou Henson, whom Knight disliked—a lot. Knight was in a buoyant mood and happily signed away. As he did one of the autograph workers turned to Feinstein and said, 'Hey, Coach, can we get you, too?"

Feinstein, who obviously had been mistaken for an IU assistant, shook his head no.

With that, the autograph seeker turned to a friend and said, "Get this, Knight signs, but this asshole won't."

Knight roared with laughter when he heard that one. As it turns out, it would be about the last time he cracked a smile at anything involving Feinstein.

Knight was always picking on somebody. If it wasn't Feinstein, it was Russ Brown. If it wasn't Brown, it was *Sports Illustrated's* Curry Kirkpatrick.

Kirkpatrick made the mistake (at least, in Knight's eyes) of appearing on *60 Minutes* and offering a less favorable view of the fabled Knight. And although the program hadn't been aired when Kirkpatrick attended an IU game on the final day of the season, Knight acted hostile, as if he had been told the content of Kirkpatrick's taped interview with Rather.

This was the year (1980) that IU won the Big Ten championship on the final day of the regular season. Kirkpatrick was on deadline, but decided to attend Knight's post game press conference and then return to his typewriter at courtside. Bad move.

Kirkpatrick had just settled into his seat when Knight stomped into the room. The coach began to discuss the game and Kirkpatrick, head down, began scribbling notes. A few moments later he heard, "Kirkpatrick, what are you doing here?"

Kirkpatrick looked up and smiled. How nice of Knight to notice him, he thought.

Problem was, Knight wasn't smiling back. In fact, Knight began a profanity-laden speech that was directed entirely at Kirkpatrick.

Knight wanted the writer out of the room. He even threatened to end the press conference if Kirkpatrick didn't leave immediately.

"I want you all to know that I'm not saying one more word until that asshole leaves and you all know who I mean."

Kirkpatrick gathered his things. "In deference to my colleagues, I'll leave." He said. "I'm leaving, but I'm leaving for those people's sake, not yours."

"You're leaving because I told you so, asshole," Knight said.

Kirkpatrick made his way to courtside and started typing his story on a machine borrowed from another *Sports Illustrated* writer. The computer happened to have an SI logo on it. As he typed, several Indiana fans noticed the magazine logo and began heckling Kirkpatrick and throwing debris at him.

"Hey, SI, what do you think of that?" one of them yelled.

Another IU fan walked by and began slapping Kirkpatrick with a Hoosiers pennant. Tough day at work.

Sports Illustrated wrote a letter of protest to the Indiana University president, but that was about it. Kirkpatrick didn't mention the incident with Knight or the fans in his game story, which explains why Knight hugged him a few weeks later at the Final Four in Philadelphia. Knight, Kirkpatrick was told, apparently respected the writer's restraint enough so that he later sent Kirkpatrick an autographed copy of a book entitled, *All I Know About Coaching Basketball.*

The pages were blank.

All was well between Kirkpatrick and Knight until the 1984 Olympic Trials. That's when Knight, coach of the United States team, turned the try-out camp into a security stronghold. Guards, wearing suits and packing guns, patrolled the areas during practice. These were not pleasant people.

Somehow, Kirkpatrick lost his media credentials, but still managed to attend one of the workouts. As he stood talking with the other basketball writers, two of the armed guards approached him.

"Can we see your credentials?" asked one of the guards.

"Well, you see . . ."

The guards grabbed Kirkpatrick and tugged him away. They took him to a small room near the courts and kept him there.

"Who the hell are you guys?" said Kirkpatrick.

No response. At last one of them made a phone call, nodded, and led Kirkpatrick out onto the courts and to a tower occupied by, you guessed it, Knight, who used the vantage point to observe workout.

Basketballs stopped bouncing. Drills ceased. Knight looked down at Kirkpatrick and then tossed him the missing credentials.

"Fucking Kirkpatrick," he said, "you're just lucky I'm a nice guy."

The writers of *Sports Illustrated* always have had mixed success with Knight. Depending on the day and the most recent story about him or his IU program, Knight could be steamed or gracious. You never knew for sure until the moment he looked into your eyes or opened his mouth. Then the secret was out.

Jack McCallum once was sent to Bloomington by his SI editors to do a story on Hoosiers stars Ted Kitchel and Randy Wittman. Of course, any piece on any player at IU meant having to speak with Knight, which is easier said than done.

McCallum, who had never met Knight, began the process of arranging an interview with the famed coach. After about a dozen phone conversations with the school" sports information department, McCallum was told Knight would see him.

And then it hit McCallum: He would actually have to talk to Knight. The Bobby Knight. The great and all-powerful Knight. The Knight who had molded young men into whatever he wanted them to be, which takes one hell of a strong mold. That Knight.

The interview took place in the Indiana dressing room. McCallum asked his questions about Kitchel and Wittman, and much to the writer's surprise, Knight answered them. And politely, too.

McCallum let his mind wander ever so briefly. He wondered why he had ever been nervous about speaking with Knight in the first place. This guy was a pussycat, as soft as cashmere. Any more accommodating and he'd have to send Knight a thank-you note.

Knight started to describe each player on the Indiana roster. It was when he reached the name of Jim Thomas, a guard, that Knight's disposition took a turn for the worse.

"If I only could get Jim Thomas to . . ." said Knight, searching desperately for the right word, "To . . ."

Unable to adequately describe "killer instinct," Knight reached over and without warning grabbed McCallum's shirt and, with it, McCallum's necklace and a small handful of chest hairs. McCallum didn't know whether to cry or scream for help.

"You know, I want this from him!" said Knight.

"Hmmm," McCallum said, wincing.

It is hard to retain your dignity when valuable chest hairs are fluttering toward a locker room floor. But McCallum did his best. He had done nothing to offend Knight, yet the coach, in his own unmistakable way, had sent a message. Knight wanted McCallum to know that this was his domain, that McCallum was merely a guest and only marginally welcome, at that.

McCallum understood immediately.

For a number of reasons, the story on Kitchel and Wittman never ran. And for a number of reasons, including the amount of time Knight had given him, McCallum felt compelled to call to apologize.

"Bobby, you're not going to believe this," McCallum said, "but after all the time you gave me, the story isn't running."

McCallum expected a tempest. Instead he received a gentle breeze.

"I understand your business a lot better than you think I do," Knight said calmly. "I understand this happens all the time."

McCallum hung up the phone that day freshly intimidated and thoroughly confused. To this day, he understands Knight not one bit.

Knight is an Indiana treasure. They might as well designate his IU office a historical landmark, such is his appeal in Indiana and the surrounding region.

For example, when word leaked that Knight might accept an offer to coach at New Mexico, people went bonkers. They couldn't believe that their beloved Bobby would leave IU for anyplace else.

There were skeptics, including *Louisville Courier-Journal* columnist Rick Bozich, who thought that Knight was simply using the New Mexico offer to secure his standing at IU, to say nothing of having his ego enriched by concerned Hoosiers fans. So convinced was Bozich of Knight's intentions that he told a radio audience that very thing.

They take their basketball seriously in Indiana and Kentucky. Bozich had been threatened in anonymous letters and phone calls before, and there was little doubt that his comments about Knight might prompt similar action. And don't think his friends and neighbors didn't know it, either.

As Bozich pulled into his driveway after appearing on the radio show, he noticed a large cardboard sign attached to the utility pole that stood between his house and his neighbor. "Bozich lives here, "read the top of the sign, complete with an arrow that pointed toward the Bozich residence. "not here," read the bottom half, this time with an arrow pointed toward the neighbor" house.

You expect the unexpected when dealing with Knight. For instance, Rick Reilly of *Sports Illustrated* once was supposed to meet Knight for a 9:00 A.M. interview session. Knight was visiting Denver at the time, so Reilly arranged to be at the coach's hotel a little before nine.

The appointed hour came and went and Reilly, standing in the middle of the hotel lobby, began to worry. What if he had missed him? What if Bobby Knight, one of the country's most recognizable sports figures, had walked right past him? What would Reilly tell his editors?

At 9:45 Reilly raced to the house phones and called Knight's room. No answer. He hopped on an elevator and then knocked on Knight's door. There was the clicking of locks, soon followed by the grand sight of Knight in his birthday suit.

"C'mon in, I'm taking a shower," Knight said, "Talk to me now."

So Reilly, his glasses fogging with steam, sat on a toilet bowl and conducted an interview as America's most controversial coach lathered up.

Knight thought I was too snoopy; at least that's what he wrote in his diary

John Feinstein

In 1986, a young writer wrote a book that catapulted him and the Indiana basketball program to national prominence. The writer was John Feinstein, the book was A Season on the Brink. *The result was a thoroughly irritated Coach Knight who surprisingly, as a result of the book, had more admirers than ever before.*

Word circulated that Knight was upset that Feinstein had failed in his promise to seriously limit profanity and never thanked Knight for the incredible access granted.

The always erudite Feinstein was generous with his time as he addressed these accusations and other Knight problems.

You just have to understand Knight's psyche. I wasn't surprised that he was upset at me. Knight was just going to find something to be upset about because that's just the way he is. I was certainly surprised when he chose to make an issue out of his profanity because that's the least controversial thing about him. Everybody knows he uses profanity. That's just Bob; that's just the way he is. I was not surprised that he found something not to like; I was surprised by what he chose not to like.

My time in Bloomington was fascinating, very interesting because I was around people who are the best, or among the best, at what they do and I'm a basketball fan, and Knight's a great coach so it was an interesting experience. Fortunately I was single at the time so it wasn't as if I had to leave my family. Or move my family. It was just me. In Bloomington, I lived in a place called Dunnhill Apartments, right across from Assembly Hall. I've said often that I thought there were three coaches in the country who were interesting enough at the time to be worthy of a book like that: Knight, Dean Smith and John Thompson. I knew all three and knew of the three the only one who would even consider such a project was Knight. That's why I approached him.

Knight is one of these people who, he's a very black and white character, if he likes you, he likes you. If he doesn't, he doesn't. He liked me. I had a good relationship with him, and I think he honestly thought, correctly, that an inside look at his program would get the response that many people did ultimately have. It gave many people a more positive attitude about Knight. He's certainly got his flaws but he also has very positive things going for him.

On the other hand, no matter how many good things you do, it doesn't give you the right to break the law, to hit people, abuse people in any way. Bob seems to think it's okay, and one is not connected to the other. It's like the guy who owns the Washington Redskins. Dan Snyder got upset with me because I said he was a bully. He called me up and said you don't know how much charity work I do. I said, "so what does that have to do with anything?"

In regard to Knight supposedly being upset with profanity in the book: Number one, as I said a million times, when we discussed the issue of profanity, I said to him very specifically, "Bob, writing a book with you without the word 'fuck' would be like writing a book about you without the word 'bastard'." And he said, "Oh, I understand. I can go along with that." And I said, "no, because I want the book to be shorter than *War and Peace.*" And I left out eighty percent of his profanity and I never even used the word "cunt" which he uses all the time so in many ways. I did leave out a lot of profanity but I had to include some because otherwise people wouldn't take the book seriously. As far as the 'thank you note' was concerned, I never heard that one before to be honest. That's a bunch of crap. When the book first came out, I sent him a copy of it, before the book was published with a note saying "Here it is, hope you're happy with it. I think it accomplishes what you and I set out to do and obviously I couldn't have done it without the access you gave me." When I got the phone call, he didn't even call me himself, he had one of assistants call me, to say he was upset about the profanity, I wrote him another note saying "Look, Bob, if you're upset about something in this book, given everything you and I went through together, we should sit down and talk about it face to face, man to man. At the Notre Dame game that year, which was the first Indiana game I attended, Bob Hammel, who has been Bob's right-hand guy for years, came up and handed me an envelope. He said, "Bob wanted me to tell you that he refused to open your letter." As far as I was concerned that was the end of it.

Bob Knight is Bob Knight. I'm certainly not going to spend the rest of my life worrying about it—you move on. The only time I've made any attempt to contact him since then was when I wrote him a condolence note when his mother died. He did, six years ago in Hawaii, walk up and shake hands with me in a hotel and ask how I was doing and seemed to be very cordial. Since then whenever, I've seen him, we've exchanged hellos and kept going and that's been pretty much the end of it.

I don't know anybody who doesn't like Steve Alford. Bob can't stand for anybody's star to shine brighter than him. I got close to several players when I was there. I'm still good friends with Steve. I was pretty close to Daryl

Thomas and Todd Meier, certainly. Those were probably the three I knew best and I still keep in touch with Todd and Steve.

I was 28 when I did the book. This year I did another college basketball book called *The Least Known Division One Conference in America,* the Patriot Conference, which consisted of seven academic-oriented schools. I really got so tired of writing about 'pros in training,' I wanted to write about kids who really do go to college and play basketball and aren't gonna be pros and aren't gonna get rich off the sport and play the game because they love it. I had a very good time doing it.

When I was younger, I think I fantasized about someday writing books for a living, but I don't think I expected to have the success, especially right out of the box, based on the things I did. I know I worked hard, but I also have been very lucky. It's a matter of trying as a reporter to get to know how the people you are writing about think. I always try to be able when I finish a project I like to think I understand the people involved and know the subject involved as well as anybody. That's sort of my goal; I may not achieve it, but that's my goal. If I come close to achieving it and I can write like that, then I've done what I set out to do.

At the end of the book, when I left IU, I was on good terms with Bob Knight.

The NCAA changed the rules as a direct result of *A Season on the Brink*. The book described how Indiana kept practicing once they were eliminated from the NCAA Tournament . . . to get an early start for the next season. Technically, you could practice until the champion was crowned on the first Monday night in April. I think Knight was the only coach who understood that it was legal or might have been the only coach who saw the loophole. Once your season has ended these days you may not conduct practice. Before that, the rule simply said that no team could practice after the conclusion of the Final Four. They changed the rule because of Knight. Once your team has completed its season and played its last game you cannot hold formal practices. He felt it was legal; Knight would never break a rule.

In spite of plenty of evidence to the contrary, Bob still thinks he did absolutely nothing wrong. He is totally defiant, and he is not repentant. I don't see how you could expect anything different from Bob Knight. This is who he has been for 35 years as a head basketball coach. You know it was the chair's fault back in 1985. If you talk to Bob Knight about it and that's the whole problem. That's the crux of the problem There's never been anybody born who didn't do anything wrong. But because of the people around him, his friends/enablers who keep telling him that it's never his fault. Somebody else did something wrong. Someone's out to get him. In this case it's now Myles Brand. Bob honestly believes that he hasn't done anything wrong.

What do you think the chances are that Myles Brand wants to be remembered as the President of Indiana University who fired Bob Knight? If he builds the greatest library, the greatest history department in the history of higher education, he's gonna be remembered for one thing—He fired Bob Knight, and students burned him in effigy on the front lawn of his own home. He knew that something like that was gonna happen. That's why he didn't fire him in May. That's why he tried very hard to avoid firing him because he knew what was going to come down on him if he did. He tried everything he could, and, by the way, Myles Brand is as complicit in this as anybody because he never disciplined Bob Knight in any way before May nor did anybody else at Indiana. But he didn't want to fire Bob Knight because of what's happening right now.

Bob Knight never believed, nor did I, that it was really a zero tolerance policy; in fact it really wasn't. Because if it was zero tolerance, he would have been fired the minute he refused to deal with Clarence Doninger. He would have been fired the minute he raised his voice to that female lawyer. If you believe for a second, by the way, that he didn't raise his voice to her, then I've got some ocean-front land in Nebraska I'd really like to sell you. He believed that Indiana would let him continue to be Bob Knight and that every time something happened it would be someone else's fault. Frankly so did I!

For crying out loud, we're now into the semantics of what of what is zero tolerance. I'll tell you one thing zero tolerance is. It means you don't grab a kid you don't know. And now some of the Knight apologists are saying "well that was really no different than you know, patting a kid on the back during the course of a game." In another week, we're gonna find out that Knight was really inviting the kid into his office for tea and cookies.

If it was my kid, I'd be very upset. I'd be upset with my kid for addressing someone of that age and that rank disrespectfully, and I would tell him that. But I would also say, Wait a minute. If you want to turn around and say something in response, I don't have a problem with that. But the minute you put your hands on my kid, I have a serious problem with you, no matter who you are.

Bob's been taking cheap shots at people for years. The whole problem is this. Bob Knight is three things, without any debate: one of the greatest coaches ever, a guy who cares as much about academics as athletics in a time when that's very rare, and a guy who never broke an NCAA rule. But the fourth thing is: He's a self-righteous guy who thinks he can do no wrong and has a double standard for behavior. You behave one way toward me—respectfully, never be rude, always show me respect and loyalty, but I don't have to return any of that to you because I'm Bob Knight and you're not.

I think he could end up in a major program, and he absolutely will end up in a major program, if he takes the advice—and I thought Digger Phelps showed some guts by saying on television that he had advised Bob Knight to seek anger management counseling. Because if he had more friends do that before this occurred, he would still be the Indiana Coach. Because if his friends can get together and all those people out there he respects can convince him to do that, then there's no reason he can't get a major job. But even if he doesn't, he'll get a job, and it'll probably be a pretty good job because the president of a major university will stand up and will cite all that I have just cited that is positive and he'll say that Bob Knight has pledged that he will control his temper, and here's our new coach. And he'll sell lots of tickets and get lots of attention.

Even if he was being baited, under the terms of this alleged policy, he has to just walk away. The year I was with Knight, the one real bad blowup we had occurred on a Friday morning in Minneapolis when we were walking out of breakfast and a friend of Knight's had come to breakfast and he said to me, "So what are you going to do all day?" I said to him, "I'm going to do what I do every day; I'm going to follow Knight around." Knight was walking a couple of steps in front of us. I was not speaking to him, and I was not being disrespectful. He whirled on me, came back, put his finger in my face, and said, "Don't you ever address me that way. You can call me Coach, Coach Knight or Bob."

You see, this is the lunacy of him—lecturing anybody about manners. He doesn't have the credibility to lecture anybody about "manners and civility." His boorish behavior is well documented. He has no credentials on this.

If the run-in with the IU student is true, he didn't even get out of his own gym. It wasn't a question of what sportswriters would say; it wasn't a question of going on the road; it was on-campus, and he couldn't get out of his own gym. Time and time again, Bobby Knight said, "I can handle this. I know what this is about, and I'm not gonna screw it up on any level." And right out of the box, and again I think it smells because of the people involved, but still you cannot put your hands on students.

Even if you believe Knight's version, which I don't happen to. It's still too much. He still had his arm on the kid. He's still in the kid's face. I would bet you that he honestly believes he didn't use profanity on the kid. I guarantee you that he did use profanity on the kid.

Going back to when I was doing the book, the first question I was always asked was, "Will he have a Woody Hayes type ending?" You remember Woody Hayes, the great Ohio State coach whose career ended when he slugged Charlie Bauman, a Clemson player, during a bowl game in 1978. My answer was, "I hope not." But clearly, even though it wasn't on national television, this is that kind of ending. It's embarrassing. It's humiliating. Bob Knight, with his record, should have left coaching, to a standing ovation, after his last game at Assembly HalI. Instead he leaves this way, completely humiliated by what he has done.

This will be part of his legend. I think it's in the first sentence. When you write about Bob Knight's career, you have to say, "Bob Knight, the brilliant but constantly self-destructive basketball coach, who won three national championships but 'caused his own firing by grabbing the arm of a nineteen year old student, ...

I wouldn't be surprised if he coaches again. He desperately wants Dean Smith's record of 879 victories which he's 117 short of right now. That's why he fought to save his job in May, because he wants that record because he believes to be credited as the greatest coach of all time, which he thinks of himself as being, or close to it, he needs that record. I can see him doing television for a year or two. Every failed coach, whether they're failed because of incidents like this or lack of victories ends up in TV or radio, he would be very good at it. And I can see a big-time program on the skids hiring him in a year or two to come back.

This was a brutally difficult for Indiana. And even though I've been critical of President Brand for not taking this step earlier, it's still a move that takes courage because he is going to receive threats from people at Indiana who are still loyal to Coach Knight, and it's going to be a very difficult time for Myles Brand because he took this step.

What will have been Knight's greatest positive contribution? The fact that he always stood for the right things in college basketball. His players graduated. He never came close to violating a rule. He was always standing up and saying, "There's a right way to do things in college basketball and a wrong way." I've always said about Bob Knight, "When it came to the big things, no one was better, but it was the little things that always brought him down, and this was another example."

Which makes this an even sadder episode.

It's a terribly sad episode because a great coach should not be brought down by small things.

Actually, if you play that tape backwards, it looks like Coach is helping Neil up and showin' him on his way

Terry Reed

Terry Reed has watched the roller-coaster ride of his son, Neil, through stardom at Indiana University to banishment from the team and death threats following CNN/SI's expose of Coach Knight choking Neil Reed

This whole thing has just wiped us out. We're devastated; there's nothing we can do; it just keeps on. I can tell you from a legal standpoint it was very, very difficult first of all to prove that the choking or something like that—before the tape. By the time the tape came out, the statute of limitations was up. Legally, there have been a number of people from coast to coast try to initiate some sort of effort to see what can be done. Up to this point, nothing has.

Ever since he was a little kid, my son Neil wanted to play for Bobby Knight. It's a long story. Neil is the only person involved in this whole thing who has lost everything. Everybody else went on about their business—kept their jobs—making bookoos of money up there at IU, assistant coaches, a kid that wouldn't have got to play for three years got to play for three years—the (Michael) Lewis kid. Everybody involved, the AD, the assistant AD, who knew about it. Every single person involved has continued on with life in a merry way. The only person that it's hurt—there's no monetary gain, not any gain, has been Neil Reed. It's a sad thing. You don't know half of it—the blockage at the end there. It's like there's a wall up; it is over! It's an amazing thing. We've been through so much with this, and I know it needs to be out there. Every day since all this happened I get a call from someone, many I know in the media. Not a day goes by that somebody doesn't call and bring this up—not one day. Tell me you'd like to live that life—it's difficult.

Against Kentucky, the sixth game of his freshman year, he had an outstanding game; Pitino said some great things about him in Sports Illustrated, but we can go through all that. I'm telling you we're wore out. The Knight group, I'm telling you my son lived it. My son played up there. One of his assistants—the one who's suing him right now, Ron Felling, was like a brother to me. You can't get any closer to that program than we were; my daughter was his secretary when my son was a sophomore. We were living up there and she was a freshman. People don't realize all this stuff. Neil didn't even visit any place else; he was going to IU. It just didn't matter. You talk about, as a father, I'm a sick son of a bitch. I'm not gonna go and jump off a bridge over it, but this kid did exactly what I asked him to do. He didn't smoke, he didn't drink; he trained like a son of a bitch. He did every single thing and he went through as tough a high school situation as anybody—moved from town to town. Nobody ever said I was easy on kids but I didn't choke them. I don't hit them. And despite what people might say or think I might have threatened, I might have said a lot of things, but I don't do that. When Neil left IU, I was moving from Iowa State to Southern Mississippi. The choking thing was bad, but the slander has been horrible. There are some attorneys in Philadelphia looking at that. Hell, Knight ripped my ass in the Chicago paper just about a year ago—just ripped it—ripping at me. This is a long roundabout thing, but I lost a job over this deal. And he's raising hell about that and about me and how bad I am and he turns and fires his assistant two days before they play Kentucky. He's ripping my ass and he don't have his facts right. But he don't have to. You see Bob Knight doesn't understand the truth. He don't know the truth and doesn't give a shit. All he knows is what he wants. He gets away with it because he owns them—because he owns them lock stock and barrel. You rest assured, from zero tolerance on down, he told them you figure out what you got to say, but he owns them. He's the cash cow, and they're not running him out.

They always slander. You see, anybody who leaves up there at IU, they just rip. You cannot leave up there on good terms. You cannot. That's an unwritten rule. It's a good thing that Neil didn't have a background that was shaky 'cause had they had one it would have been awesome. It was bad enough as it is, but the kid didn't do anything. Anyway, on the slander thing, when he left up there, obviously if you think you're gonna continue to play ball you just have to bite your tongue. As a coach, I'm in this business, I also understand how powerful Bob Knight is, and I don't know if there's—you see I've got good friends, coaches and head coaches, at different places, and they said, "Well, this'll get him." I told everybody, including Ron Felling on the morning they had the big press conference to announce Knight's fate, "It isn't gonna work; he's gonna win it." Understand, I've got a little insight into this deal; he owns them, and when you own them and intimidate people like he does, there's nothing that can be done. We had to stay quiet. Now you try to prove slander—three years later. Now you've got a deal—where were you when it happened. The legal aspect, everything was wrong, maybe we handled it wrong. There are people now looking into the slander issues.

This has been very difficult with my family—just a killer. It has made it very difficult on our relationships. We've spent three years trying to nurture a kid that was so positive, so upbeat. You don't want to say—because it sounds like you're bragging about your kid, but how many kids do you honestly know that don't drink—train right. He did everything. One thing they forgot to say—this was the captain of Indiana's basketball team. You don't make the captain a bad guy do you, but when all this happened—the slander, you go back to that. But I don't know—it's extremely difficult. I don't know if it can be done—I don't know.

Neil has been approached about a book—even talked about a tremendous sum of money. On the morning of the zero tolerance press conference his literary agent got a call and said it was over, dropped it, and wouldn't sign it. I have no idea to this day what happened—nothing. I don't know. It's the same damn thing. Oh, I've got it all—I know what the hell's going on, I've been there.

Knight felt like he could do anything to Neil because—you know you sometimes feel you can be a little bit tougher to your own kid than you can others and he did. Neil took it and never said a word. If the big guys didn't rebound, it was Neil's fault; if somebody was late for practice, it was Neil's fault—he was the one who rounded them up and did everything. But the deal is, the first time, when threatened with this scholarship thing Neil Reed's the first one that said "Fuck You!" and walked out and that's why this has gotten so volatile and so personal between them. He walked out on Bob Knight. Luke Recker waited 'til Knight was out of the country and faxed in a transfer—how about that?

Now you got to remember, one of the assistants was like a brother. I was there every day. I hung around in that department, I mean in an unofficial way, and I'm not the only one, I can name you ten other guys so I mean there's no cleanliness there. The only rules they follow up there are the rules that Knight wants to follow. Do they cheat for players? No, not necessarily. They cheat for Bob Knight. They don't do anything that helps kids. Now Recker's situation—they went out on a limb. They couldn't afford another major deal right then. But like I said, Recker, when he did transfer, faxed it in when Knight was out of the country. Now that takes a lot of nerve huh? He was the only one, assistant coach, any of them, all the others. You know what they do when the assistants leave—they phone Knight or leave him a message to call or something of that nature. They don't do it face to face; they haven't got enough nerve.

Felling, after fourteen years, is suing for age discrimination and assault.

I feel quite sure it will never get to court. Can you imagine Indiana University allowing Bob Knight to get on a witness stand? Now they have got it into federal court, which means you've got a larger jury pool and you're gonna have judges that maybe didn't graduate from Indiana. But you're fighting in the state of Indiana, and it's gonna be a monster.

I'm stupid enough but I will admit I made a mistake. I don't know if you would say—worse than a false god or whatever. I always thought Knight did more good than bad but I'm way, way wrong. Now, does he do all bad? No. There are some things he does good, but I get sick of hearing them saying about his contributions. I've seen him twice contribute when he's starting to have a bad year. For them, and he contributes nothing—$250,000–$300,000. Well, you know what's going on in college basketball. There a lot of professors wouldn't have a job if they weren't contributing a lot of money. That's part of the deal. It's in their contract; they've got to give back a certain amount of money. Knight is their No. 1 giver. He's their No. 1 fundraiser—on a yearly basis. I know you're gonna have Lilly Corporation and some of the others up there, but I'm talking about individual givers. They don't have anybody. He always uses that. For a guy who doesn't want it to be a big "celebrity" thing, he does it at halftime of a ball game in front of seventeen thousand. So you see the irony in it. But look, it helped Neil, and he has given up a professional career—that's money today. I don't know. Neil's a good kid, but the emperor doesn't say he's sorry. Knight's not sorry. He hadn't even admitted that he did it. That's a test for him that means he can't take credit for it. But there's a twisted mind; he's crazy. He's vulnerable. Kids like that are vulnerable too. Neil, when he was there, and this is what happened every time. It's what happened to Alford, to Recker, what do Indiana fans like the most? Knight would bench Neil—take him out. Two or three times he won ball games for him after he was trying to be—course Knight will put you in when games are on the line. You know how hard it is to sit there under that kind of pressure and then go out and perform in the final few minutes? And he did it. And you know what that would do for him—get him deeper in debt, because the fans would go nuts over him. He was the little hero. And what it's all about was—this is why Krzyzewski's sideways with him—this is why all of them are. Knight's ego is such he will not share—his players can't be bigger than him or even close or on the level which is stupid 'cause they're not even trying to be. They aren't trying to be in competition with the man.

The first people that came to Neil turned down his proposal after reading—what is it you write when you give them your proposal?—synopsis or something because they didn't want to hear that—they wanted the negative and Neil said I'm gonna tell what happened. 'cause there was a lot of good up there; there was a lot of bad.

Everybody's intimidated. You watch the tape in slow motion. Felling slows but he kinda goes on. Now see, what people don't realize, the two kids that stepped up to the podium and said their thing—that they didn't see it. Well, one of them was guarding Neil, that was Lewis, so you know he saw it. The other was even closer. It was A. J. Guyton. On top of that, they said the coaches didn't break them up. For people who don't understand the videotape—that was spliced. They cut out where the assistants had to go into it. It goes from Knight hitting him or choking him to Neil immediately starting another play. This is the way they splice game tape all the time and practice tape. That's my opinion. They accidentally left it on 'cause generally they go right back up to "on top at half court" and they go right into another thing. Well Knight goes and does his thing. Then Knight and Neil ended up down there at the free throw line on the other end and that's when the other coaches had to come in. But the coaches, in order to keep themselves out of it, spliced it. So I know there's some tape missing. So now Knight's deal was that Neil Reed even lied—Neil said they had to break it up when it doesn't show that on the tape. You can see on the tape they didn't have to break him up so but he still hasn't addressed that he choked Neil. But I understand and I know where it was and if you had to put somebody on the witness stand, they, too, would say "Yeah we did break it up." But as it is now, that's the only thing they can say that ever that Neil said that can't be proved or hasn't been proved. It can't be proved at this point in time without going to a witness stand because they took that out to protect themselves.

A lawsuit would get sticky because there's four people, Knight being one, who would have to go up and say they saw this. Now, Knight, you can believe this or not, has already given a "reward" or would you say "bonus money" immediately following this incident—all of them got raises. Now that's the truth. You see Felling's been fired half a dozen times and every time he got fired and come back, something would go wrong and here'd come a new washer and dryer; next time it would be a bedroom suite, or here comes a big screen TV. Knight buys his support and love. That's what he does. He don't say, "I'm sorry." You just get a new car. You get a new this. I'm talking about secretaries on down.

Knight, even in the face of the tape, he has refused to admit it. That isn't the only thing. I've seen crap myself; that's why I'm so sick. I'm the one who put my son at IU—what a huge mistake as a father, but there's nothing I can do about it; I've got to go on. I made a mistake. He didn't even visit Kentucky; he didn't visit Carolina and Kansas. He was going to Indiana.

Our whole family has gotten very little sleep for three years. There's a lot of nights where we're up all night long.

Indiana University is Bob Knight's University. He loans it to the University so they can have tailgate parties and some other times when they need it. It is not Indiana University; it's Bob Knight University, and I believe that now.

Bob Knight does not understand the truth. He only understands and says whatever he thinks fits. That's the way it is.

Knight finally said something good—when he said goodbye

Murray Sperber

IU professor Murray Sperber was forced to take a leave of absence from his teaching post in the fall of 2000 because of the Bob Knight furor.

Sperber has written the definitive books on the tenuous relationship between universities and their athletic programs. His latest release is Beer and Circus *on how college sports are crippling undergraduate education. Earlier works include* College Sports, Inc. *and* Shake Down the Thunder.

This whole thing is ancient history. I've moved on with my life. That's my position. I am a serious professor. I don't care what the perception is. I have a sense of what I do, and what I want to do with my life and one of the things that I really don't want to do anymore is talk about Bob Knight. I don't care. His fans hate me. Some people think I'm a great hero.

Sadly, his saga-and what has become my own small role in it-will continue. In the past, I have publicly criticized Knight's conduct, but nothing ever happened to him, or me. This spring, however, everything changed.

On March 14, 2000, I appeared on a CNN/SI television news report about Knight. Because I am a long-time faculty member on Indiana's Bloomington campus and have written extensively about college sports, the CNN/SI interviewer showed me videotapes of some former basketball players charging Knight with misconduct, and then asked me: What would the university do?

Knight has a history of questionable behavior. He has been accused of intimidating and abusing players and athletics directors, hitting a Puerto Rican policeman before a practice session at the Pan American Games, and throwing a potted plant against a wall in a temper tantrum at a secretary, to name just a few of the incidents. But the university had never reprimanded him, I told CNN, "I call him the Emperor of Indiana, and there is no one in this state who will stand up to him and certainly no one in this university who will.

. . . If you are the Emperor, you are allowed to do what you want."

Privately, I wanted to call Knight "the former Emperor." But I could not ignore the historical record of the administration and trustees' pandering to Knight, in their relentless quest to have a winning and successful basketball program.

The program aired at 11 p.m., and before I went to bed that night, I had received 14 e-mail messages, most of them condemning me for my comments. By noon the next day, the number of messages approached 50; most were negative, although a few congratulated me for my remarks. Faculty members sent the bulk of the positive responses, but-to give a sense of the tenor of such support-one colleague wrote in capital letters at the bottom of his message, "Murray, whatever you do, don't use my name."

The following day, Knight held a press conference on ESPN and denounced every person who had spoken against him on the CNN/SI report, including me. That prompted many more nasty e-mail messages, as well as telephone calls from newspaper, TV, and radio reporters.

My main point in the interviews? The *Chicago Tribune* quoted me verbatim: "There's a very well spelled out, very strict code of conduct for every person at Indiana University in authority: faculty, staff, everyone. But Bob Knight, because of his great fame as a coach, seems to be getting an exemption. I don't feel that's right. I also feel it makes the university look very bad."

Hardly a radical pronouncement, but it unleashed still more denunciations of me.

In the past, as a critic of big-time college sports, I have been involved in a number of controversies, but none of them ever affected my private life or daily routine in the way that the most recent one has. In fact, because of my scholarship on issues involving college athletics, sports journalists and others have frequently asked me to comment about Bob Knight and his antics. The recent occurrences, however, have pushed me into the spotlight-and into an uncomfortable and odd symbiotic relationship with the infamous coach-in ways that I certainly never imagined or desired.

Before the CNN/SI interview, I had made enemies, but no one had ever physically threatened me or launched ad-hominem attacks on my appearance, dress, speech, religion, or politics, or had spread malicious rumors about me. Beginning on March 14, insults along all those lines arrived in my e-mailbox, on my answering machine, in letters to the editor of newspapers, and on the Internet.

For example, at a Web site maintained by Indiana basketball fans, the "report" appeared that I never showed up to teach my classes after spring break! I had thought that I understood the frequent antagonism between the athletics department and its supporters on the one hand, and the academic aspects of the university on the other. But suddenly, in just the past few months, I have faced a steep learning curve.

Often the vilification has come from people who have no direct connection to Indiana University but are rabid fans of its men's basketball team and coach. In addition, the people who write letters frequently know nothing about me but assume that I fit their stereotype of university professors. Indeed, the most depressing element of the attacks has been the revelation that anti-intellectualism is alive and well in Indiana and probably elsewhere in America, and that although many faculty members spend many years in college towns, a segment of the local population detests them.

The daily newspaper in Bloomington printed a letter that stated: "After viewing Sperber on the CNN Enquirer gossip hour, It seems obvious to me that Sperber has never worn a jock strap. So the next time somebody . . . claims to be an expert of something they know nothing about . . . say that he or she is a 'Sperber.' Or, if you hear a child spinning a tall tale, you would call that child a 'Sperbie' . . . By the way, would somebody let Murray know that Staples is having a sale on pocket protectors."

In fact, I played basketball for many years, including two years as a semi-professional in France, but that does not make me more or less qualified to comment on the current charges against Knight-particularly after CNN released a videotape in April that showed the coach grabbing the player, Neil Reed, by the throat. I need only vision and a reading of my university's code of conduct to form an opinion about that incident.

In the wake of CNN's airing of the Reed tape, more journalists asked me for interviews about Bob Knight. I found myself on national TV uttering such profundities as "A university is more important than any of its sports teams or coaches, and it must not lose sight of that fact." Yet even that comment sparked controversy; many fans berated me for not realizing that the Indiana University men's basketball team was, to quote one, "far more important than the English department" or any other academic part of the institution.

Many fans also argued that English departments and positions like mine exist only because universities can support them with the profits from college sports. My first book about intercollegiate athletics, *College Sports Inc.*, demonstrated indisputably that almost all athletics departments lose money annually, and rather than contribute to the university treasury, they suck millions of dollars from it. But, alas, no one can drive a silver stake through the myth of college-sports profitability.

In recent years, I have studied and written about fan behavior, and I am very aware of its irrational component. Nevertheless, the best preparation for my current experiences was teaching George Orwell's *1984* numerous times. For example, in the original CNN/SI report, in March, Neil Reed described Knight's "choking" him and then said that two assistant coaches had separated them. But when CNN released the tape of the incident, in April, the tape didn't show the assistants approaching or separating Reed and Knight. I immediately started receiving e-mail from Knight's supporters claiming that "the tape proves that Reed is a liar-you don't see Felling and Dakich (the assistants) separating them." Similarly, in reading the e-mail from Knight's supporters, and also scanning their comments on Web sites, I have sometimes detected the same fervor toward their beloved "Coach" as the people of Oceania felt toward "Big Brother."

As Orwell explained, in the world of true believers, "War is peace," "Ignorance is Strength," and "Hate is love." College athletics produces strong emotions, but before my recent experiences, I never realized how antithetical the mindset of the sports fan is to the university tradition of reason, inquiry, and open discussion.

In an e-mail message to me, one writer commented, "Years ago, I heard an interview with you and Larry King where you confessed that you had never met Bob Knight. I find this disturbing. You would have people believe that as a member of the I.U. faculty, you were an authority on Indiana University basketball."

I replied that I have never claimed expertise on Indiana basketball, merely on the university's code of conduct. But the writer raised an interesting point: In my 29 years at Indiana, since 1971, I have never met Bob Knight, even though he arrived in Bloomington exactly the same semester that I did.

Like Larry King, many interviewers have asked me about meeting Knight. I explain that I have seen him in person only at games in Assembly Hall, the university's basketball arena. However, the premise of the query intrigues me: The interviewers are clearly envisioning a small college, or a bygone era, where the faculty members actually meet and greet the coaches. In the more than 40 years that I've spent at large, public universities, I have never encountered such a situation.

Nevertheless, in the 1980s, I attempted to meet Bob Knight. While doing research for *College Sports Inc.,* I tried to interview him, but I never got past his secretary. I did not take the rebuff personally-I had not yet published any criticisms of intercollegiate athletics, and he knew nothing about me except that I was a faculty member at Indiana University.

To this day, the question about meeting Bob Knight keeps recurring, and a number of years ago, it motivated me to take a poll of Indiana faculty members. I work in a nine-story building that houses many academic departments, and I went down the hallways, knocking on office doors and asking faculty members whether they had ever met Bob Knight. I had two criteria for my poll: first, meeting him was defined as being introduced and shaking hands; and second, the respondent had to have worked at Bloomington for at least 10 years. I polled 45 tenure-track faculty members, and of that sample, only one had had the opportunity to meet Knight, an English-department colleague, Chris Lohmann.

At the time of the possible encounter, Lohmann was president of the Bloomington Faculty Council and had been invited to a luncheon with university officials and members of the state legislature. Knight was the featured speaker, and according to Lohmann, the coach "made all sorts of denigrating and insulting remarks about the faculty. . . . I was so angry that I almost walked out." As a result, no meeting between Lohmann and Knight occurred.

The final score of my poll: 45 to 0.

Such an outcome prompts the conclusion: When and how would the average faculty member at Indiana University, or at most big-time college sports universities, meet a famous coach? Even a professor who studies college sports cannot easily gain access to a celebrity coach.

Basic geography emphasizes the point. At Bloomington, Knight's office was in the athletics-department complex on the far northern edge of the campus, a long distance from my building at the center of the University. The same symbolic and geographic separation between intercollegiate athletics and academics exists at many other universities. In addition, big-time college coaches are in the entertainment business, a very different endeavor from higher education. Those coaches often amass incomes of more than $1-million a year, whereas the average faculty member earns a fraction of that amount.

Finally-and my current adventure proves the case-power coaches like Bob Knight often regard themselves as separate from higher education-indeed, superior to it-and they do not believe that regular university procedures, including collegiality and codes of conduct, apply to them. Some of those coaches frequently say that they are "teachers" and boast of the graduation rates of their players-Bob Knight certainly does. But, in reality, many power coaches regard sports as war and believe that the end-or winning-justifies any means to arrive at that victory.

When coaches persuade universities to accept one standard for their behavior and another for professors and anyone else in authority, immense problems result.

Important additional questions also remain, most notably: How did people in authority at Indiana University allow Knight to become the Emperor and to do and say whatever he pleased? For the sake of the university's current and future health, the trustees should thoroughly investigate such questions and find the answers.

I was flown to New York recently by 20/20. They had originally wanted, and we're talking the fifth-rated TV show in America, to come to Bloomington and do a thing on me. I said, "Absolutely not." They wanted to come to our house and my wife said, "Absolutely not." They couldn't believe that anybody would turn them down. I guess in America where everybody wants to be famous, nobody had ever turned down 20/20 before. My publisher was upset; I did not give a shit. I just simply would not do it. What I agreed to do, mainly because my publisher's gonna send me out on a big tour, is agree to be a talking head, talking about college sports. So ABC did a piece about this woman at Tennessee and the academic fraud scandal there. They flew me to New York. We went up to Fordham at their football stadium. Now I knew these people are weasels, and my agent said, "These people are weasels, and they're gonna ask you about Bob Knight." I said, "yeah, I know that." And whenever they do I'll just say I will not answer that. And they did, they tried to work it in to Bob Knight a couple of times and I said, "Look I told you beforehand I would not answer those questions." So that's really my position.

That's why they call it "Done" Meadow

Pat Williams

Pat Williams is Senior Vice President of the Orlando Magic and has served as General Manager of the Chicago Bulls, Philadelphia 76ers and the Magic. Raised in Delaware, educated at Wake Forest, in 1967 he was the baseball Minor League Executive of the Year. He and his wife Ruth are the parents of 19 children, 14 of whom are adopted. Williams has written 19 books, his latest being Marketing Your Dreams, *an account about Bill Veeck, baseball's master promoter. Pat Williams starts or ends every conversation with a metaphor on life—even on his answering machines.*

Courtesy of Orlando Magic

Pat Williams

Let me go way back to the Olympic trials, Colorado Springs, 1972. I'm the GM of the Chicago Bulls out looking at the trials, and Bobby Knight had just taken the IU job. He comes over to me, introduces himself, we have a nice visit. He asks me if I would be willing to help whenever possible on recruiting, which in those days you were allowed to do. You could have alumni and outsiders talk to players or put in a good word or call them up. You were allowed to do that, I think up until the '80s, and then the NCAA stopped that. I got my masters degree at Indiana so I had an IU background. And we had mutual friends, so I told Bobby "Yes, I would be very pleased to do that." But it never took place—he never called on me.

The next time I saw Bobby was four years later—I'm the GM of the 76ers in Philadelphia—at the Olympic trials in '76 in Bloomington at the old field house. They had set up bleachers for the scouts and all to watch. I was standing watching a scrimmage and I remember Wayne Embry, who was then with Milwaukee, was close by. Bobby came—almost stalking—over and I turned as if to greet him, and it was, "These blankety-blank bleachers are here for you to sit on. If you're not going to sit on the bleachers, get out of

In 1962, NCAA semi-final, Ohio State versus Wake Forest, Billy Packer had 17 while Knight failed to score. It was Knight's last college game as he did not play in the title game.

here." "That's just Bobby, you know," Wayne said as he was there trying to help me gather myself together.

Two years later in '78, I was invited to speak at a luncheon in Jacksonville, Florida. The Gator Bowl week was going on there, and they have a basketball tournament in conjunction with the football game. The University of Florida is playing, I think, Jacksonville. Indiana is one of the teams. It's a community lunch, and the basketball teams are all invited. The coaches are sitting up at the head table and Bobby Knight is off to my right at the far end of the table. I'm sitting next to John Lotz who at that time was Head Coach of University of Florida. The coaches are sitting at the head table; I get up to speak. As I'm speaking, Knight is there—I could see it out of the corner of my eye—he was reading a book. I deliver my address, and afterwards John Lotz came over and apologized for Bobby. I said, "John, what was that all about?" He said, "Well, I talked to him, and he said he wasn't going to listen to a phony." He said, "You sign high school kids—he wasn't gonna listen to you." Well, in 1975, we had drafted and signed Darryl Dawkins, "Chocolate Thunder," out of Maynard Evans High School here in Orlando, he was our number one pick. That was Bobby's explanation to John on why he was reading a book. We had signed a high school kid, which in Bobby's eyes was wrong. This was pre-now when high school kids are coming out all the time. Moses Malone had signed in '74, then we had drafted Darryl. This was not common, and this was Bobby's view. Apparently he was not gonna listen to me because we had signed a high school kid. That was over twenty years ago, and I've had no contact with Bobby since.

Who knows what and how the guy—tracing back into his past, and his roots—got this way?

Life's like a roll of toilet paper. The closer you get to the end, the faster it goes.

Hoosier Daddy

Clair Recker

Clair Recker is the father of Luke Recker, Indiana's Mr. Basketball in 1997. After two years at Indiana University, Luke Recker transferred to the University of Arizona. In the summer before his first year there, he was involved in a horrible automobile accident near Durango, Colorado. After a long recovery, he since has transferred to the University of Iowa to play for Coach Steve Alford. Ironically, Clair Recker has lived in Iowa the last six years and welcomes the opportunity to see his son play more often.

A Luke Recker story: On August 2, 1996, Alice Irene Girardot, ninety, lay dying in DeKalb Memorial Hospital in Auburn, Indiana. It was between 11 a.m. and noon when Marti Recker, a nurse at Memorial, realized the end was near for the beloved area resident who had twenty-one grandchildren, forty-four great-grandchildren, and seven great great grandchildren. She loved Indiana University basketball, DeKalb basketball, and Marti's son, Luke. Oh how she loved Luke. Was it possible, she wondered, to meet him? "Of course," Marti said, and phoned him at home. Luke was there and came right over. The tall kid was taken aback when he reached the doorway of the hospital room, for suddenly he realized the gravity of the situation; the room was crowded with hospital attendants and family members. But the way was cleared and he was ushered to the woman's bedside. She took his hand. It was five minutes before noon. "I'm going to be with you," she said to him with a smile. "I'll be watching you." She died at 12:13.

Luke Recker

I'm just nervous about saying anything at all because Luke's still playing and will still have to go up against Coach Knight. Coach Knight has his following of rabid fans who look at things from the perspective that Coach Knight is right. If he says it's right, it's right, regardless of what other people might say. Or even if things point to it not being right, it still doesn't matter. I think that was proven out when Knight was able to retain his job after the investigation. If that would have been me in my job, I wouldn't have lasted very long, and I can't imagine that anybody else would either.

I grew up in Ohio. I spent my whole childhood in Ohio and most of my young adult years there and when Luke was in the fourth grade, we moved to Indiana. When Luke was very young—preschool—he was already doing sports things that to me were amazing. Throwing a baseball, swinging a bat, which was the sport that I thought would really be the sport he would excel at and maybe make a living at. Right before his high school years, he made a choice to concentrate on basketball, after completing his eighth grade. He said he was going to start on the varsity basketball team as a freshman, and that was his goal at that point in time which seemed pretty audacious, and I said "Just be happy if you start reserve and get a little bit of varsity here and there." And it wasn't long into the season before he was starting varsity. He was no slouch. By the time he hit tournament time his freshman year, he was a very complete basketball player already—playing like a wing or a forward position, and I think it may have been as early as his sophomore year already, they were playing him at the point. He was fortunate to have a lot of good ball players around him. That's what he had always worked at—his ball handling. Even as a youngster, before he went to school, he was going toward those types of things.

As a father, I am exceptionally proud of Luke—obviously have been a Luke Recker fan ever since he was a young toddler. I really saw early on. I played at a small college back in Ohio, Bluffton College. Luke was just very good; it's hard to describe. I knew he was gonna be an exceptional ball player. He's a very good student, very intelligent kid, got a good head on his shoulders. He's got a sense of direction about him; he knows where he wants to go. He knew back in high school what his goals were—pretty far-reaching. He said in high school he wanted to play in the NBA.

Luke and I are about the same height—he's maybe a little bit taller.

In high school, Luke didn't really consider going to any other school but IU. The recruiting process happened so quickly with Indiana that it was just kind of a real quick whirlwind. Somebody evidently put Knight on Luke's trail and he saw a couple of tapes of Luke playing—never did come down and watch a game in person to my knowledge. After just viewing a couple of tapes said "Yeah, this is the kid that we need." Luke committed when he was still a sophomore. I think maybe that might have been the first time Knight was seeking a commitment from a sophomore. There were other players that I am sure he was watching at that time. As I understand it, the story is that Luke is the youngest player he ever recruited.

I've never talked to Knight very much. Our conversations weren't very long. The last time I had any communication at all with Coach Knight was the

Varsity is the British short form for the word University.

day Luke committed as a sophomore in high school back in '95. We had been invited to watch Indiana play Iowa, their last home game right before the NCAA tournament, and all the recruits were coming in on that day. But we didn't really know that Knight wanted a commitment. Luke was invited down as a recruit so obviously we went and saw the game. Indiana won. It was a fun atmosphere. We had great seats. It was something I enjoyed and we had a good time. We spent some time with Knight at that time. He asked Luke how he enjoyed it. Luke said, "It was great, we had enjoyed it." But we didn't know that the express reason for Luke being down there was for Luke to make a commitment at that point in time to go to Indiana. We didn't know that.

It came back to us, what's the matter, doesn't Luke like Indiana? They said he didn't commit. We said, "What's the deal?" So we went down two weeks later and met with Knight and his staff and at that point in time Luke committed to the program. We'd had no clue earlier that they wanted him to. We had no clue that was the reason he had Luke down there. We thought that he was interested obviously but didn't know how interested he was at that time. That is the last time I talked to Bob Knight.

There were other schools interested. John MacLeod at Notre Dame was very interested in Luke because I sent Luke to a basketball camp there when Luke was going into seventh grade. Luke wanted to go to camps before that but I had said, "No, your camp will be in the back yard." I had put in a real nice court back there and I said, "I think I can probably teach you as much as you need to know" because I not only played collegiately but I coached in high school; until I got out of education and went into industry. I said, "You just work out here and when your time's right, we'll send you." Then Notre Dame had a camp and he asked about it. I said, "Okay, I think you're ready for it now." Then he went and John MacLeod called and said, "Hey, your boy's a good ball player." I thought it was a friend of mine just playing a prank on me. Then when I finally realized that it actually was him, I thought "Holy Cow," you know. Notre Dame wasn't a real solid basketball school at that time but MacLeod was serious about trying to build a program and get them back on the track and get them back to the level of success they'd had previously when Adrian Dantley and Kelly Tripucka and Laimbeer and Paxson and those types of players were there. But it was close enough to home that when

Of the top twenty individual scoring games in NCAA Tournament history, only one name appears more than once: Austin Carr of Notre Dame. He has the top, three of the top five and five of the top thirteen.

he left Indiana in '99 he thought he would at least be courteous enough to take an unofficial visit there. So he did, and he really kind of agonized over that a little bit.

IU was just a situation for him where Luke felt he wasn't getting the opportunity to develop like he felt he needed to develop to try to get to the next level. He could have had a great career at Indiana. I mean he had a great career at Indiana in the two years he did play and did very well.

If Luke would have been playing the off-guard for Indiana, I'm sure he would have stayed. I'm sure he would have completed his career out there. It was a matter where he really didn't feel he was getting the chance to develop his skills and Luke didn't blame Knight or anything like that because Knight was doing what was best for his team. And I don't blame Knight for it either.

After his freshman year, Luke went to Knight and said, "Coach, I want a situation where I can actually talk to you where I can have a relationship with a coach who will talk to me, who would say, "Hey Luke there's a game coming up, what do you think?" Or talk to me during the course of the game and say, "What do you think?" Just have a relationship you know. Luke said, "I really want to play guard. I want to get to the NBA. I made no secret about that when I came here, and I don't think I'm gonna get there playing small forward." So Knight promised him his sophomore year, he would give him a minimum of half of his minutes at guard so he could start showcasing or honing his skills as a guard. It never happened. It never happened. In fact it appeared that Knight was going out of his way many times to embarrass Luke with a situation. It was like he said "Okay, I had to agree to do it, but by God I'll tell you what. I'm gonna just show you the kind of man I am, I'm not gonna do it." Luke was still kinda willing to grit it out, but the thing of it is, it became very obvious from the reports we were getting back from people who really were concerned about Luke's future saying, "Luke, you can't stay. If you stay, you're going to . . ." I mean it's like Damon Bailey—his junior year. It was just like he lost all confidence. It was a lost year for him—he probably was in Knight's doghouse. Damon did have a good senior year, but by that time it was just like the pros said, "Hey," and they gave up on him. If you're gonna make the pros, you've got to progressively get better, you can't sit back there and have a relapse.

Damon Bailey played thirteen years in grade school, high school and college and lost at home only twice.

The information we were getting from sources that we know were saying, "Playing forward is not helping you at all, in fact quite the contrary." You've got to trust some people. These weren't malicious people. These were people who were genuinely concerned for Luke and his well-being and saying what's important to you. And it's not that Indiana wasn't but again if Luke was going to reach his goal, and again Luke's not shy about saying it, Luke wants to play in the NBA. He doesn't only just want to play; he wants to be a very good player in the NBA. In order to get to that level, he needs to start competing and practicing in a situation where he can really hone his guard skills and that just simply would not have happened at Indiana. So it was more of a business decision than anything else. It was a tough decision, a very emotional gut-wrenching decision because he really did enjoy his teammates and playing for Indiana. But by the same token it was just almost strictly a business decision. Now, unfortunately, that's the way college athletics are for players who have the capability of playing beyond that level. You've got to look at a situation that's going to be best for you.

Now there's a lot of players that will never have that opportunity. There are a lot of players who simply going to IU is a great situation for them—playing four years for Indiana, having four years of notoriety, probably a nice job offer when it's all complete. But in my mind, for kids who really aspire to achieve greatness, there's probably other programs out there that are better suited. Like a Duke, obviously, or a North Carolina or Florida and, hopefully, soon here at Iowa, that can get you to that level quicker.

At the end of his sophomore year, Luke didn't want to go through it all again. It was a bad situation. It wasn't too long ago that Knight had the number one recruiting class in the country. That's when Neil Reed and Andrae Patterson and Charlie Miller and all those guys came in. Andrae was the man, he was chiseled and stuff and Charlie was a good ball player. And by the time they were done, Andrae was sitting on the bench and Charlie was hardly ever getting off the bench, and of course Neil went someplace else. Richie Mandeville, another story, never got the opportunity. Were all these guys overrated in high school? I don't think so. It's just that I think Coach Knight tried to break them down and build them back up again in the way that he wanted to build them back up again and today's ballplayers are different in that regard. If you're a really good ball player, you've got to really think twice about whether or not Indiana is the right place for you.

Andrae Patterson and Charlie Miller are not bad kids. I met those kids, great kids. That's what they were—they were kids. I think there have been some kids who have had some real issues with that, trying to determine—who struggle with "Am I really as bad as Coach makes me out to be, am I really that bad of a person?" I look at the situation and think there's different way of conducting business. I've never been a Coach Knight fan ever. When Luke told me he was leaving after his sophomore year, I said, "Are you doing it for sure this time?" And he said, "Yes, I'm doing it for sure." I said, "Well, good." Because Luke and I had a lot of conversations and I didn't want him going to Indiana in the first place. That was his choice to do that. I didn't know at that time where I would have wanted him to go, but I told him, "Luke, you're going to be such a fantastic ballplayer, you can literally go anywhere in this country that you want." But being from Indiana and being an Indiana boy, basically he became kind of a folk legend at the age of sixteen. It's pretty hard to tell a kid when you're dealing with that kind of adulation from everybody across the state saying, "Hey, don't go someplace else." Because we all know what happened to Eric Montross when he decided not to go there. That kid was vilified.

On the website, on the Indiana Independent Basketball Forum, there was a statement by someone when Luke first announced that he was leaving IU that they hope he never gets to play again just because he's left their program (this was before the accident). I used to go onto it and read it just to see what people were saying when Luke was playing. I never participated; I was just kind of a 'lurker'; I guess is what they're called, where you sit back and read what other people have to say. Sometimes it's pretty aggravating stuff that they write and the only way you can respond is if you have a password and I'm not a techno so I didn't get into that. They said he did the unmanly thing—he at least could have faced Coach Knight and told him what his concerns are and tried to work it out. They don't know he had done all that the previous year, but that did come out later. Luke won't comment to that regard and I think that's good.

People who reside on this basketball forum are just Knight fanatics where Knight can't do anything wrong. But unfortunately I was reading the bad stuff; I wasn't reading much good stuff. They got an issue on there you are not allowed to say anything good about Luke Recker, you're just can't say it; they'll delete it. They'll delete the post.

It was not that Luke couldn't play for Coach Knight; it wasn't one of those deals like Neil Reed or Jason Collier got involved in. It was just one of those things where it boiled down to "Is this the best thing for me, in regards to my future?" And did a lot of things happen while he was there? I suppose they probably did but that wasn't the issue. I'm sure things happen all over the country and in different programs. It strictly was kind of a business decision for Luke to make and I think he made the right one. I think it was necessary for him to go to a different program so he could get himself ready to have a real legitimate chance to further his opportunity to have a career in the NBA.

I'm sure Knight had a difficult time when Luke transferred. But there again, he didn't communicate anything about it. I think for a while it was kinda sad in a way—I think there was some talk afterward. Luke, I think, was very gracious in saying "I appreciate the chance for playing here, and I have a lot of respect for Coach Knight," which he does. And he said "I have no one to blame but myself for my lack of development but I want to go to a program where I think I can develop better." Again in regards to Luke, after his freshman year, he really was considering a transfer at that point in time. And it wasn't a pleasant face-to-face meeting that he had with Coach Knight. He didn't want to go through a situation that was difficult for anybody at that point in, Knight himself, or anybody associated with the program so he faxed Coach his transfer. I know people really give Luke a tough rap on that one, but again they don't know what he had experienced the previous year. They said he took the coward's way out. But he just didn't want the confrontation and stuff because he knew it would be confrontational and that's not a healthy situation.

After Luke's automobile accident, he heard from a lot of people, including some IU people. Keith Smart called and talked to him. Luke's teammates called and talked to him. He got cards and stuff from IU. To say that IU wasn't supportive of him, that's not true. There's a lot of people from IU who were wishing him a speedy recovery. I don't think that any of the coaches contacted him but I don't know that that was a directive or not. He has a lot of fondness for the people back at Indiana and it was not anything malicious that he did. It was just him looking forward to the future and what was in his interests and frankly IU just didn't figure in his development, or his plans to develop as a ball player anymore. Because it was pretty apparent that he was gonna be relegated to a small forward position for his whole career there, and that would have seriously hampered his chances. He felt he really had to transfer.

Keith Smart's shot to win the 1987 National Title came at the very same minute that the movie "Hoosiers" was up for an Oscar. Keith Smart was an usher in the Superdome as a Boy Scout, the arena where he made the shot to win the title.

But the way it worked out, Luke decided on going to Arizona instead and really it was one of those deals where I was hoping that he would go to Iowa. Even though I knew he was gonna be not on scholarship anymore, I really felt, 'cause I went to both Arizona and to Iowa visits with him. It really boils down to they were both great coaches and both great programs. Arizona obviously was the better program, as far as talent-wise, but I really think that Coach Alford is going to put something together at Iowa and Luke could be an instrumental cog in making that happen. So anyhow he went to Arizona and then he committed to Arizona and then the accident happened.

After the accident, my son-in-law called me and said Luke was in Colorado and was in a bad accident and thought he was close to Durango. I had my lady friend get on the phone and call Durango to see if there was a hospital there. She got the hospital and they wouldn't tell her anything so I had to go on the phone, and they confirmed he was there. I had my friend call the airport in Cedar Rapids and had her get me a flight reservation at six o'clock in the morning. I didn't even—I just threw stuff in a bag and drove up and waited at the airport for four hours.

I had to fly into Denver, then to Durango so this was not an easy trip at all. I was there at the hospital in Durango when Luke finally woke up. A male nurse asked him at that time, "Luke, you need to wake up." They got him to awaken. "Luke, do you know this man?" Luke looked at me and said, "That's my Dad." Then he closed his eyes and was out for the next couple of hours. For the first couple of days he was only lucid for a matter of minutes—maybe fifteen-twenty seconds at a time. He absolutely doesn't remember anything of the accident and doesn't remember his hospital stay or anything like that.

Lute Olson was very classy. Luke has nothing but total respect for Lute Olson. Because Luke just, I feel pretty confident in saying that Coach Olson looked at the situation and, being the type of class person that he is, I know he really wanted Luke to stay at Arizona because he felt that Luke was kinda the missing link for another championship team for him. And maybe he'll still get one without him but it will be more difficult without him than it would have been with him. Really Lute is the type of guy that he put an individual's well being in front of his own fame and fortune, if you will. He said, "Luke's got to do what is in his best interests, and I don't think Arizona is the right situation for him in regards to everything that's transpired at this time."

The last ten years, the University of Arizona has the best winning percentage in college basketball.

Iowa ended up being a better situation, and I didn't know it was going to happen. He called me and said, "Dad, this is what I'm thinking about doing." I said, "Well, I think that's fine," and I'm certainly appreciative of Coach Olson for going to bat for Luke and telling the NCAA that "hey this kid's been through enough. Let's don't penalize him any more by making him sit out a half season" just because he knew, too, if the accident hadn't happened, Luke would have been there.

It wasn't so much a basketball decision. He needed to get back to a comfort zone again and have some support, more emotional support than anything else. I have another child who plays basketball in the Big Ten as well—a daughter, Maria, a sophomore, who plays at Michigan State.

Luke doesn't have a scholarship at Iowa because the Big Ten has a rule that if you transfer within the Conference, you cannot get another athletic scholarship. I think it's to keep kids from jumping to another team in the Big Ten or having the opportunity to load up a team, I'm not sure. He qualifies to get in-state tuition because I'm a resident of Iowa and have been for almost six years and Luke's my dependent, and I claim him on taxes and all that. He's recovered from his accident.

Alford says there's no problem. He's never said anything. He doesn't want there to be a problem. I think part of the situation is that Luke obviously hasn't helped matters by deciding that Iowa was going to be the team that he would eventually end up with so that's not Steve's fault that Luke decided to come here

I think it's like anything else. It's no different than a lot of coaches. They're busy people. They're constantly recruiting and working on other issues so I don't think—I don't know if it's unusual or not. Do I ever talk to Steve Alford? Yes, I do. I just don't call him up on the phone, but I'm close enough. Last December, Coach Alford had asked Luke what he was doing for New Year's Eve. Luke said, "My Dad's taking me out for dinner at the Iowa Athletic Club." Coach Alford didn't need to do it, but he made sure he stopped by at the Athletic Club at least for a few minutes to say "Hi" and to talk a little bit. I'll be around Iowa City on occasion looking for Luke, and Luke will be out with the team playing softball or something like that which Coach Alford's a part of, too.

It has been interesting because a lot of people around here don't yet know that Luke will be playing at Iowa. We had a bit of a party here on Sunday. My girl friend sells real estate and she had some clients who had bought houses from her so we had them in. I was talking with a friend of mine and we were talking about Luke and this guy is a huge Iowa Hawkeye fan.

"Well it's a good thing we're about to football. Once football starts, basketball's right around the corner." I said, "Yeah, man, I can't wait. It's time for Luke to get back out on the court again and start playing some ball. I miss not seeing him out there because it's been a while." This guy said, "Are you talking about Luke Recker?" I said, "Yeah." He said, "Do you know Luke?" "Heck, yeah." He said, "How would you know Luke?" I said, "Well, he's my son." He looked at me and said, "Are you kidding me?" I said "No." I don't think he knew my last name at that time. Finally he said, "I can't wait till I go back to work so I can tell people where I was at." I said, "Well, you're in for another big surprise. Luke's actually going to show up with a couple of his friends, and you're going to get a chance to meet him." So when Luke came, the guy's eyes actually bugged out.

Cliff Hawkins, Luke's high school coach, is a good guy, too. He's been a huge support for Luke as far as somebody that Luke can actually talk to. In fact I think Luke thought that would be the kind of relationship he could expect in college, where you could actually call your coach and talk to him and spend a lot of time with. I know they still do that with Hawkins; he's a real good guy. Luke has a lot of respect for him and it's not just because of his coaching abilities but just because of his concern for his players. I wouldn't want to discredit Coach Knight or anything like that. He's like the Teflon coach; nothing will stick to him

I think Luke will do well because he's more mature and will be more relaxed. Not for anything that Knight might do or fear or anything like that, it's just that Luke's been through a hell of a lot. He had to grow up in a hurry and I think all the experiences he's had have not been all pleasant or all positive but they certainly, I think, have made him mature to the point where he can say, "I can deal with anything pretty much now."

I know you'll get maybe more information. I could probably say more, but again I'm not trying to assassinate anybody or anything like that, anybody's character.

Rodney King Probably Said It Best When He Said "Stop Beating Me"

Jose de Silva
Buddy Bonnecaze, Jr.

I told Bobby, "Hell, for 50 bucks, get the translator," but nooooo . . . he's a man of his convictions

Jose de Silva

Jose became famous as the policeman in San Juan, Puerto Rico, who arrested Bobby Knight at the Pan American games in 1979. He is now retired from the police force and is a lawyer in San Juan.

I was working that day because I was working security. I had been working since eleven o'clock in the morning, and this happened after one o'clock in the afternoon.

Well, what happened—it's been so long. Whatever happens, it's time the story be written with the truth. All these people, the politicians back in the United States they know everything that happened at the Pan American games in 1979. They know that Knight hit me. They know that he was extremely abusive in practice, and he punched me in my face. He did it because I called him over and asked him to please leave the basketball arena. The Brazilian women's team was there waiting to take the court, and it was long past their scheduled time. I called Mr. Knight over and asked him to please leave the basketball arena. He got my attention and told me he could continue to play, and the other people, the Brazilian women's team, could leave. His hour of practice was over, and he was using very bad language in front of those Brazilian girls. He said, "Get those dirty whores out of here." I remember, I said to him, "Watch your language because they speak English. Those people study in the United States, too. They don't need to hear stuff like that." That's what I told Mr. Knight. Mr. Knight said, "You take your ass out of here, too." I said, "Give me your name 'cause I'm going to report you." When I told him I was going to make a report, man, he just told me his name, and I looked down to write it in the notebook, and he hit me. He hit me with a closed hand that went to my face. When he hit me, I just jerked my head up and told him, "You're under arrest." I started to walk around the basketball arena. I asked him to come with me because, "You're under arrest." He said, "Listen, kid, get your hands off me, – – – – –." Because I had decided to mention him to the Committee of the Pan American games because that was the order that we had—to report things like that to the committee—the decisions that had been made by any participants of the games. So I asked Knight, and this guy first and this guy doesn't come out, and he hit me. At the time, I didn't know who he was—just a coach from the American team, but I didn't know who he was at that time. I know who he was after that and know he is Coach for the Indiana University. I played a little basketball and am a basketball fan. I was 34 years old at that time.

I don't expect it. I was writing with my head down, writing in my notebook his name, and I got hit, and he hit me really bad in my face. I had to go to the hospital. They told me to rest for a few days.

There were no other policemen there that day, I was alone. There were other civilian people around in the basketball arena looking for a place to practice, and they saw when Knight hit me and they called for more police because they believed that I needed some help there. The patrol came around and that's when I arrested him and put him in the patrol car. When I told the patrol that he hit me and I got assaulted, and Knight was arrested and Knight came to walk round the arena, and walk around and walk around, his helper, his assistant came around and told him, "Come on. The police say you have been arrested and let's go with him." I put him in the police car. I handcuffed him. He didn't fight back at that point. I just took him to headquarters and my commander called me and asked me what happened. I put him in the cell right there and waited for him to be in the front of the judge. The Chief of Police came to the headquarter to see whatever happened to Bob Knight and that was the whole story.

They told me to take him to the front of the judge to decide if he was guilty.

People here in Puerto Rico think Mr. Bobby Knight is a man who has no respect for the police, no respect for the Puerto Rico people, no respect for the human things—no respect for nothing. That is the opinion of the Puerto Ricans. He was in a cell by himself, it wasn't long, he wanted to take some bodyguards. I saw him again on TV that night. They gave him a chance to participate in the games and be in the basketball arena that night.

But before that he was bailed out and then the judge said he had to take charge of his team and he left him without bail with a representative and after that when the game was over, he left Puerto Rico. He never came back. He was in the cell in police headquarters about fifteen minutes

This other night, back in '79, Knight went to another guy of his home team, Isiah Thomas, he was a player on the Indiana team. When they were practicing in another basketball arena, Knight grabbed him by the ears . Other people were in the basketball arena that night; a representative of the team of Puerto Rico saw him doing that and said he picked really bad. In fact, Knight talked to Thomas really bad and picked him up by his ears.

I've been a policeman since 1966, and have retired from the police already in 1994. I'm a lawyer right now in my country.

I don't want to remember anymore that happens with Mr. Knight. I believe that somebody has to cut it out.

Then Coach Knight stuffed the accountant like a Thanksgiving turkey; go figure

Louis "Buddy" Bonnecaze, Jr.

Buddy Bonnecaze, Jr. is an accountant and investor in his hometown of Baton Rouge, Louisiana

This was 1981 at the Final Four in Philadelphia. I'm there with the LSU Alumni Association. LSU played Indiana in one of the semi-final games and Indiana won. It just so happened that the Alumni Association was staying in the same hotel in Cherry Hill, New Jersey as the Indiana basketball team. We go back to the hotel after the game and we're out on the porch having a couple of drinks and a couple of friends of ours came up, and I said "Well if y'all want a drink, I'll go get you one." So I go into the bar and order them a drink

And as I'm walking out of the bar, Bobby Knight walks in, so I just said one word. I said, "Congratulations." Of course, I had an LSU shirt on, so we just kinda pass. Then I hear this voice saying, "Well, we weren't your goddamn Tiger Bait after all, were we?" You know LSU has a cheer about "Tiger Bait," the LSU Tigers you know. I just turned around, 'cause the way he said it was obnoxious, you know how everybody calls him an ass-hole. So I said, "Well you are an ass-hole." We were about fifteen—twenty feet apart; he had walked on into the bar. He gets this mean look in his eyes, and he said, "You care to repeat that?" No, that's not what he said. He said, "What did you say?" I said, "I said you're an ass-hole." He comes running over to me. You know he's six feet, five inches tall. And he puts his nose about a half-inch from mine. He says 'You care to repeat that." I said, "Yes, you're an ass-hole." Course I didn't think the guy was gonna do anything. You know this guy Neil Reed that he choked, and then Knight said, "I never choked anybody." Well, I know he's a liar, because that's exactly what he did to me. He grabbed me by the throat and he shoved me backward and he squeezed on my neck as hard as he could. In fact, I went to the doctor just to document it 'cause I had some contusions all around my neck. I mean it scared me. I didn't think the guy was gonna hit me. And he just squeezed as hard as he could and he pushed me down and there was a big plastic garbage can. And when he pushed me back, choking me, the garbage can just kinda crumpled behind me. Of course, the story was embellished about throwing me into the garbage can. Luckily, there were a couple of Indiana assistant coaches who grabbed him as soon as he grabbed me. It was just about a second or so that he squeezed me, but he squeezed my neck as hard as he could. It hurt, and it startled me, and I couldn't breathe for just a second or two.

The reason he was staying at the hotel was a friend of his owned the hotel. So somebody from the hotel came up and started giving me a hard time. I said, "Whoa, wait a minute, I was just assaulted here." They said, "No, no." I said, "Well, I'm gonna call the police then. This is ridiculous! Y'all getting on my case about bothering Bobby Knight." So I tried to get an outside line; they wouldn't even give me an outside line to start with. I said, "If y'all don't give me an outside line, we're gonna really have a problem." So they gave me an outside line and I called the police, and the Cherry Hills, New Jersey policeman came. He got statements from several people there, and it was obvious that Knight had assaulted me. The policeman told me if I wanted to have him taken downtown and booked for assault, he would do it. To be honest with you, I didn't want to get my name in the paper and all that kind of stuff so he said, "Well, let's come into a room."

So the policeman, Bobby Knight and I went into a room. Knight was still just defiant. So we go into the room, and I had a couple of friends of mine who were attorneys who were on the trip with us. I don't remember for sure if they went into the room with us or were just outside. But anyway, we go in the room. So then the policeman is telling Bobby Knight that he had taken statements from independent people and they said that you assaulted this Louisiana man and I'm trying to see what y'all want to do. Knight just looks at me and said, "Do what you want to do." I came within a hair right then of saying, "Take him downtown." And if I'd have known my name would have gotten in the paper and all that, I would have done it, but at the time I said, "Aw, I don't know." We just kinda talked it out, and then Knight got a little more mellow as we sat there; we must have been in the room twenty or thirty minutes. At the end, he was more civil. He knew then, I think he realized he could get in a lot of trouble so then he started being a little nicer. Then he kinda got, "Well, I just thought you were one of those guys who were doing this or that . . ." I said, "All I did was say one word—congratulations."

The next morning it hit the newspapers, but the first ones I read didn't have my name in it. My wife and I went on a sightseeing trip that day, and when we came back, I just had a zillion messages in the hotel room, and my name was all over the newspaper and on TV. The local TV station interviewed me and several other people wanted to talk to me. I tried to be fairly low key about it and not get too involved in all of it. But just a zillion, I mean, every reporter in town wanted to talk to me, and I had a stack of messages.

Then, of course, we got all kinds of stories. Friends from all over the country—I got newspaper clippings from every newspaper in the country. Some of them were kind of humorous like "Two-fisted drinker"—that sort of thing. One of them said, I got stuffed in the garbage can but I never spilled a drop. All this kind of stupid stuff like that 'cause obviously that wasn't the case. The only thing I didn't like about it was it was almost like 'drunken LSU fan accosts Bobby Knight after LSU loses, or something like that, which was totally ridiculous. We had just had a drink ourselves and all I was doing was going in to get drinks for friends.

Knight had a press conference the next day and he said a bunch of LSU fans were outside their windows the night before hollering "Tiger Bait," "Tiger Bait." Could have been, I don't know, but I wasn't one of them.

When we got home, my wife and I have an office in the same building as an architectural firm, good friends of ours. They had a big banner put up, 'cause all those guys are artists, too, showing me getting stuffed in a garbage can. I took a lot of ribbing. I had to tell the story till I got sick of it.

From time to time, usually when Bobby Knight has an incident, people begin talking about my run-in with him.

I can't say I'm glad it happened but it has been a source of some humor in my life. Let's put it like that.

What Heisman Trophy winner has made the most money? The 1959 winner, Billy Cannon of LSU, was arrested for counterfeiting in the early '80s and spent almost three years in jail. Technically he is the only Heisman Trophy winner to ever "make" money.

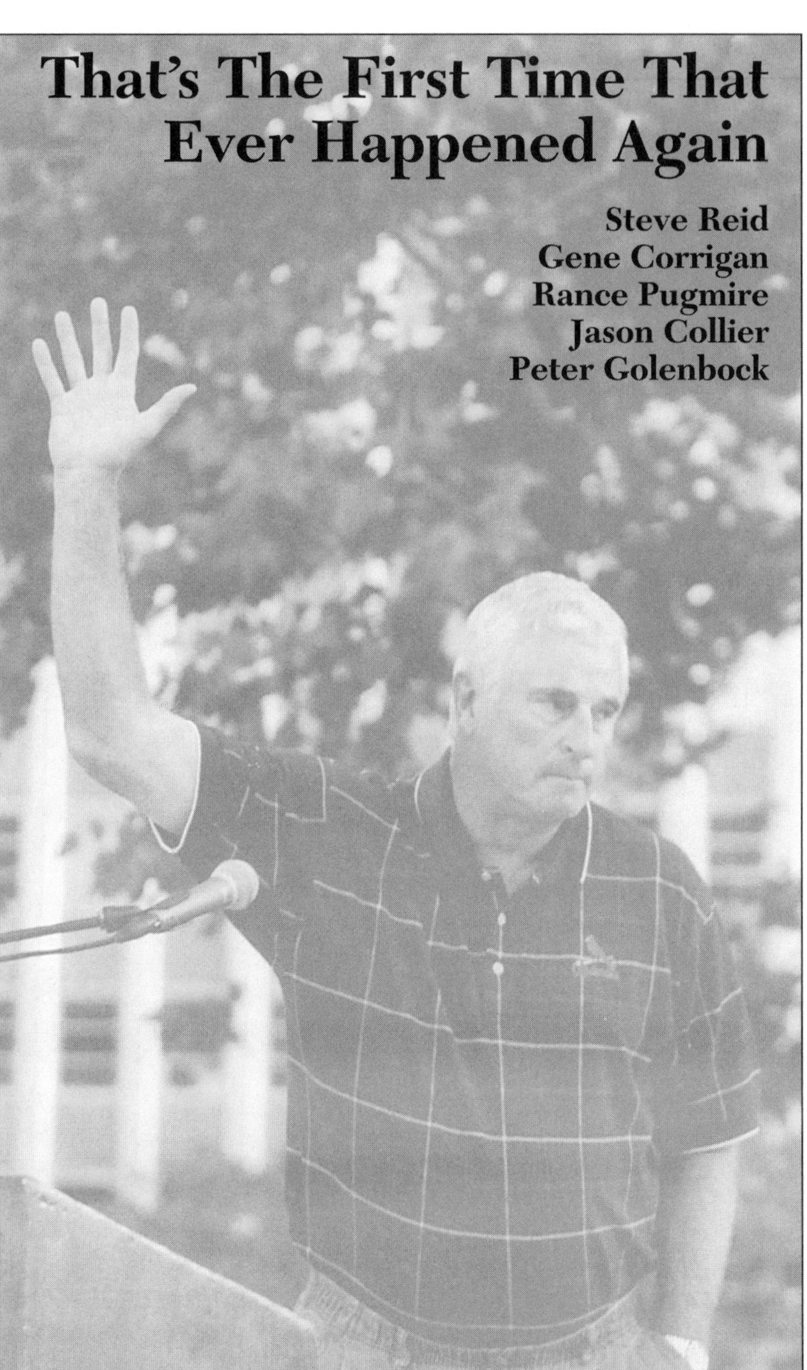
That's The First Time That
Ever Happened Again
Steve Reid
Gene Corrigan
Rance Pugmire
Jason Collier
Peter Golenbock

© Steve Bush/Spurlock Photography

A gentleman always gives up his chair

Steve Reid

Steve Reid is a footnote in college basketball history for the unlikeliest of reasons: He was preparing to shoot a free throw for Purdue early in a game at Indiana's Assembly Hall in 1985 when Bob Knight launched his plastic chair across the floor to protest the technical foul that had just been called on him.

Steve's father, Duncan Reid, is one of the most successful coaches in the annals of Illinois Prep Basketball. Seven of his former Rock Island Rocks played Division One basketball last year. Steve's brother, Bill, also played at Purdue.

For the last seven years, Steve Reid has done color commentary on the Purdue Basketball Radio Network. He is Vice-President of a Lafayette (IN) Trucking Company

What happened was I didn't see it coming. I had no idea the chair was coming. I had the ball in my hands and was going through my free throw routine and all of a sudden this red thing came out of the corner of my eye. My goodness, what was that—and saw it was a chair. I was just getting ready to shoot a technical—the first of two free throws at the time. The chair came flying across. The first thing that went through my mind was to go pick it up. That's one of the things my Dad taught me growing up. If you want to get "brownie" points with the officials, if there's a loose ball go get it and bring it to them and don't make them have to chase it down. My instinct was to go pick up the chair and as I was running over, I thought what am I going to do with it if I get it? Oh, probably just take it back over there. Fortunately a security guy was there and said, "No, we'll take care of it." As I was going back to the free-throw line, I thought that's got to be two more technicals. So that's six free throws. We've got a chance to get a pretty good lead here. That was the first thing that went through my mind. After that I got six free throws. I make the first two, miss one, miss the next one, turn around and Coach Keady is yelling at me—"Get off the line, let somebody else shoot." I kinda did one of these "No, I'll make these." Turn around and miss the next one—number five. The crowd is going berserk. I'm thinking I've got a couple of choices. I can somehow make this next one or I can miss it and go in the locker room with Coach Knight and watch the game 'cause I do not want to face Coach Keady. Next one went in somehow and that was it.

I get calls from friends every once in a while saying "you were on TV again last night." One called to say "you were on David Letterman last night."

I said, "That had to be the chair throwing incident." About three or four days after the game, when it had gotten so much coverage in the newspaper, controversy and everything else, I knew this was one of those stories that was gonna stick and be told over and over. I guess it's better to be remembered for that than for nothing but there's a part of you that says. geez, you play basketball from the time you're five years old and you're always trying to get yourself and your game in shape, and improve and be a good player, and hopefully do some things that people will remember you for in your playing and then in a matter of about five seconds, that's pretty well swept out the window because the one thing they will remember first and foremost is you being at the line when Bobby Knight threw the chair. I have never talked to Coach Knight.

My brother Mike has a great story. He tells it, I wasn't there so I can't attest to it, but supposedly Mike was a junior at Colorado at that time. Colorado was hosting one of the NCAA regionals there in Denver. He was in the coach's office and one of the assistant coaches was talking on the phone, and Mike goes, "Who you talking to?" The coach said, "Coach Knight." I guess he had called there to get some tickets for somebody who wanted to go to that particular regional. Mike grabs the phone and says, "Coach Knight, I'm Mike Reid. I just want to tell you I don't appreciate you throwing that chair at my brother." Knight says, "Well if I didn't respect the son of a bitch, I would have hit him with the chair." That's the story my brother tells.

The one reason I would not go play for Coach Knight is that most of the time by the time you're a senior, only one out of five seniors make it to that level without being in the dog house. It is incredible the number of guys who look great as freshmen and sophomores at IU and you go "Man, this guy's gonna be good." Then by the time they're a senior they play five to eight minutes a ball game. I think he mentally beats the heck out of them. Or he's also one who, like some bosses when they hire a new employee, think that employee's gonna be the guy who's gonna take that department and turn it around and make it the success that it hasn't been. Then, two years later, they're disappointed 'cause that guy's not doing anything right either. I think he's got that syndrome of guys coming as freshmen and getting a lot of playing time 'cause he sees their good qualities and thinks he can build on those. Then by the time they're seniors, there are some new freshmen or sophomores he's gonna give the minutes to. It happens a bunch.

Wilt slept with 20,000 women; these guys haven't even peed that many times

Gene Corrigan

Gene Corrigan is a graduate of Duke University who later became Athletic Director at the University of Virginia, then AD at Notre Dame before becoming Commissioner of the ACC. He and his wife are currently enjoying retirement in the Charlottesville, Virginia area. Corrigan was present at the press table during Bob Knight's famous outburst in the 1987 NCAA regionals. Knight's banging of his fist on the table and causing a phone to fly into the air became a celebrated picture in sports.

I was sitting at the press table. Bob Knight had just gotten a technical, which really shouldn't have been called. I was making the point that the thing with Bobby was he thought he was right whatever he did because he was wronged. It doesn't make a bit of difference what you do—he should have gotten another technical. He was yelling and walking around. He was on the court; he was everywhere—just kind of embarrassing. Finally he came over to the table where Schultz, Hank Nichols and I were sitting. He looked at me. He said, "I don't know why I got the technical. I never cursed; I never did anything." And I said to him, "You'd better go ahead and sit down and shut up or you're going to get another one." So that's when he got mad and he banged the phone. He said, "Screw them or fuck it,"—I don't remember exactly what he said. He did use profanity.

Then we fined him ten thousand dollars, and I was disappointed—very disappointed—when he appealed the fine because the basketball committee couldn't allow coaches to come over in front of the committee and scream and yell and bang the table. For some reason, he felt, because the technical shouldn't have been called—you could argue that it should or shouldn't have been called, and I felt it shouldn't have—he was allowed to do whatever he wanted. It was just kinda Bobby. He just never understood why we were doing what we did. I guess we were the first ones who ever did anything like that to him.

The fact that it was on TV and everybody saw it—the media didn't really do anything more than we did. Once it was seen and everybody in the world saw what happened, that Bobby Knight, the coach at Indiana, could come up in front of the committee and act like that, we just felt like we had to do something with it. At halftime, he came over and thanked me for telling him to go sit down. He said, "I probably should have gotten another technical." Bobby was—when he'd get mad, he'd get mad. He changed so much, though. Now it seems he always tries to put the blame on someone else.

I've known him for a long time; we weren't good friends or anything, but I was at Notre Dame then and he was at Indiana. Being on the basketball committee, we were with him a lot. I didn't know he had been considered for a Notre Dame job before he went to Indiana. I don't think he would have been Bobby Knight at Notre Dame. I think he would have been a very different guy. They wouldn't have put up with all that. It probably would have been the best thing in the world for him to have gone there; he would have gotten all this out of his way and just coached. I think all the things that happened with him—they kept getting worse because he was allowed to continue to act the way he was acting, which was in so many ways improper.

Knight doesn't like playing the late games, and I don't think that game started until close to ten o'clock. Like all games, it was two hours or more because it was on television, and this was the first year of the drug testing—not anything the coaches wanted anyway and so nobody was particularly happy with the fact that we had the drug testing. Then we went in a special room, and three of their kids, the three best players, Keith Smart, Dean Garrett and Alford, couldn't pee. They were dehydrated. It went on and on. I was concerned. So I called Tom Jernstedt at the NCAA and I said, "Tom, it's 12:30, quarter to one, can't we just let these kids go?" And he said, "No, we can't. You gotta go back there and do it," and while I'm out of the room, Knight goes in and I come back, and there he is sitting in the room (No coach is supposed to be in there. But think about it, it's really late. He's got to play the day after and he wants the kids to be able to go get something to eat.) So I said, "All right, out of here, I want you out of here now. You're not supposed to be in here. Get out." He did; I got his trainer or manager and said, "I want him out of the building; get him out of the building; nobody is going to be able to pee with him around." He's just so high-strung. We found out the guy conducting the pee collection in there was a Purdue guy, too, which made it a little bit worse. He got out of the room. So probably the whole team was in the bus waiting for these guys. Then they all left and went to get something to eat, and then these kids, within ten minutes after he left, were out of there. It seemed to me to be an hour—a long time. I felt really bad for those kids.

Ralph Floyd, the Athletic Director at Indiana, called me the next morning. Bobby and these players were supposed to be at a press conference at eleven o'clock that morning, and he said, "Bobby isn't going to come." I told him, "Yes, he is going to come. That's part of being in this tournament. That's what you've got to do. There's not going to be any excuses." Poor Ralph. He said, "Oh, God." Five minutes after eleven, he walked in with the players. I walked up to Knight and said, "Now look, I know you don't want to be here, but just go up there and be charming." He started laughing. He went up there, and for over an hour, he was terrific with the media. He was unbelievable. He could surprise you that way. I had never experienced anything like that. They were playing in the Hoosier Dome. The next game they played, I happened to be standing in the entryway when Knight came out and we were chatting for a second. Then I said to Knight, "There's 40,000 people out there and 30,000 of them are in red—the noise is just deafening." Whenever Knight walked on the floor, the noise got even louder. I said to him, "Coach, let me walk out on the floor with you; I want to know what it sounds like to have 40,000 people cheering for me."

He just looked at me with a little smile and said, "Gene, you'll never know." He winked and walked through the overhang onto the floor and 40,000 people went crazy.

In July of 1984, the first basketball game was played at the Hoosier Dome before a United States record crowd of 67,596 people. It was Bob Knight's Olympic team versus NBA Stars such as Larry Bird and Isiah Thomas.

The DOs and DON'Ts of dealing with Bob Knight—don't

Rance Pugmire

One of Bob Knight's most famous rantings—and most replayed on TV—was at an NCAA Tournament post-game press conference in Boise, Idaho in 1995. Indiana had just been eliminated by Missouri.

Rance Pugmire, now the Athletic Director at Utah State, was the moderator of the press conference and the recipient of Knight's tantrum. At the time Pugmire was the Regional Development Director for the University of Idaho.

Courtesy of Utah State University

Rance Pugmire

Boise . . . Let me try to remember back. Each school is assigned a volunteer as a liaison with the media room I had been the SID there for four years.

Looking back, it was an 8–9 game (referring to NCAA Tournament seeds)—one of those real close ones. One of the Simeon twins from Missouri tipped one in at the buzzer to beat Indiana. At the end of a game, you have a ten-minute cooling off period. Then the losing coach comes for ten minutes. Then the winning coach comes for ten minutes. The media come in, you have the sports comments, then you have to get them back out to the court to cover the next game. Then the next game starts approximately thirty minutes after the previous one

Ten minutes comes around—no Indiana. Finally the volunteer shows up and says, "They say they're not coming."

Locker rooms are open to the media after that ten-minute cooling off so I just made the announcement "It appears Coach Knight has been delayed. There is some difficulty getting them here." I didn't say, "Coach Knight refused to come." I didn't say that. I just said, "There's been some confusion

The NCAA did not start seeding teams until 1979.

and some delays getting here. But the locker rooms are open to the media, and I'm sure he would be happy to take your questions there."

In the meantime, I'm looking down the hallway, and Missouri Coach Norm Stewart, and his players are standing there and he is looking at his watch as if to say "What's going on?" So we get Coach Stewart up, and he makes his statement and the players talk. They're part way through, and I look down the corridor again and there's Coach Knight. So we excused Missouri. By now it's well past, way over for the time allotment, almost time for tip-off for the next game. I go down the hall to meet with Coach Knight and say, "Hey Coach we apologize for the mix-up. I'm gonna tell them It's our fault. We'll handle this thing." And he was upset and got after me then, and that's fine, it didn't bother me.

Knight comes up and I had made the statement, "We appreciate Coach Knight sticking around and coming. There was some confusion on trying to get coach and players out here, and Coach, again, we apologize and are glad you're here." Knight makes an opening statement. About halfway through, he turns and goes off on me, and I don't remember to this day what he said.

But I do know that I said, "Again, Coach, we apologize. If we could just turn our attention to the questions, please." He gets through another one and takes off again, and I don't remember at that point if he did answer another question or two and then away he went. That was the extent of it.

One good thing that came out of this though is that the rule has been changed. The winning coach goes first now, which works better. If you think about it, this would have to be the last game of your season, you're in there saying goodbye to your seniors. It's always emotional. Your season's over. We're going home. What are we doing? It's hard to get in and out of there and get your wits about you in ten minutes. Whereas the winning coach comes in, "Hey, great job guys! Let's clean this up. Okay, let's eat at ten, practice tomorrow at three, now let's go watch half this game. Way to go." They're in and out.

So now they've switched it. The winning coach goes in, and gives the losing coach more time with his team before they come in. So that's a good thing to come out of it, and that's the way it should be.

So yeah, Knight knew he had to be at the Press Conference, and Indiana was notified, but it's tough to do. I was SID from '85 to '95 and have had that experience a lot in a number of different sports and a number of different sit-

In 1985, the NCAA expanded the tournament field to 64 teams.

uations. It's tough after a loss to be in that locker room with those kids—tears are flowing and you're upset. The fact that he was late—yeah he was supposed to be there, and that's what the rules say you've got to follow them, but I'm glad the rules changed because it makes it easier for everybody.

When you look at the whole thing, the real error that was made was when he went off on me—twice—and it's carried on satellites all over the country. That's how high-strung the guy is; he's intense; he's very, very competitive. Did he need to go off? Absolutely not. Did I take it personal? Absolutely not. He'd have done the same thing to anybody else. Honest to goodness, it didn't bother me.

There's only one camera in there. Maybe the clips have been narrowed down to where there's only him in it, but as you open you see me and as you close you see me. If you see the whole thing, you can see me, because I got calls from my buddies all over the country that day, about ten at home that night. You know, people sitting in a restaurant or bar and look up and say, "Look what Coach Knight's doing. Oh my god, that's Rance."

I got a lot of calls; they were kidding me. I got a lot of "Hey, this is Coach Knight calling. Do you want to go fishing?" Or, "Coach Knight said to drive you off a cliff." They were all from different area codes in the country.

You hope these aren't the things Coach Knight is remembered for because he's had a tremendous record for winning, tremendous record graduating players and doing things the right way. Unfortunately, there's these other incidents that seem to take precedence over anything else you talk about when you talk about Coach Knight.

There are only five Division One schools without University in their names: Boston College, Georgia Tech and the service academies.

• • •

The rights to "Ramblin' Wreck from Georgia Tech" are owned by Paul McCartney. The rights to most Beatles' songs are owned by Michael Jackson

• • •

In the 1998–99 season, the leading scorers for Georgia Tech, Rutgers and Southern Mississippi were all former Indiana University players.

Notre Dame, Indiana, Georgia Tech.—this guy doesn't know what a bad fight song is

Jason Collier

At Notre Dame High School in Springfield, Ohio, Jason Collier was Mr. Everything. He was arguably the highest-rated recruit Bob Knight ever got out of his home state.

Collier played his senior year at Georgia Tech and was drafted by the Milwaukee Bucks and traded on draft day to the Houston Rockets.

The University of Notre Dame sued Collier's old high school for using their leprechaun's likeness—a tactic that didn't open a lot of recruiting doors for the Irish.

Jason Collier

I went to IU because it was basically close to home. My parents could come to see me play. It was just a good area for me to go and it was the biggest basketball place so a good place for me to go. I was recruited by Knight. At about the beginning of my sophomore year, a little bit at the end of my freshman year, was when things started to fall apart for me. I left there after my junior year. I read *Playing for Knight* by Steve Alford.

I remember one time when Knight came to my house on a recruiting trip. My grandmother, who is a no-nonsense kind of lady, grabbed his face—his mouth, shook it from side-to-side, and asked him why all those dirty words came out of his mouth. I'm going "GRANDMA!" Knight's face got beet red, and he turned and looked at her and said, "Well it won't matter what kind of words come out of my mouth, but what good things I'm gonna do for Jason."

The difference between Bobby Knight and Bobby Cremins, my coach at Georgia Tech, is "night and day." There's no pun intended.

Gee, where did Mike go?

Peter Golenbock

Pete Golenbock saw up close what happens when a highly touted Indiana player transfers. While writing a book on Jim Valvano and North Carolina State Wolfback he got to know and like a young man named Mike Giomi.

Golenbock has written over 30 sports books and has Mickey Mantle, The Last Autobiography *scheduled for publication in 2001.*

Giomi had been selected Ohio High School Player of the Year in 1982, and as sophomore at the Indiana University he had helped shut down Michael Jordan and then hit the clinching free throws in the Hoosiers' 78–68 win over North Carolina in the second round of the 1983 NCAA tournament.

Bobby Knight had dropped Giomi in the middle of the 1984 season, and though he looked a little rusty, everyone at State was figuring him to be a strong rebounder and an enforcer for the Wolfpack.

Giomi's departure from Indiana had been something of an enigma. Giomi was such a picture-perfect forward that Coach Knight had used him in his instructional films.

The official story on Giomi's departure was that Giomi had broken Knight's hard-and-fast rules about how many classes a player could skip, so Knight dropped him. Giomi had a 2.4 grade-point average at the time.

Giomi disdained talking about his experience at Indiana. When asked about Knight, his usual reply was, "I see things differently from him, and I'm going to be happy here."

One thing Giomi did comment on was the difference in approach between Knight and Valvano. At Indiana, Giomi once observed, "Some days we'd go to the gym without a ball. The whole two-hour practice was defense." At N. C. State, it seemed that the only time Valvano practiced defense was as punishment.

After reading *Season on the Brink*, John Feinstein's book about Knight, a N. C. State teammate asked Giomi, "Man, how can you take that verbal abuse so much?"

Giomi said, "You wouldn't dare grab him, because he's so fucking mean-looking and he's big. He's six-foot-five, two hundred twenty. You wouldn't dare challenge him."

The one story Giomi did tell was about the day he and one of his Indiana teammates had played badly against Minnesota. Knight refused to let them fly home with the team. "We had to fly back on a charter jet with the alumni." Giomi said.

Gee (Giomi) was a fundamentally sound, hard-working player. He ran the floor well and was tireless.

After one practice during which he was really struggling, one of Giomi's teammates had asked him, "Do you think Bobby Knight is checking the boxes on you?" Giomi said, "Yeah, he always checks on his former players." He looked sad. He said, "Coach Knight has seen all the boxes on me, and he's saying to himself, 'I was right about Giomi. I did the right thing.' "

Some of his more sympathetic teammates felt that the system had failed, rather than Giomi. "I knew he wasn't a failure," said a teammate. "Gee got ruined by Coach Knight, by Valvano, and by the NCAA that makes a player sit out a year when he transfers, even when it's the coach who forces him to transfer.

"Gee was a good guy, but he wasn't able to stick out four years of abuse by Bobby Knight, so he quit. And when that happens, it's Knight's fault, because he better know enough about each kid he recruits before he signs him to know he can pull his shenanigans on him and he'll still be there at the end."

"And then Mike comes to N. C. State, and everyone is thinking, 'He's a Bobby Knight product, he'll score thirty a game,' and he never comes close to that, and so the fans dogged him, booed him, called him 'slow' and 'flat-footed,' without remembering that he hadn't picked up a basketball in a year and a half."

"All he needed was someone to work with him. But Valvano wasn't the coach to do it, so Giomi was consigned to a seat at the end of the bench, disgusted and rejected."

Giomi's whole life would have been radically different if he went to a different college out of high school. Read the Mickey Mantle book when it comes out.

Hoops—There It Is

Dale Brown
Bill Frieder
Norm Sloan
Mike Krzyzewski

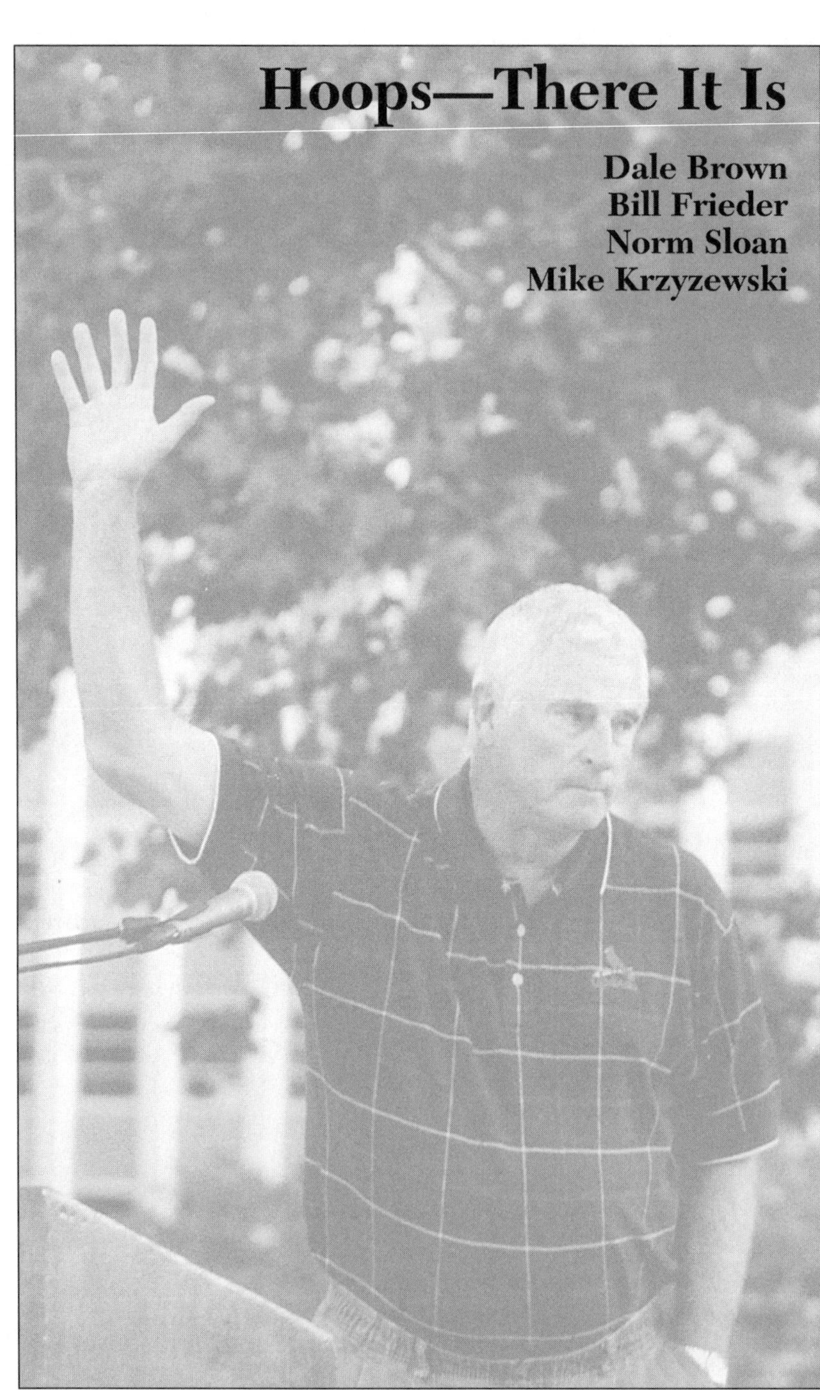

Personally, I think Knight has Post-ESPY Syndrome

Dale Brown

Dale Brown is a native of Minot, North Dakota and is the winningest coach in Louisiana State University history. He has traveled the world extensively and has written about it in various publications. He currently heads Dale Brown Enterprises in Baton Rouge, Louisiana.

Dale Brown

Tex Winter is one of the nicest guys in the world and he's now at the Los Angeles Lakers and was with the Bulls. He's in his late seventies maybe, and he used to be on a committee with Knight, and he would say "Knight always had to get the first hurt." Knight would come in and say, "Goddamn, Tex, where'd you get those damn clothes you're wearing—Salvation Army? They're shitty looking." Then he'd laugh, and people would go along. But, if you said that to him, he'd flip out.

I wasted a lot of time during the last decade doing something I really regret: feuding with Bob Knight. I should never have let the situation get to the point it did, but I'm glad to say that it is all behind us.

The first time we played against Bob was in 1981. We were in the Final Four and were playing them in Philadelphia. When one of the referees was running down the court, Bob stood up and said, "Get those guys off our back." The referee never said anything to Bob. The referee came down to me and said, "You sit down or you're going to get a technical." That told me this wasn't going to be a fair situation. The referee wouldn't say anything to Knight, but didn't hesitate to threaten me; I even ended up with a technical foul.

I just chalked that one up to experience. But in 1987, we played Indiana again. This one was for the right to go to the Final Four. We were twelve points ahead and the situation repeated itself. It all fell apart because everyone was afraid of Bob Knight. First, he got a technical foul for going out on the floor. Then he came over to former Notre Dame athletic director Gene Corrigan, who was at the official scorer's table as a representative of the

NCAA, and said, "You've got to do something about these blind bastards," pointing to the referees. Then he took his fist and pounded the phone sitting on the scorer's table so hard that the phone receiver popped up in the air. I looked at the NCAA people. They just sat there with their arms crossed.

I said to myself, "If I would have done that I would have been banned from the game. There would have been headline stories." Then Bob actually grabbed one of the referees by the arm before our player shot a technical foul. He kicked his bench, and the only reason the benches didn't fall over was because they were all attached to each other.

From that point on, those officials bellied up to Coach Knight. The rest of the calls in the game were in his favor. I went back and watched the film. Sure enough all but a couple of the next seventeen calls went for Indiana. On one play toward the end of the game, one of their players grabbed our ball handler and got a lot of body and a little ball. The referees called a jump ball. The ball went to Indiana. On another play, one of our guys got hit four different times while he was dribbling the ball near half court. They called him for five seconds. Coach Knight was later fined $10,000 by the NCAA, but Indiana went on to win the national championship in our home away from home—the Superdome.

I had a quick decision to make and my thought was not to shake the man's hand after the game, but just go on to the press conference. Then I realized I would be a poor loser. They beat us and I knew there would be a time and a place where we would get it back. I went on and shook his hand. I knew, however, that I had to do something about this. I went to the press conference and did not say anything about his tirade.

When I got on the team bus my daughter, Robyn, was there. She was very emotional. I said, "What's wrong, Robyn? We lost a game, big deal. We'll be back." She said, "That doesn't have anything to do with it, Daddy. What Coach Knight did, that was wrong. Especially for that old man." That sent a red flag up to me. I said, "What did he do?"

She explained it very thoroughly. She said, "I know he probably didn't recognize me, but when he came through the tunnel, he stopped and looked up into the crowd. With a diabolic look on his face he said, 'Hey, you LSU people. I stuck it to you again.' Then he turned to run into the dressing room. As he did there was an old man on the other side of the walkway. I don't even know if he was an LSU fan. The old man yelled to Coach Knight that he didn't think Coach Knight should talk like that, especially after winning the game. Coach Knight turned back and yelled an obscenity at him. too."

I took off out of the bus and headed for the Indiana dressing room. By the time I got down there, they were gone. I ran down the hallway just in time to see their bus drive off. As I headed back to our bus, Hank Nichols, the head of officials at that time, was coming out of a room. I called him aside and I said, "Hank, enough is enough. That conduct out there was ridiculous. You're the head of officials and you let him get away with that. Somebody's got to stop this man." Hank looked at me and shuffled his feet. "Well, Dale," he said. I interrupted him. "Don't give me that. It's the way you guys all start your sentences—'Well, Dale.' He's wrong and you know he's wrong." Hank said, "I'll admit he's wrong." So I asked, "why don't you say something about it, Hank?" He just walked away.

I went back and got on our bus, determined that I was going to face Bob with this. The next week at the Final Four in New Orleans, Bob Costas had me on his radio show and he said, "We understand you don't have a lot of respect for Bob Knight." I felt sure he was setting me up..I just said "Yeah." And Costas said, "Well, Bob Knight made a statement about you, too. He said that when Indiana was twelve points down, and it seemed as if he might lose the game, he looked over at the bench and saw Dale Brown was coaching. He wasn't worried anymore."

I said, "The way to settle this would be to put me and Coach Knight in a wrestling room naked and whoever came out first would be the best man. I'm sick of him bullying and kicking people around."

That made its way around pretty quickly. Then it got to be a name-called deal. He would say smart things about how he was not worried about LSU or Dale Brown. I would say something back. It was like two kids, and both of us resisted attempts by mutual friends like Pete Newell and C. M. Newton to get us together.

A year later, I was at the Final Four talking to Coach Bob Boyd. He was sitting at a table in a hotel restaurant and I was down on one knee beside the table. Over to one side were several of Knight's former assistants, Dave Bliss, Bob Weltich, and Don DeVoe. All of a sudden, I spot Knight. Man, my ears got red. I figured he was going to come over and talk to his assistants, so I would have a little confrontation with him. I was staring at him as he got near, but he wouldn't look at me. Knight walked by and he hit Bob Boyd on the back, but he did not say anything to me. I stuck my leg out as far as I could, hoping he would trip over it. I figured I would just deck him and get it out of my system. I looked like that old cartoon figure, the Plastic Man, with my leg stretched out as far as I could get it. Somehow he stepped over my leg and nothing happened.

Shortly after I hired Tex Winter, who was later an assistant with the Chicago Bulls, he told me a story. Tex said that one year he head tried to nominate me for the National Association of Basketball Coaches board of directors. Bob Knight was on the board of the NABC. He had mentioned to Knight that I would be a good choice for the position on the board. Bob said to Tex, "I don't want that cheatin' son of a bitch on this board." I got really mad. What he was saying was that we had to cheat to win, but Indiana doesn't have to. I had that in my craw for a long time.

Just as my disdain for him was really getting to be too much, a twenty-eight-year-old girl was killed in Baton Rouge. She was driving home and somebody threw a brick through her windshield and killed her. I was reading the story in the paper, and thinking about how painful it must be to lose your daughter like that. If that happened to our daughter, Robyn, I would probably become a vigilante.

A few days after the incident, a follow-up article was in the Baton Rouge newspaper. The police had found the killers. The newspaper interviewed the girl's father, a doctor by the name of James Upp. His wife had died of cancer prior to this happening, now his daughter was dead too. In the interview, the reporter asked Dr. Upp what he thought when he saw the picture of the young boys on television. Dr. Upp said, "Well, they certainly look like clean-cut youngsters and I have no malice or anger toward them. I am sure they did not mean to kill my daughter, and I forgive them. I only wish they could have met my beautiful daughter. I think they could have learned from her."

I read that story, and it just took everything out of me. I thought to myself that I wanted to live my life as Dr. Upp. I cut the article out and I was going to put it up on the bulletin board in my office. As I started to do so, I realized I was being counterfeit. I sat there knowing how much I disliked Coach Knight. I could not put that on my bulletin board as long as I had all that anger for him. That father could forgive those boys for taking his daughter's life, and I could not even forgive someone for something so trivial as our conflict. I put the clipping down on my desk and I opened the coaches' directory. I looked up Indiana University, and I dialed the number. The secretary answered the phone and I said, "Bob Knight, please." She asked who was calling and I replied, 'Dale Brown." I could hear her swallow hard on the other end.

Bob picked up the line. I started, "Bob, you can hang up anytime you want to but I want to tell you something. I want to tell you about an incident that happened here in Baton Rouge." I told him all about the girl, and then what Dr. Upp had said. Then I explained to him, "I was getting ready to put his clipping on my bulletin board, but I knew I couldn't because of my contempt for you. I'm going to tell you right now, if I'm going to put this clipping up, I want to bury the hatchet with you. I want to forgive you. And if I did something to ask for any of your actions, I want to apologize.

Suddenly, it was as though the whole slate was clean. He said, "Dale, I'm sorry." He apologized for the incident that had upset Robyn. He said, "I appreciate your call and I want to bury the hatchet. Maybe we can work on a friendship." From that day on it was as if a cross was lifted off my back because I'm not a hateful person.

A year later, I tried to reach out again, calling Indiana and offering Bob's son a scholarship to LSU after Bob suspended him from the team.

Calling him was one of the hardest things I have ever done. First of all, I didn't know what I would receive from the other end. And I wasn't humble enough to do that naturally. I'm sorry that it took a death to teach me that lesson. But anger and hatred only weigh you down and kill a part of you. By hating, you are really losing twice.

There's a difference between religion and spiritualism so I've always tried to be spiritual and do what was right. I do a lot of corporate speaking and one of the parts of my speech is that being a human being is so complicated that none of us can get it right and we're living under the false impression that God wants perfection. He doesn't. All he wants from us is to do our best and never give up—never give up, and he'll take care of the rest. You grow into spiritualism, too, I think you think you're more spiritual than you are. When you get out of the arena, you then look back and have more time to concentrate and ponder things.

The most powerful probing answer about, "What'd you think about Bob Knight getting fired?" came from Krzyzewski. He used one word—remember what it was? It was "tragic." And I think in that one word he was including Knight in it. Tragic how he acted. Tragic what happened to him. Tragic the Indiana situation. I think that was probably the most probing thing with only one word describing the situation but I don't think there's any question he needs help, and he'll probably never get it.

When the NCAA calls, ya gotta accept the charges

Bill Frieder

After an outstanding high school coaching career in Saginaw and Flint, Michigan, Frieder joined Johnny Orr's staff at the University of Michigan in 1973. He became head coach and put together Michigan's 1989 NCAA Champions before leaving for Arizona State. After Athletic Director Glen Schembechler was told Frieder was going to the Valley of the Sun, he wouldn't allow Frieder to coach the Wolverines in the Final Four. After being forced out at ASU in 1997, Frieder runs an investment company in Paradise Valley, Arizona. He is banned from most casinos around the world because of his extraordinary ability in playing Blackjack.

People make too big a deal out of Bobby Knight. You'd think he was the only coach, or maybe the only person, in the league. Whatever Bobby's doing is always the biggest news in the Big Ten. The only thing that comes close is what his team is doing.

The fans at Michigan's Crisler Arena were always their loudest and most involved for Michigan's games with Indiana. And whose face was on the Midwest editions of all the pre-season magazines? They even had a full-page ad for some investment company or something, half of which was a picture of him, in our own Michigan basketball program! I told our people to get it out of there.

I don't agree with everything Dale Brown says, but the former Louisiana State coach was right when he said Bobby tries to get his way by intimidating people—referees, other coaches, his players. Mort, my friend, says this is because he's (Bobby and Mort both, really) an only child and a Scorpio and that's the way they are. Mort pays attention to that kind of stuff; I don't. It wasn't gonna help me win games.

Maybe it's only the media that make too big a deal out of Bobby. With them, it's more like a manipulation. He gets his tail beat but the whole story is not the game. The whole story is something else, and then nothing happens to him. I saw that for fifteen years.

I remember Iowa was beating him in Bloomington one year and the whole story was about Wayne Duke and the officials. It was the game where he went to Wayne during one of the timeouts and ripped Wayne on the officials.

He picked that fight with me in 1984 after I beat him, or I should say my team beat his team—see how easy it is to fall into that, and here we go again. Here he was getting beat and the whole story is whether he did me a favor and his breaking into my press conference, and nothing about my players winning a great basketball game. They were young kids, and they had no business beating Indiana that day, but that's Bobby Knight.

And that's always what it seems to come down to. We beat Indiana in Bloomington by 12 points one season and the story was how this was Bobby's worst start ever at Indiana and the program was in ruins and "What's Wrong with the Hoosiers?" and all this bull.

Mort says Hank Hersch of *Sports Illustrated* told him that Knight is like the pivot that the league revolves around. Coaches are judged on how often they beat Knight, or whether they're pro-Knight or anti-Knight, and so on.

And, sure enough, after we beat them again, this time by 20 in Ann Arbor, the story was how I was now 8–8 against Bobby and I had won five of my last seven against Bobby and I had swept Bobby for the second time in three seasons. See? It was like now I was a good coach because I was .500 against Bobby.

Bobby liked me just fine when his teams were beating mine all the time. The trouble started when my teams started beating his. He and Johnny Orr were supposedly such great friends, but you notice Bobby beat Orr's butt more than Orr beat his. Now they're still great friends, but they don't play each other, either, do they? I don't think Bobby has too many friends among the coaches he plays regularly.

Some people say he just loses control of himself but I don't agree. He's setting the agenda and it's calculated. This man knows what he's doing. I don't think Bob Knight has ever lost control.

It's a fact that the Big Ten isn't going to discipline him, and neither is the NCAA. But what would happen if you worked for The University of Michi-

Big Ten Commissioner Wayne Duke and John "Duke" Wayne were once Co-Grand Marshals of the Rose Bowl Parade. The Rose Bowl Parade had nothing to do with roses. It was to celebrate the end of the orange-picking season.

• • •

Johnny Orr is the winningest basketball coach in the history of two schools: Michigan and Iowa State University. Bear Bryant, Dick Tomey and George Welsh have accomplished the same feat in college football.

gan or Arizona State and you threw a chair, or hit a policeman, or pulled your team off the floor? I'll tell you what, you wouldn't do it again. If you were lucky, you might get one warning, but I doubt it. How did it come about that Knight and I had a falling out?

It's funny that incident with him ever happened. If we'd had the coaching box back then, it probably wouldn't have. I would have had to work another official to get that other official to do what he had to do. I never would have gotten close enough to him for him to hear, or think he heard, what I said.

Even at that, there were a lot of coincidences involved.

First, there was the fact that I was at Crisler the Friday morning before the Indiana game, which was on a Saturday afternoon. We had lost to Ohio State, a team that hadn't won a game in the Big Ten up until then, at the buzzer Thursday night, so I didn't go to the office at all. I was at Crisler until five or six in the morning, might have gone home for a couple of hours, then went right back. Now maybe in another situation, I wouldn't have been at the arena at 11 in the morning, but I was.

Second, Indiana had played at Michigan State Thursday night, so they were there for like a noon practice. Normally, it's 5:30.

And third, John Viges of the *Ann Arbor News* shows up. So for this whole situation to happen required an unusual sequence of events. Usually I would come a little later, usually they would practice later, and usually Viges wouldn't be there, but it all happened.

So I walked out to say hello to Knight and Viges was out there. This was when Knight wasn't talking to anybody in the media, and Viges asked me if I could get him an interview with Bob. He must have found out somehow that they were practicing at noon, so he came over.

So I went out and Bob and I sat on the scorer's table. We got talking and I said, "Bob, they're on my butt because I didn't start Tim McCormick." Viges ripped me for not starting McCormick and the *Daily* ripped me for playing him 28 minutes because I knew he was sick.

McCormick hadn't been playing well. He got one rebound the game before Ohio State. So I said, "Yeah, they're rippin' my butt for changing the lineup."

He said, "Well, I've changed the lineup 17 different times already this year. What the hell has that got to do with it?"

I said, "Well, my guy's out there right now. He wants to interview you. Why don't you talk to him about it?"

He said, "I will."

That was it. That was the favor, okay? That was the favor I asked of him.

He said, "What kind of guy is he?"

I said, "He's a good guy. I want you to do the interview with him." So that was the favor.

Now, during the game, he was up berating the officials; intimidation, like he always does. None of that bothered me, except that my guy was waiting to shoot a free throw, and we're waiting and we're waiting and we're waiting for the referee and Knight to finish their conversation.

Finally, I said, "Either sit the SOB down or give him a technical." Probably five or ten seconds before I said that, the Ref had given him a technical, but I didn't know that. I must have been looking back at our end of the floor to see what was going on. Whatever it was, I didn't see it.

Knight claims that I said, "give him another technical," which I didn't, but it doesn't really matter what I said because he shouldn't have been taking up the time. We should have been playing. Let the kids decide the game, not him.

Then Knight came after me, calling me a chicken-bleep SOB and that kind of stuff.

He chewed me out all the way into the tunnel at halftime, calling me every name in the book, just like I read he calls his players. My biggest thing then, when I walked in-we were four ahead at the half-was, hey, we're gonna win this game. We are not letting his commotion detract from what we've got to do as basketball coaches. We did a great job in that locker room, putting all this behind us and coaching our team, instead of going in there bitching and complaining about Bobby Knight, which is what he probably wanted.

It's the same old thing. Bob Knight, if he gets beat, he wants to find a way to distract from his loss. Purdue's beating him, he throws a chair. Michigan beats him, he does something else. The Russians are beating him, he pulls his team off the floor. So that when he gets his tail beat and walks into a press conference, the story isn't the game, the story is what Bob Knight did, the story is some of his antics, and that's what happens all the time.

I started off the press conference by asking for a vote on throwing out Jim Spadafore of the *Detroit News* because he had written a story misquoting my players. I wasn't really serious-Spad's a good guy and I just wanted to have some fun with him-but I like to keep the press a little off balance and I wanted to relieve the mood.

I didn't even know there was a back door to the room where we have the press conferences at Crisler, but during the vote Knight storms in. It was quite a shock because like I said, Knight wasn't talking to the press then, or going to press conferences.

Well, he not only came to this one, but he also started off by making some sarcastic remark about how he didn't like to hear the media criticized. I said I hadn't realized Bobby was there and I'd let him talk and come back later. And then he laid into me, calling me more (but not very different) names, saying I had used him, talking about how much he had done for me, and so on. Lynn Henning, who was covering my team then for the *Detroit News,* wrote that "to anyone there, the whole ugly scene felt like a punch in the stomach." That covers it pretty well.

After he was finished and I came back, they all wanted to talk about Bob Knight. No one wanted to talk about the job my basketball team did in beating Indiana when they had lost by 27 points in Bloomington the year before.

When I got home that day, I told Janice, my wife, "You know, this is so ridiculous. As badly as I feel, and as upset as this guy has got me, I wish we'd have lost the game. You shouldn't have to go through something like this."

I honestly felt that. I felt that, hey, I don't want to go through this nonsense. If you can't compete against each other and then be friends afterwards, then who needs it? I was upset because I thought the guy was a friend, and a friend does not act that way.

He called me at my house that night. He called me at my house the next day. I didn't even want to talk to him, but I did, and I tried to defend myself. You could see that he was upset, that he was not going to bed, that he thought I was entirely wrong and disloyal or whatever. I think he wanted an apology.

He was upset at some of the things I said at the press conference, I forget exactly what. He said I lied to the press. I tried not to discuss it, but he had on tape everything that I said. He was upset that I did not admit that he did me a favor, that was the crux of it. We just kind of got into it again, so it just never got settled.

I don't remember ever calling him after that. I answered his calls a couple of times within the next year or so, but I didn't talk to him at the press conferences and meetings. We really haven't talked since then, and that's fine with me.

He did get a hold of me after many attempts in Charlotte at the NCAA tournament in '87 because my manager screwed up and said I was there after I had not taken the call. He wanted to congratulate me for beating Purdue. I was going to prove to the world that I don't need favors from him to have a successful program.

He's the type of guy who, when this happened, called everybody. Everybody. He called coaches. He called media people. He called mutual friends. He wanted to tell them his side of the story and get their support.

I never called anybody to discuss the matter but when I would run into a Sparky Anderson—"Oh, Bob Knight called me"-or if I'd run into a coach- "Hey, Bob Knight called me about this." He called everybody, because now he's trying to get support and justify what he did. I think if he did do me a favor, it's not a favor when you call a press conference and talk about it.

If I do anything for anybody, they can stab me in the back but then I don't go tell other people what I did for them. If I do somebody a favor, it's a favor, and it's over.

I made a mistake my third year as head coach when I let him come into my locker room and talk to my team. It seemed like a nice thing at the time because I had great respect for the man, but I would never have allowed it to happen if I knew he was going to call a press conference and tell about it.

He said, "I can't believe Frieder did this to me, when I went into his locker room and talked to his team one time."

Former coach, Jim Dutcher, told me after I did that that I made a mistake. He said, "You should never have let him go in there, because you'll owe him. You'll owe him the rest of your life because he thinks he did you a big, big favor. You're as good as basketball coach as he is. You don't need him."

What it amounts to is, he's your friend as long as he beats your butt every time you compete. And as soon as you start beating him, you're no longer his friend. At least, that's how it was with me.

Knight and I had a great relationship before that incident. I first met him when we were on clinics together when I won the state championship at Flint Northern and he first went to Indiana, which was 1971 or '72. Then I came to Michigan in '73. I always respected him. I always thought he was the finest coach in the country. I knew he was doing a great job. He knew that I liked him, that I was observant of what Indiana basketball was accomplishing and how they were accomplishing it, and that I was trying to learn from him.

You know, we had Orr's 50th birthday party and Janice, my wife, invited Knight and he came. I don't think he'd have come to many assistants' houses.

When we went to Bloomington, Janice went over to their house. We had a pretty good friendship going. When the game was over, he'd be patting me on the back, telling me how my kids were coming along, and to hang in there, we're getting better.

Knight paid me a great compliment once, and maybe that's why he got so upset with me. He sent me a picture of the two of us at the national championship in Philly in 1981 from when I went down and wished him good luck before the game. In fact, they were all amazed that I could get down there, because I didn't have any pass or anything.

Then somehow there was a picture taken of it, of me wishing him good luck before the game. So he got it laminated and wrote on it. "Some day the positions will be reversed" or something like that.

In all honesty, that' a great compliment-isn't it?-from a great coach when I'm a first-year coach. I don't think he would do that for too many people. Now because of all that, maybe he felt that I was in a special category of one of his lieutenants or whatever. I think that's what he imagined. Now all of a sudden these incidents come up and it's something that he can't take because he thinks he's been betrayed. Maybe he's going back to the war or something and he's been betrayed by one of his men, and he can't cope with that. I think that's what he went through with it all, and that wasn't the case at all. I was just trying to win a basketball game.

I think our relationship would probably still be good today if he had just called me afterward and said, "Hey, I think you made a mistake. I'm talking to the official and you shouldn't interfere when I'm talking to the official." I would have agreed with him then. I'm an easy guy to get along with.

He's accomplished too much, but if the United States had the guts to let him coach in the Olympics and nothing happened, maybe he'll make it. What guts that took, huh? And they stood by him, but thank God he won. Thank God something didn't happen where he was getting beat and there was some bad incident.

You can tell by his book *(Season on the Brink)* that he doesn't like me or Michigan. What poetic justice it was to beat him in the first Big Ten game of the 1986 season. Going into that game, he's telling his team we haven't played anybody, and our last nonconference game was who? Cleveland State, who beats them in the first round of the NCAA tournament. I never thought I would see the day when Knight didn't respect opponents, but evidently he didn't respect Cleveland State if he would tell his team we hadn't played anybody and we're fat and lazy.

What an honor it was for me and my team that he prepared for Michigan during his Christmas tournament. That's in the book, about how he didn't worry about San Jose State and all of them, he worried about Michigan, prepared for Michigan, and then we beat 'em down there. That was satisfying, if he put that much into the game.

But see, then he lost the next game to Michigan State. That's what happens if you put too much effort into one game. You cannot do that at that level, and he made a serious mistake there. It was extremely important to me to get the best kids in Michigan to commit to Michigan. I thought that was a real weakness in the program when I took over, that there wasn't a single Michigan kid on the team, but do you notice how few Indiana kids there were in Knight's program near the end? Part of the reason for that is the jaycees he's taking.

That shows there's a lot of two-face in Bobby Knight. When I was an assistant, you cannot believe how he ripped the schools that were taking jaycees (Junior College transfers). How they cheat. How he will never take a jaycee kid because they've got bad attitudes. How there's a reason that they're in junior college, that they can't do the work academically. He went on and on and on, but he went and got jaycees when he had a bad season.

Well, what kind of person is that? He compromised. I don't like people who compromise their principles. And then he wins the national title and he goes out and gets more jaycees. It's almost like once he acquired the taste, he forgot about his principles.

Also in *Season on the Brink* is a scene where Indiana is playing Iowa at home and the referees give George Raveling a technical. Knight comes over and asks them to give him another technical.

That's the same thing he said I did that got him irritated, and it's another example that if Bobby Knight decides to do it, it's okay, but if someone else decides to do it, you're violating the code. It's just like the jaycees. If someone else takes jaycees, it's not good, but if he takes 'em, then it's okay.

And don't ever let him tell people that Michigan fans are the worst because his fans haven't been that nice to me, even though I entertained 2,000 of them in New Orleans at the national finals in '87 when I saw them up and down Bourbon Street. They were all shaking my hand and being nice to me because we beat Purdue for them to give 'em the co-championship and the number one seed. I mean, I just set the whole national championship up for them.

All those fans were nice to me and promised me a standing ovation in Bloomington, and I did get some cheers when I got introduced that next year—I think it was my boys I met on Bourbon Street-but when I go off that court, I get stuff thrown at me. I hear 'em talking.

How's he think the people are gonna treat him when he walks out there after the way he acted? You know what I mean? What the hell does he expect?

May the best team win and your team lose

Norm Sloan

Norm Sloan led the North Carolina State Wolfpack to the 1974 NCAA title. The Wolfpack were led by David Thompson, Tom Burleson, and Monte Towe. Sloan now is enjoying retirement in Newland, North Carolina.

Bobby Knight doesn't want to be called Bobby any longer, sort of like when Lefty Driesell wanted to be called Charles. It didn't work, and he finally gave up. Bobby may get upset about it, but he's still "Bobby" to me. I don't mean any disrespect, but he's been Bobby all of his life, and suddenly he thinks that isn't proper and wants to be called Bob.

You're going to get along fine with Bobby Knight until you recruit against him and beat him, until you compete against him and beat him, or if you ever have the audacity to challenge him on any of his regular pronouncements.

I am fortunate in that I have a wonderful marriage. I married a marvelous woman, a tough lady whom I respect immensely. I would no more demean her in public than I would sprinkle salt and pepper on Michael Jordan's sneakers and try to eat them.

We had breakfast with Bobby and his first wife in the coffee shop of one of the big Las Vegas hotels while we were at the Pizza Hut Classic in the mid-seventies. Joan and I came away from that breakfast with queasy stomachs. Bobby had demeaned his wife over breakfast, talking down to her and about her in front of her so viciously that both of us were stunned.

Later, we were playing in the Hoosier Classic right after Florida's football team had been put on probation. There was Bobby's wife—the same gal we had felt so sorry for in Las Vegas—sitting up there screaming at Vernon Maxwell and cursing like a sailor. Shortly after that the Knights were divorced.

I was on a clinic with Bobby in Louisville at a time when women's athletics and Title IX was just starting to gain momentum. Several women coaches were sitting in the audience. Before that time, you just didn't see any women at coaching clinics.

Bobby couldn't deal with that. He started off, first of all, by jumping on the women and belittling the Title IX movement. He said they wanted the same money without the same pressure that men's programs were under. "I think if you're going to get the same money that we do," he told them from the podium, "you ought to get your ass fired just like the men do."

He told three of the foulest jokes I have ever heard in my life, even making a point of doing it because of the women in the audience. He told them that if they were going to come with the men, they'd have to be treated like the men. I think what he did was unbecoming and unnecessary.

Bobby and I got into a tiff that was completely my fault. At the 1987 trials at the Olympic Training Center in Colorado Springs for our various national teams, Vernon Maxwell did not make the first cut-down for either the Pan-Am Games or the World University Games. When asked about it by a reporter, I noted that two of Bobby Knight's players—one a nondescript junior college player—were invited to the World University tryouts that his bosom pal Mike Krzyzewski was holding at Duke. I also said that there are more ways to cheat than giving a kid illegal aid. You can also cheat by promising a kid a tryout or promising a kid a place on one of these national teams if he signs with a certain coach.

Little did I know the reason Vernon didn't make the team was that he had flunked a drug test. When I made my statement, Bobby angrily called Bill Arnsparger, told him about Maxwell's drug test, and threatened to go public with it, breaking the confidentiality that is supposed to exist around Olympic drug tests.

I called Bobby, and he wasn't in. He called back. It was summertime, and we had a young part-time worker named Amy Tyner in the office. Amy took the call and told him I was at our beach condo in Daytona Beach. He asked for the number, and she said she couldn't give it out. She offered to call me and advise that Bobby was trying to reach me. Typical Bobby, he began showering her with profanity.

After a moment, Amy broke in and said, "You know, Mr. Knight, my mother raised me a lot better than your mother raised you. I can tell by your language."

When we hooked up, I apologized to Bobby for reading into the player selections something that apparently wasn't there. I even followed with a letter of apology, explaining that I didn't know about Maxwell's failed drug test.

When I was forced to retire at Florida, Bobby was quoted as saying college basketball was "better off without people like Sloan."

Bobby likes anybody he can beat or browbeat. He doesn't like anyone who will stand up to him and yell back. I think Bobby is an excellent basketball coach, but he is a bully. I don't like those who try to dominate people, but

I would like to think I would never say the game would be better off without Bobby Knight. I don't know that you should say that about anybody in any profession. Everybody with enough ability to stick around for any length of time makes a contribution of some sort.

Though we had a good relationship at first, Bobby and I started falling apart when we beat him in head-to-head recruiting for a big kid named Glenn Sudhop, a seven-foot, two-inch, center out of South Bend, Indiana. When we signed Sudhop at North Carolina State, Bobby started accusing me of all kinds of recruiting irregularities.

The truth was that Sudhop didn't go with Bobby Knight because he didn't think he could take Bobby's kind of pressure. As it turned out, he couldn't take it from me, either. Glenn and I didn't have the best of relationships at State because he didn't want to work hard. I used to tell him he was going to wind up as the tallest used-car salesman in South Bend. I was wrong. He would up as the tallest milling machine operator at International Harvester.

Bobby has always done a fine job wherever he has been. He was a good selection for the Indiana job. I was one of the people who interviewed for that job the year Bobby did. I always considered Indiana to be one of the best jobs in the country because of the great basketball tradition in the state, the pool of talent, and the school's commitment. Also, football wasn't a threat like it was at Ohio State or Michigan. At Indiana, Bobby Knight was the Bull Gator.

Krzyzewski is Scrabble for Triple-Word Score

Mike Krzyzewski

Mike Krzyzewski was the captain of one of Bob Knight's early Army basketball teams. Krzyzewski later became an assistant coach at Indiana before Coach Knight helped him land the head position at Army, which in turn was a giant step on his way to becoming head coach at Duke. Krkzyzewski and Knight have had a falling out in recent years which was detailed in A March to Madness *by the talented John Feinstein.*

Mike Krzyzewski

Mike Krzyzewski had no idea how he felt at the end of his team's four-game run in the 1996 preseason NIT. The Blue Devils played very well in their two home games against St. Joseph's and Vanderbilt, winning both games easily. They struggled, but survived, in their semifinal in Madison Square Garden against a very good Tulsa team.

That victory put them into the final against Indiana. Like it or not, that was going to mean a difficult, emotional evening for Krzyzewski. His relationship with Bob Knight was a complicated one, dating back to the first time Knight had come to his parents' home to recruit him in 1965. Much of what Krzyzewski had become was because of Knight. He had taught him toughness as a player and a system he believed in as both a player and a coach: hard-nosed, man-to-man defense; a motion offense tailored to allow smart players to make smart decisions, and a no-nonsense approach not only to games but even to practices and meetings. He had gotten him started in the business as a graduate assistant at Indiana and had played a role in getting him both of his head coaching jobs, at Army and at Duke.

They had remained close friends for years, doing clinics together in the off-season, talking often on the phone. Krzyzewski had never forgotten what Knight had done for him, and more importantly for his mother, when his dad had died during his senior year at West Point. In 1986, when Krzyzewski took

Duke to the Final Four for the first time, he had Knight speak to his team prior to the semifinals. Knight walked around Dallas that weekend like a proud father, wearing a Duke button everyplace he went.

When Duke lost the final to Louisville, Knight was on the phone with Krzyzewski every night for a week. "Are you OK?" he kept asking. Krzyzewski was fine. He takes losing hard, but he has never taken it as personally as Knight. Still, he appreciated his old coach's concern. A year later, the student and the mentor met in the Sweet Sixteen. Duke, a decided underdog, played Indiana tough before losing to a team that would go on to the national championship. After the game, Knight's first comment was "It's hard for me to enjoy this very much thinking about Mike."

But the relationship now wasn't what it had once been. The 1992 Final Four in Minneapolis had been the turning point. By then, Krzyzewski had won a national championship and became arguably, a bigger star in coaching than Knight. He won just as consistently—in fact, he had been to one more Final Four at that point-and he did it without any of the baggage that Knight brought to the table. Knight was uptight about the match up and told friends before the game that he believed that Krzyzewski had changed with his success, had somehow become less loyal to him.

Krzyzewski heard all this but ignored it. He was convinced Knight was playing a mind game with him, trying to soften his approach to their semifinal. The game was a war, Indiana jumping way ahead, Duke coming back. Knight hurt his team's 'cause with an ill-timed technical foul in the second half and Duke pulled away and appeared headed for an easy win. Then the Hoosiers rallied, actually getting to within three points, with the ball, in the final minute. But Duke hung on for an 81–78 victory.

The post game handshake was not what you might expect between student and teacher. In fact, it was more along the lines of what coaches call a "blow-by," a handshake so quick that no words are exchanged as one coach blows by the other. Krzyzewski was surprised, but not shocked. He knew how much the game meant to him and he assumed it meant just as much to Knight. He hadn't expected a blow-by, but he was prepared for something less than warm and fuzzy.

What he wasn't prepared for was what happened twenty minutes later. At each Final Four, the NCAA curtains off a walkway between the locker rooms and the interview room so coaches and players can walk unimpeded from one to the other. As the losing team, Indiana went to the interview room first. Krzyzewski was walking into the interview room with Christian Laettner and Bobby Hurley just as Knight was leaving. Knight stopped and shook hands with both Laettner and Hurley and wished them luck in the championship game. OK, Krzyzewski thought, he's got his emotions under control, now we'll shake hands like men and talk for a moment about the game.

Wrong. This time, Knight didn't even look at Krzyzewski. Instead, he looked past him as if he wasn't even there and walked right by him without so much as a nod. Krzyzewski was devastated. Intellectually, he understood what was going on. Knight was a bad loser; always had been. The list of coaches who have turned from good guys into bad ones for having the audacity to beat Knight-especially in a game he really cared about-is a long one. But even knowing all that, Krzyzewski was blown away by the blow off.

He stumbled through his press conference, barely able to keep his mind on the questions. When he walked back to the locker room, he found Mickie, his wife, and his daughters waiting for him. When Mickie put her arms around him to give him a post game victory hug, she was shocked to find him racked with tears.

"What is it?" she asked, completely baffled. "Knight" was the only answer she got.

While his players dressed and answered questions in the Minnesota Twins locker room, Krzyzewski sat in the back with his coaches, his eyes still glistening. "There are days," he said, "when life's not fair."

His team had just qualified for a third straight national championship game and a shot at back-to-back titles and Krzyzewski was completely undone emotionally by his old coach's behavior.

By the next day, he was fine. A number of former Knight players and coaches, having witnessed the initial blow-by in the arena, came by the Duke hotel that night to make sure Krzyzewski was all right. When he told them about the incident in the hallway, they were unsurprised, but nonetheless disappointed in Knight. To a man, they told Krzyzewski to ignore it. "Coach will get over it," one friend said.

"I don't really care if he gets over it or not," Krzyzewski said. "That was it for me."

Ten months passed before the two men spoke again. When word began to leak to the media about a Knight-Krzyzewski schism, it was Knight who took most of the heat. Knight will never admit a battle is lost, but he is always smart enough to understand when it is time to cut his losses.

Shortly after New Year's 1993, he called Krzyzewski. Krzyzewski wouldn't take the call. He kept calling. Finally, on the afternoon that Duke was to play North Carolina in Cameron, Krzyzewski took his call. They talked for about an hour. Knight never said, "I'm sorry," because he never does. What he did do was "explain" to Krzyzewski why he had behaved the way he had. The story was lengthy and convoluted, full of imagined slights, most of which led back to Krzyzewski having had the audacity to win the game in Minneapolis.

Krzyzewski listened and didn't argue. What was the point? He knew this was as close to an apology as Knight would ever come, and he appreciated the effort. "I'll always love Coach Knight," he said later. "I will always appreciate everything that he did for me. But I think the time has come for us to go our separate ways in life."

Which is exactly what they did. Krzyzewski made a point of never criticizing Knight publicly. In fact, whenever Knight got into trouble one of the people his media sympathizers ran to looking for pro-Knight quotes was Krzyzewski.

Duke and Indiana had played in November of 1995 in the semifinals of the Great Alaska Shootout. That had been Krzyzewski's first weekend back on the bench since his illness the previous season. Duke had won the game 70–64 and had gone on to win the tournament. Facing Knight again-and beating him again-had been cathartic for Krzyzewski. There had been no blowups or blow-bys. Of course, a preseason tournament played in near privacy in Anchorage is a lot different than a Final Four. There was almost no media, and Knight had been cordial.

This was also a November game, but it was a little different. New York was a long way from Anchorage and both teams were nationally ranked. It still wasn't the Final Four by any stretch, but it was important to both coaches as an early-season test of where their teams were and how good they might become. And it was important because they knew the whole country would be watching.

"This is the kind of game you came to Duke to play," Krzyzewski told his team during their afternoon shoot around in Madison Square Garden on the day after Thanksgiving. "Did you see *USA Today* this morning? Banner headline: Duke-Indiana. Anyone who cares about college basketball will be watching this game tonight. That's good. That's the way we like it. That's where Duke basketball is supposed to be."

Indiana was 4–0 and Duke was 3–0. Neither school had won an NCAA tournament game since 1994, which, for these two coaches, represented a major drought. Each suspected that his team was better this year than it had been and each was eager to find out how much better that evening.

This was the match up that NIT officials had hoped for when they put together their sixteen-team draw in the summer. The preseason NIT was twelve years old and, on a number of occasions, attendance in The Garden on Thanksgiving weekend had been embarrassing, with, announced crowds of under 10,000 that looked a lot more like 5,000. That was not a problem for this final. The attendance was 17,930, just shy of a sellout.

Krzyzewski had decided that he was going to take the high road with Knight before the game. He would play the role of dutiful student and greet his old mentor when he arrived at his bench. Knight likes to come out of the locker room at the last possible moment. Krzyzewski knew that. With about two minutes left on the pregame clock, he walked to the Indiana bench to wait for Knight to arrive. He talked to the assistants, even sat on the bench briefly to make things look as informal and comfortable as possible.

The clock ticked down to zero. Still no Knight. The PA announcer began introducing the lineups. Krzyzewski was squirming. Part of his pregame routine is to kneel in front of his bench and give each starter a pat on the back as he is introduced. Still, he waited. Knight finally emerged, walking with famed horse trainer D. Wayne Lucas, a pal of his who was in New York hanging with Knight and the Hoosiers for the weekend.

Krzyzewski was now standing next to the Indiana bench, almost at attention, waiting for his old coach to show up. Knight saw Krzyzewski, stopped, threw an arm around Lucas, and launched into a story. Then he made a point of shaking hands with a few people. By the time he got to Krzyzewski, the teams had been introduced.

Krzyzewski put out his hand. "Good luck," he said,

"You too," Knight answered, turning away quickly.

If it wasn't a blow-by, it was pretty damn close to it. Krzyzewski walked back to his bench angry, but forced himself to forget about it and focus on the game at hand.

Both teams were tight throughout the first half, shooting the ball poorly. Both coaches were on the officials early and Knight, showing what the game meant to him, drew a technical with 5:11 left in the half. That led to a four-point play for Duke and a 28–22 lead. They were still clinging to a six-point margin at halftime, even though Indiana's Andrae Patterson had been virtually unstoppable, scoring 27 of Indiana's 31 points.

"If we get him under control, we'll win the game," Krzyzewski told his assistants at halftime. "None of their other guys are hurting us."

But they never figured out how to stop Patterson. What's more, in the second half, he did get help, most notably from freshman point guard A. J. Guyton, who consistently beat Duke's defense into the lane and ended up with 16 points, six rebounds, and five assists. Patterson had 39 on one of those nights college players dream about.

No one from Duke came close to matching Patterson or Guyton. All five starters shot less than 50 percent and as a team the Blue Devils shot a miserable 35.6 percent. The second half got uglier and uglier. Indiana opened with a 10–2 run to take the lead. Krzyzewski picked up a technical of his own during that stretch, arguing over starting center Greg Newton's fourth foul. "You got the second foul," he kept yelling at referee Joe Mingle, implying that Newton had been fouled first. Mingle ignored the comment and ran down the court. "Joe, you guys missed the first foul," Krzyzewski insisted. "You got the second one. Come on!"

For some reason, Mingle decided that comment was worth a technical. When he made the signal and walked to the scorer's table, Krzyzewski really lost it. "Oh fuck you!" he screamed in complete exasperation, loud enough to be heard at least ten rows up. That line didn't earn Krzyzewski a second technical, no doubt in part because Mingle knew he had been trigger-happy on the first one, but also because officials are loathe to toss a coach (two technicals and you're gone), especially a famous one, in front of 17,930 people and a national television audience.

As it turned out, Mingle would have been doing Krzyzewski a favor if he had sent him to the locker room. The Blue Devils were awful down the stretch. Trailing 50–49 with ten minutes left, they managed to get outscored 35–20 the rest of the way. Krzyzewski was on the officials right to the end, but his tone was more plaintive than angry. He knew his team was being outplayed. He just didn't want to concede until he had to.

"What makes me angry is you were outfought," he said to the players when it was over. "I can live with losing if the other team is just better than we are. But you let yourselves get outfought. That's not acceptable."

He didn't get angry or even raise his voice very much. He was frustrated. The entire evening had been frustrating. Sitting with his assistants after he had said all the right things about Indiana in his press conference, he shook his head. "It could be a long season. That just wasn't very good. But we can't afford to jump this team too much. They can't handle it. We've got to almost baby them right now."

The subject of Knight's pregame behavior came up. Krzyzewski sighed. "I'm almost glad it happened that way," he said. "It lets me put a period on the end of the sentence. The end. You know, it's really kind of sad. He keeps turning his friends away. I'm not the first or the last. I tried to do the right thing. I'm over it now. Five years ago, that would have hurt me. It doesn't hurt anymore."

In fact, the most painful part of the evening had much more to do with what Knight's team had been able to do to Krzyzewski's team than anything Knight had done himself to Krzyzewski.

"We play like this," he said finally, "and it's going to be a very long winter."

Experience is What You Get When You Don't Get What You Want

Chris Foster
London Bradley
Butch Carter

Chris, Chris: Maybe it was just the Heimlich Maneuver

Chris Foster

Chris Foster has been a life-long resident of Bloomington, Indiana and led a rather peaceful lifestyle until the Spring of 1999 when he had a fateful encounter with Coach Bob Knight. Foster is a noted guitar maker who has fashioned instruments for some of the top country artists in America

I build musical instruments for a living and I've met a lot of celebrities. When this whole thing came out, I read in the paper that I'm out for my fifteen minutes of fame and that I'd met my first celebrity and was seeking to exploit it. On web sites, I was accused of putting the marks on myself.

It's a long story. Essentially I was in a restaurant and he was at a table in a little town next to Bloomington, called Ellettsville. I overheard comments Knight was making. When I went up to pay my bill, he came up behind me and, basically, I told him that I was offended by some of the things he'd said. He said, "What things?" I told him I didn't think profanity was called for in a public restaurant and that I was particularly upset by his racist comments. The statement that he made that I thought was racist was, "When I have a black player, and he comes into some money, I tell him to buy his mother a house and hang onto the rest of it because when one of those people comes into some money, the rest of them come out of the woodwork." He said that wasn't racist. We were by this time walking out the door; he was ahead of me and I was behind him. I said, 'I'm sorry. But you obviously don't know a racist comment when you make one."

That's when he exploded. He whirled around and grabbed me by the throat, left marks on my neck. The guy I was eating dinner with knocked his hand off my throat and I went in and tried to call the cops. The restaurant people didn't want to tell me where the phone was, but I finally got them to tell me where it was and called the police. I had to say, "Look, I'm calling the police. Where's the damn phone?" They reluctantly did tell me.

Knight has a huge, huge following of fans, and they are religious—bordering on fanatical about it. In fact if you looked at the web sites, especially *The Star,* and *The View* web sites where you have forums where people can discuss whatever, Knight's fans are referred to as lemmings and Kool-Aid drinkers, making reference to Jim Jones.

If you go against Knight, you get your death threats; you get your nasty letters. I've called like the local ReMax realtor to list a property for sale. He comes out, looks at it and never calls me back. He knows I'm the guy.

Knight will lay out a rash of words at you that you won't believe and then tell everybody that he didn't say anything profane and that he didn't raise his voice. He's really loud. The only time he's not loud is when he's telling you "I said it in this tone of voice." That's the only time he's quiet. And he's profane enough that I don't even think he's aware of it when he is doing it. As far as he's concerned about our run-in, he was just talking "goddamn it, bitch and everything." Nothing really major. But when I first went in, there was a table behind me that had children at it. And so I had thought about what he was saying not really being appropriate. But about halfway through the meal those people left, then one guy came and was sitting there, and he left. So that left Knight's table and mine and when. . . . He was with his wife and her sister and some other woman—three women and him.

The women went outside. I guess as we were going up to pay the bill, they went on out the door and then he's left remaining to pay his bill behind me. I thought his bill had already been paid so I don't know what he was doing behind me—maybe leaving a tip or something. But the women were outside so it wasn't like I walked up to his table and embarrassed him or that anyone overheard what I said. So it was pretty minor. What I kinda wanted to do was clue him in—when you're in public like that and you're making these diatribes that maybe not everyone else wants to hear it. I was just kinda letting him know that I was offended by it and it was loud enough for me to hear and maybe when he's in public or whatever. . . .

You can get all the police reports. Bear in mind—I'm shaking from adrenaline, just been attacked, the police give me a pen and paper and I'm supposed to write down what just happened. One of the errors I made in trying to whip this thing off so I could go—while waiting for the cops to show up in the parking lot, the manager comes out and is talking to Bob Knight. Bob Knight says, "Look if the cops want to talk to me, tell them I'll be at home." And he gives him a card with his number on it and leaves. All the rest of us are still there in the parking lot. He gets three or four days before he finally gives his statement to the police.

I had taken pictures of my welts at a friend's house. I called the cops, then I read that either the prosecutor, Carl Salzmann, is gonna charge him with assault or charge me with provocation. This goes on for a week to ten days. Here in Indiana, no one that I know of has ever been charged with provocation; it's a vaguely upholdable law—I don't know that they use it because you can't uphold it. If I had been black, since I'm white, people chose to look at it as if I were looking for a fight. It was bizarre. After this, the prosecutor walks way out on a limb by defending Knight and not pressing charges. You can't do anything about a prosecutor. You can't sue him. He's an elected official, right, and he knew a lot of Indiana people wouldn't vote for him if Bob Knight was charged. I can only imagine it was a political choice. Who's not going to vote for him because he threatened to charge the guitar maker? Nobody.

But you go over and try to press charges—I mean look how many IU presidents, like Tom Ehrlich have been run out of town because of Bob Knight. He reprimanded him when he walked off the team with the Russians, and Bob Knight started shopping his resume around. The next thing you knew Tom Ehrlich left town rather than Bob Knight. I saw an old clip on TV where Knight was giving an interview to business people about how he uses choking people as a means of manipulating their behavior.

There was the thing with J. D. Maxwell. When I first had the cops come to the restaurant, they called in the state cops. J. D. Maxwell is an evidence technician for the state police and he also teaches at Bob Knight's basketball camp. He works for Bob Knight, as well as the state police, evidently. He came and the first thing he did was—I was in one state trooper's car, he went up to the guy I was having dinner with and asked him where he worked and told him he knew his boss—as if trying to intimidate him. Then he comes over to me and tells me "No prosecutor's gonna touch this. What did I do to provoke him? Why didn't I just talk to the management? I don't really want to press charges, do I?" I talked to the other state trooper and said, "Look, that other cop's really intimidating and you know I don't know if I should press charges." That trooper said, "Well somebody needs to, he's been getting away with too much." So I said, "Well, let me check with my dad and stepmother, both of whom work for the University." I checked with them and made sure their jobs could handle something like that. Then I called the next day and went ahead and pressed charges.

I called the Superintendent of State Police, Melvin Carraway and told him, "Look, one of your officers was really good, but the other one was completely out of line." He said that he was not investigating officer on this case and that I would have no further problems with him. A few days later, J. D. Maxwell's doing the lead into Bob Knight's press conference saying, "As sure as there's a God in heaven, I knows Bob Knight is no racist." That earned him eight days of suspension, and he was also charged with funneling information about the case to Knight. I believe, and this is totally a guess on my part but, I tend to think that he was involved with locating a witness that didn't exist. Because the prosecutor waited about ten or eleven days to try and decide what he should do. It was when this witness who was a preacher from a town twenty miles away, who said he was at the table next to Knight, but there was no one at that table. So I don't know where this guy came from but he said he didn't hear Bob Knight cussing but he said he left a couple of minutes before we did. I don't know how he knows when we left if he wasn't there! How could he? Then the "preacher" supposedly had a massive heart attack and is in the hospital and nobody can go talk to him—but we have his statement here, right? Salzmann, the prosecutor, said it was the defining thing. He does claim that Knight grabbed my shirt. It's really unbelievable. I'm forty years old, and first lived in Bloomington in 1962. We've peacefully coexisted for a reasonably long time. Maybe because I deal with so many celebrities, I did not defer to his "celebrity." I thought, "Hey you're a person, you're standing next to me. As far as I'm concerned, you're a person; you just stepped on your dick. I'm gonna let you know you did it. Maybe you'll learn."

This all happened about a year and a half ago. I did get my share of threats and whatever, and it was a big thing and in all the papers. I pretty much didn't give those any more mind than that they were threats. I don't know—there are a lot of people who refuse to see Bob Knight doing anything wrong. They talk about his honesty and his integrity, and he's against hypocrisy. But these are all things he's guilty of.

Theoretically, he got onto this kid for not respecting elders, you know and saying "What's up, Knight?" Yet, this is the same guy who cussed out a 64-year-old woman and threw a potted plant at her. He said, "Oh I might have knocked that plant over accidentally." They accept that—that's true.

When Knight gets ahead of himself, before he realizes the ramifications of his actions, he's already acted. So he immediately goes into damage control mode.

Look into almost any incident with Knight—watch how he handles it. The first thing he does is he gets his lawyers and he gets out of town. He buys himself time—in almost every instance that's what he does. He gets out of town and lets his lawyers deal with it. When he shot the guy in Wisconsin, he didn't take him to the hospital; he got in his car and went straight to his lawyers; the 'chair incident' he goes to Kansas on a recruiting trip; last May on the day of Brand's "zero tolerance" press conference, he left to go fishing; the weekend he got fired, same thing.

John Mellencamp lives here; he's a celebrity. When was the last time you read anything about him encountering people in Bloomington and making national news? Never. You never heard it. It never happens. Joshua Bell lives here, there's I don't know how many accomplished world-class musicians associated with the University and scientists that are celebrities in Bloomington. None of them have this problem. How many coaches are there? If it smells like a rat, it's probably a rat.

Is there a conspiracy against Bob Knight? Either the world's biggest conspiracy or there's got to be some truth to it.

If you look at the kind of guy Knight is. . . . His generation of people—they don't go to a shrink. That does not happen. They don't apologize to you whether or not you just took a beating you didn't deserve or not. There are certain things that I just would describe as "old school mentality." Bob Knight seems to be pretty much the type who subscribes to that. I'm not sure that there aren't a bunch of people who affiliate with those values in some way or see him as some sort of father figure or something to where they're defending something that—most of these people have never been in the same room with him.

Athletic Director, Clarence Doninger said "Tough luck, Coach." After the Ohio State game last year. That's when Knight went off on him. They theoretically have not spoken since. The kid he grabbed, that got him fired, all he said was, "What's up, Knight?" That's all he said. It's really strange.

This spring I watched IU totally defend him. Back when he assaulted me, IU said "This didn't happen on University property and we are gonna stay out of it because it wasn't a university matter." Then when he gave his press conference, he did it out of Assembly Hall, draped with all of IU's prestige. Oddly enough, this was the first one since this press conference from the thing in Puerto Rico.

It's very frustrating. The only avenue left me is to civilly sue Bob Knight. Well, I can't get my lawyer fees back from that because Bob Knight didn't threaten to charge me with a crime. All I can get is my hospital bills and it's just not worth going up against him. I offered to his lawyer, "Look, if he pays my hospital bill, I'll drop charges." But he wouldn't do that.

Our final resolution was the prosecutor couldn't determine one thing or the other. He used the mystery witness to say that he had decided that my story didn't hold enough to be prosecuting Knight and he wasn't going to prosecute me for provocation. He just dropped everything. I thought it was an obvious kangaroo court. Take a look at it. Then it turns out that the state cop was feeding all this information. Bob Knight, at the press conference, said, "If Salzmann was in charge of the Manson case, it would still be undecided and that he'd like to call the whole thing a Mickey Mouse affair except that would insult Mickey Mouse." Knight came out and proceeded to just ream the guy who had just bent over backward doing him a big favor.

You just find yourself vilified on all sorts of different levels. It becomes popular opinion. I've got a friend whose mother read the press accounts and my friend couldn't convince her, having known me for fifteen years, that I didn't do anything wrong . . . but she wouldn't believe her own son. He hasn't talked to his mom since.—which is the biggest personal thing that I've seen happen as a result of it. She bought the media account.

"Chris Foster is no stranger to law enforcement." Then proceeded to list stuff, the most current of which was fifteen years old. That's hardly means I'm well acquainted with law enforcement. An AP photographer said, "If you piss Knight off, it's forever."

Like the last night when he did his speech to the students in Dunn Meadow after he was fired, he went off the list and litany of all the great players he's had over the years—never mentioned Steve Alford. It's real obvious. I get quite a few calls. When it first happened to me, I had two full notebook pages of media that called but I wasn't talking to them. I gave a brief interview to AP just to get my side of things out and then dodged the rest of it.

London was one of the best referees in the country—the country was Mongolia.

London Bradley

An official that Bob Knight had many run-ins with was London Bradley, now a high-ranking executive with Allstate Insurance in suburban Chicago. London was one of the first black officials in the Big Ten and paved the way for many other minority referees in this country. Bradley was the referee in the 1985 Purdue game who gave Knight the technical foul that caused him to launch the infamous chair across the court. Also, later on in a crucial game against the University of Michigan, Bradley had called a technical on Knight and later, in the eyes of many, Bradley blew a goal-tending call that went against Indiana. Knight came unglued. He was quoted in a national publication as saying, "I did everything but call the guy a "nigger." People are human. If I were a referee, I would tell a guy, 'I'm not gonna call a technical, I'm just gonna throw your ass out.' " That quote sent shock waves throughout the refereeing fraternity.

Nevertheless, London Bradley agreed to an interview for this book and was most gracious and favorable in his comments about Bob Knight. Later Mr. Bradley had second thoughts about that interview and requested that none of his quotes be used.

It's Free Speech only when it's politically correct

Clarence "Butch" Carter

For a man just barely into his forties, Butch Carter has done some amazing things in his life. While not as famous as his younger brother Cris Carter of the Minnesota Vikings, Butch was the Ohio High School Player of the Year in Middletown, Jerry Lucas's home town, before matriculating to Indiana University. He played almost every game in his four years at IU and was the co-MVP of the only NIT Tournament that Indiana has ever won. He made the winning shot with just six seconds to go as the Hoosiers beat Purdue 53–52 in Madison Square Garden. After graduating in four years, he was drafted by the Los Angeles Lakers and spent seven years in the NBA, primarily with the Indiana Pacers. In 1984, while averaging 13.4 a game with the Pacers, he set the all-time NBA record—still standing—for most points scored during overtime in an NBA game. Until recently, he had spent the last ten years as an assistant coach or head coach in the NBA. He led the Toronto Raptors to their first playoff berth ever and he is the winningest coach in Toronto Raptors history. He also holds the distinction of being the only person to become Ohio High School Player of the Year and Ohio High School Coach of the Year in basketball. Carter is the author of "Born to Believe" a book he co-authored with his brother Cris that contains universal positive messages appealing to those searching for meaning. One of the twenty chapters in the book pertain to his relationship with Coach Knight and created quite a stir when the book was released in early 2000. Carter now heads up the Carter Group, a Real Estate Investment and Management firm in Toronto and also is recognized as one of the top motivational speakers in the Ontario province.

Clarence "Butch" Carter

I'm from Ohio and basically went to Indiana 'cause it was one of the few places where all the players were graduating. I was the oldest of seven kids and it was extremely important that I came home with a degree, in my Mom's eyes. What was important to me was that Scott May was from Ohio and Scott had been successful there at Indiana University.

The year (1979) I shot the winning shot at the NIT—it was very important to make it 'cause I had just turned the ball over the possession before. I graduated in four years.

Playing for Bob Knight is tough. The guys who go there are tough guys. You are not going to be practicing with a bunch of soft guys—they're tough guys.

I went back to only one Indiana game, since I left. It was years ago. Knight asked me about being a graduate assistant. I told him things hadn't changed between him and me. He told me he had changed. I told him that he might have changed, but I hadn't changed.

He's a better politician than he is a coach and finally the politicians have turned against him.

Knight got to the point where the people that saved him all these years, the University; he's turned to lying on them. I told one man at the University, "The biggest problem I have on Bob Knight is that you guys have allowed him to use the University as a platform for his lying."

There is the ugly side of him—things that have been hidden because he would threaten to ruin people's lives if you ever exposed anything. People want to be close to someone powerful like that, but he would get on the phone behind people's back and kill people

He threatens guys that challenge him that they won't be able to work or have a meaningful life and he gets away with it.

A painful lesson to learn at any age is how to make friends and also knowing just how and why friendships and acquaintances unravel. It's crucial to make a distinction between sincere friends and acquaintances seeking to exploit the relationship for what you can bring to their lives. A true friendship is built on shared experiences to mutual benefit. A friend loves you for who you are, warts and all, through good experiences and bad, whereas a casual companion or acquaintance seems to like certain parts of you. Developing and maintaining friendships presents certain challenges when you've got a grueling travel schedule.

To complicate relationships, when push comes to shove, you have to put people where they actually are in your life. People whom you thought were friends, you understand later had befriended you, as they wanted something from you, not necessarily because they wanted to contribute positively to your life.

Many cannot and do not understand that this is a method of control and maintaining an illusion of superiority. I think these people are cowards, who will do damage to others by their destructive words and underhanded actions. But people forgive their bullying behavior because they have power.

Knight is an example of this type of person.

When I was an 18 year old freshman at Indiana, Knight gave me a copy of the wonderful Rudyard Kipling poem *If*, which illustrates the positive and negatives of the journey through life. It speaks of hypocrisy and duplicity in a friendship. It's ironic Knight handed it to me, as we are now estranged.

However, the poem remains a poignant source of strength for me. While Knight motivates in a detrimental manner and people do learn from negative lessons, I realized later that he was like many dictators—selfish and ruthless and you just can't get too close to challenging or questioning them. They always have some overt or insidious way of maintaining control and use threats to hold you back. This is different from being a mentor, as a mentor wants the best for you, but doesn't use intimidation and threats as methods to help you develop.

Although with media reports and the actions I witnessed, I don't know if Knight is a racist, but I know he does not like educated strong-willed blacks. He is the kind of man who implies a man should not stand up and be a man; should not have an intelligent opinion. I feel it would be fair to say that he does not like the fact that Cris and I are professionally successful.

This all started when "God" stopped practice early one day. I first heard my mother call Knight "God" during my recruitment. During recruitment, Knight promised he'd be fair to my teammates and me and we would not be subject to segregated behavior. When we were recruited, we thought we'd left these segregated situations behind. One bad day, Knight first threw me out of practice, then threw everyone out, but Knight called me back onto the court while the guys were heading to the locker room. He ripped me up and down. He was still in a rage in the locker room 15 minutes later, going up and down the line. Knight yelled at one of the players (Editor's note: Carter is talking about Isiah Thomas. During Knight's recruiting of Isiah, one of Isiah's brothers "got into it" with Coach Knight at Thomas' Chicago home.) that he would end up like "all the rest of the niggers in Chicago, including your brothers!" An assistant coach, grabbed Knight and pulled him from the room, while Knight screamed that "I don't have to f***** apologize!" I'll never forget looking at that assistant coach, who I greatly admired as a person, yet with Knight's outburst, he couldn't say anything.

When you tell a kid he's going to be like every "nigger" in Chicago, how far is that over the line of inappropriate and cowardly behavior? Knight felt he was at such a superior level that he could make a statement like that to a player in front of his teammates and he had no obligation to apologize to him or the rest of the black players. In effect, not only was Knight talking to that player, but he was also talking to his two captains. Both of us came from families with many children.

His words and anger affected me, because he was overtly talking about all of us; the eight black players in that locker room and essentially all the black players he had ever coached. All these players had put money in his pockets and helped win Big Ten and National Championships, yet he was hypocritical and deliberately chose to say what he truly felt about us.

We all got dressed quickly and scattered, knowing that his tirade could have been directed at any one of us. I felt sorry for that individual player, but he said not to worry about it as he had decided to leave the next year. The talented player could have chosen any college, with a scholarship, but he had chosen to go to Indiana. Knight had shown his deepest, darkest thoughts and resentment to him and everyone in the locker room had witnessed the display.

Knight never did apologize—that day, nor in the week or months afterward. It was as if it had never even dawned on him that his behavior and that incident might not only be unacceptable, but hurtful in the long run.

Even after the years have passed and I was doing everything possible to move away from that incident, it haunted me. A former Indiana teammate who was also in the locker room that day, sat down with me at a restaurant a couple of years back. Randy Wittman is now head coach of Cleveland Cavaliers and he was upset with me, saying he heard I'd been saying Knight is racist. I had never talked about the incidents at Indiana I'm describing—I've never mentioned them to family members, friends, nor discussed it with those teammates.

I asked Randy, 'You sat there in the locker room and heard the same thing I did. What part of it did you not understand?' Even if he didn't think the comment was racist, was Knight just having a bad day? How did I end up getting the blame for what Knight said? I left there thinking that here's this guy coaching in the NBA and how is he ever going to be fair to his black players if he takes that stand on that statement? He did it because of intimidation and widespread acceptance of Knight's behavior. This reminded me again of the poem's validity and especially the first two lines.

Another incident that happened after a practice in my first season was the final straw in having any trust in Knight. That year he had also denounced a former player in the locker room in front of our team, who was in his rookie year with the Milwaukee Bucks. (Editor's note: The only Bucks' rookie from Indiana that year was Quinn Buckner.) The team was visiting Indiana for a game with the Indiana Pacers and the player had taken the time to drive down to talk to Knight. He was evidently having personal problems and thought he was discussing them in private. Knight immediately came down from this meeting and talked to the team and told us the intimate details. With no thought of discretion or sensitivity, Knight shamelessly used their discussion as an example of why we needed to listen to him in making decisions to avoid making mistakes.

That's what turned me totally away from Knight—doing what he did to that man was cowardly. And it was totally unnecessary. It was self-serving—it was none of our business what was going on in this player's life and I was even more disgusted since this player had helped to recruit me to Indiana. I left the locker room in a furious state. This man had trusted Knight with the most intimate details of his personal life and Knight used it to make himself look good.

Half the guys in the locker room didn't even know the player personally and after the incident of Knight's locker room explosion at the black player combined with this, I knew I was never to trust this man with anything going on in my life. Not only was Knight clearly not a friend, he was a self-serving coward who masqueraded as a confidant.

If Knight was angry, he usually was angry at me first as I was the the team captain. With two starters out with injuries, it showed in our early record. Knight knew I was the first in conditioning, but told me I was to be the sixth man, and was not even allowed to compete for a starting spot that season. We were in a position to win the Big Ten Championship, on the strength of Isiah Thomas. Luckily, his sheer talent was so impressive that Knight overlooked situations, and it was a constant pleasure to me that he would have to bend to the will of Isiah. And, Isiah did not let Knight stop him from developing his natural talent.

Still, he'd take me out of the game if anyone else made a mistake. After one particular game where he benched me and let us lose the game, I called a friend who worked at the university. He said that if I was going to listen to everything Knight said, I wasn't going to be able to play. He was right, and I'll bet he gave that speech many times. I just decided not to listen to Knight and I overcame whatever he put in my way.

Most players were forced to play a level of basketball they might not have reached otherwise, and a lot of good players have come out of Indiana. There are no gray areas there—you're either a successful player or you're not.

How did these players—these men—swallow their pride to accomplish a more important goal of teamwork, winning and taking instruction? We buried any feelings of personal boldness and became a versatile, strong and powerful team. Some people do well in a prescriptive, militaristic environment where they adapt well to being told what to do. Some don't and bury their personal feelings, which is destructive. In this case, winning wasn't everything.

Knight always used to say, "I've forgotten more about basketball than you'll know." That's especially true since he's a better politician than he is a coach. For example, he said his practices were closed, but then we'd see his favorite trustee of the moment or the president of the university at practice, so we knew it would be easy practice and we'd get the hard practice later.

He always told us that when you win games, people continue to accept whatever you do and he has proved that over and over again. Swearing was a common way for him to express his anger but that was tolerated as well as his explosive physical actions such as throwing or kicking objects. I understood him so well because he was so predictable; one of the most predictable people who have been part of my life. He understands most people are weak and shy away from confrontation.

When incidents like these happen in life to you, or if you are an observer, you think by being quiet or with time it will go away. But it doesn't go away. Continuously throughout my process to become a head coach, in college and in the pros, people fed off the fact that I did not have a strong relationship with Knight.

One athletic director (editor's note: The University of Toledo) told me in an interview for his head coach's job that he thought he needed Knight's recommendation. I was up for a college job and it was one of the few times I've lost my temper. I specifically told him that if he needed Knight's recommendation, I didn't want the job. The guy talked to Knight and I didn't get the job because Knight discouraged him from hiring me. I played for Knight, was his captain, and I graduated on time, yet he had the power to defeat me professionally. But the way the system is set up in the United States, you can pick up the phone and assassinate someone's character, as it's the politics of the game. Interviewers don't check because it's the perception that counts.

For some reason, Knight can't acknowledge he's one of those old-style, intimidating personalities who's got seasoned athletes and coaching peers quaking in their sneakers rather than talk about him publicly. It's understandable as many bide their time and are worried about the repercussions of confrontation. The fact is, when you deny stories, you actually then are accepting and perpetuating cowardly behavior. It's a detriment to the public, the league, players, and the families of athletes being recruited. Dark private thoughts are just that, and the ones who are hurting are the people who don't acknowledge his harmful private behavior.

I don't for a moment expect others to acknowledge these particular incidents as we've all got a lot on the line, but I wouldn't be true to myself it I kept it hidden. Some people say "forgive and forget," but if we all did that, we'd forget crimes and the large acts of irresponsibility and abuse. Besides, it reinforces the best way I've learned how to deal with controversy and static; deal with it head on and move on.

I mentioned earlier that I don't believe you rise up by stepping on people; your job in life is to help people rise up as you rise. Unfortunately, there are people who stomp on you as you rise. Don't accept it. You may have to wait a few years before you understand what was happening and how to make it right for you, but don't hold on to destructive relationships or thoughts.

And, of course, beware of cowards.

The bad part about my book was that my timing was bad. I didn't know that shit with Neil Reed was coming out so everybody thought I was just piling onto what Reed was doing. That wasn't the case. We started our project the prior summer and it would have been out last Christmas, but my brother, Cris, didn't get his part written.

As far as I know Quinn Buckner never knew that Knight came down to the locker room and talked about the intimate details of their conversation. Quinn has seen my book, but he doesn't know that he is the former player I was referring to.

I had written a book involving Knight once before. It happened way back in 1988, I submitted it to a writer, Mark Katz, of the Dayton Daily News, and he begged me not to do it. He said, "Butch, don't do it—don't do it." The whole thing is everybody wants to believe there's very few cases where someone actually kisses a lot of asses and gets ahead. Mark was thinking "You're gonna hurt yourself—you're gonna hurt yourself." I held it for that long. But that's the way it works out.

That week the book came out, Marcus Camby called to say I was a liar. It wasn't the fact that he might know anything about Isiah, Knight and me. It was the fact that I had traded Marcus to New York.

I said, "To hell with this guy calling me a liar." I filed a slander suit because Marcus has already been convicted of lying to a grand jury on the UMass thing. And, obviously he had no clue about this situation as he was a toddler when it happened.

Marcus Camby's manager was the Public Relations Director for the Toronto Raptors when we drafted him and was hired by Isiah. Isiah left the Raptors and that guy left with Isiah, to manage Isiah. Then when we traded Marcus to New York, he started managing Marcus. So Isiah and him put

Marcus up to attacking me because Isiah was 'in bed' with Bobby Knight in order to get the Indiana Pacers' job. Isiah was the one who came out and defended Bobby Knight last spring because Isiah was so desperate to get back into pro basketball. The only opportunity that was available to him was Indiana and if he comes out and admits that Knight has said that to him, there's no way the Pacers can hire him. I know all that; Isiah hated Knight. But Isiah sold his soul to get the Indiana Pacer job. He sold it to Knight.

Isiah put Marcus Camby up to calling me a liar. The thing is I had to send the message up to Isiah and the next one who called me a liar I was going to sue them. The last thing Knight and them wanted was to be in court and everybody would have to stand up under oath and tell the truth about what happened.

That's what I told the NBA committee when I talked to them when they were reviewing my Knight statements. I said, "I got no problem with what Knight said. If you read my book, you'll understand that to me it wasn't the matter of that. The problem I have is that Knight is a coward—anything that goes wrong in Indiana if you don't buy into what he says, even if you go away and keep your mouth shut, he tries to destroy you. He lies and gets other people to lie to destroy people's lives. If this hadn't come out on Neil Reed, you guys would be sitting there saying it never happened and you would have hundreds of people lie to you.

This was after the whole state felt good about Larry Bird, who was one of the few people who overcame Bobby Knight. He really has. Knight, basically, didn't give a fuck that Bird left school because Knight's attitude is "If you don't go to Indiana, your life's all fucked up." Bird went to Indiana State, then goes to play for the Celtics. Bird had left the year or two before I got to Indiana.

I just knew that people in the coaching fraternity like to think of certain schools as 'family,' and that I wasn't in the kiss-ass Indiana family. That didn't bother me at all. It's just the way it works.

The Last Chapter

The last chapter of *Knightmares* is yet to be written.

It would have been written Sunday but the author watched football.

© Brian Spurlock

© Brian Spurlock

NCAA
HEAD COACH
NCAA

NCAA
NCAA

NCAA
HEAD COACH
NCAA
ERIC ANDERSON

NCAA
NCAA

© Phil Sears

© Brian Spurlock

© Phil Sears

© All Sport Photography/David Leeds

© Brian Spurlock

To Kathryn

My Real-life Barbara Jane Bookman

Contents

Acknowledgments

The people who helped me put this book together could be sorted into three groups, probably. I don't know what the three groups are or why I would want to sort them, but since everything else in this book is sorted into groups, I thought this would be an appropriate place to start. I'm sure I could figure out the three groups if I had to.

I am personally responsible for all errors, misstatements, inaccuracies, omissions, commissions, comminglings, communisms, fallacies. . . . If it's wrong and it's in this book, it's my fault.

My thanks to Special K for everything and especially to Ellen, my Oklahoma typist, who can spell strange names, decipher garbled tapes, scribbled handwriting, and "unusual" editing marks and do this in a very quick and orderly fashion.

Sincere thanks to Cappy Gagnon of Notre Dame security, Mike Kinney in Denver, Kim Shapiro at ESPN the magazine, Chris Sherrod at Cresencio, Brett Steindl, Bill Goldman at ESPN Radio, Eric Edwards in San Juan, the wonderful Heidi Day in Scottsdale, Mr. Walter B. Planner in Davenport, Iowa, Jon Spoelstra, Bill Tidd, Mark Duran at Playboy Enterprises, Ray Compton and Scott Bindley.

A very special thank you to Dale Brown, Dick Vitale, Bob Ryan, John Feinstein, Gene Wojciechowski, Bill Gildea, Jeff Mortimer, Larry Guest, Cynthia Martin, Peter Golenbock and Charles Barkley. I appreciate the help, kindness and time of these talented people.

Preface

It must have been my first day with the new brain. It was the night before the most recent Kentucky Derby, and I was at a nifty dinner party in suburban Indianapolis. After dessert was served, my "friend," a former owner of an Indiana professional sports team, suckered me in by saying, "Hey Rich, tell your basketball theory that you showed me at the SuperShow." Clearly, I must have forgotten that I was in the middle of Indiana. A few months before, my host and I were at the SuperShow in Atlanta, which is the second largest trade show in the United States, a galaxy of sporting goods and sporting goods-related items from almost every manufacturer in the world.

Taking a break from touring the exhibits, my friend and I were eating a hot dog and drinking a Coke at one of those stand-up tables with no chairs at a concession stand in the Georgia Dome, when a beautiful woman walked toward the table adjacent to ours. I noticed that she had on a brand new style University of Kentucky Wildcats' shoe-something my cohort didn't notice. I leaned over and said, "Hey, I'll bet this gal's from Kentucky, and she knows more basketball than you do." So during an animated conversation with her, she expounded on the exploits of a 1950's Kentucky high school basketball legend, Kelly Coleman, told us why Rick Pitino left the University of Kentucky, and explained what the problems were with the University of Louisville Cardinals. Then she disappeared into the aisles. My friend turned to me and said in a quizzical manner, "How did you know she was from Ken-

tucky and how did you know she would know so much about basketball?" With no mention of the shoes, I told him, "When you see a "Show Dog" the odds are great that she's from Kentucky, and what makes Kentucky the best basketball state in the country is the women there all know basketball as well as most men do in other states." That may have been interesting to him that day in Hotlanta but it got chilly fast in his Indiana home that night.

The room was deathly silent. If I had just had a private audience with the Pope and referred to Mother Teresa as a conniving bitch, I would have been more warmly received than I was by the people at that dinner table. When I finished my story, that's when the shenanigans began. This "drop dead gorgeous" woman—not "drop dead" in the way that Fred Lane's wife meant "drop dead"—this woman just looked at me scathingly, and then said sneeringly, "At least our high school heroes don't play drunk in the state tournament, Gene Keady's wife is not a bitch about wanting to move back to Kansas and Bobby Knight doesn't sell phone service or chase cheerleaders."

Then she made personal, non-basketball remarks that I won't dwell on here other than to say that sometimes I wouldn't mind being the last man on the face of this earth just to see if all those women were telling the truth.

Everyone at the dinner table broke out in a large cheer with much applause. I was ready to crawl under the table. Only later did I find out that my so-called "friend" had set me up and coached that woman what to say. But it certainly was a strong introduction to how serious and knowledgeable the people in Indiana are about their basketball.

As we regrouped the following morning to head to Churchill Downs, any man present was more likely to be struck by lightning while honeymooning with Christie Brinkley than Bob Knight was to be fired by Indiana University. The women were more likely to see a left-handed female golfer than to realize that long before fall basketball practice started at IU, Bob Knight would be standing down at the corner of What and If by himself.

One reason I was at the dinner party was that I was in the Midwest doing a promotional tour for a book I'd written on Kurt Warner, the St. Louis Rams NFL MVP. I write sports books as a hobby, and they're great fun to do. I've done books on Harry Caray, Kurt Warner and Mike Ditka among others. It was during this party that I was strongly encouraged to do a Bob Knight book, rather than a previously-planned one on Terry Bradshaw.

It was a fortuitous decision, marketing-wise, given the subsequent events. Why a book on Bob Knight? Because Bob Knight is a character at a time when the world is running out of characters—just like Mike Ditka.

Orthodox behavior has totally stifled creativity. Posturing and positioning one's image in order to maximize income has replaced honesty and bluntness. Political correctness has made phonies out of too many. Enter Bob Knight.

For another thing, we are of the same generation. I am just a few years younger than Knight; we're both on the back nine of our lives, and I didn't like it when the word "old" started creeping into descriptions of Bob Knight and others born in the Forties. "Old" is someone who is ten years older than you are. But old is never the age that you are at the moment.

For Knight and myself, and many like us, grew up in another time when Elvis was the King, Little Richard was the Queen, and Bruce Springsteen wasn't even in middle management yet. The people of Bob Knight's generation grew up at the very best time to be involved in sports: Baseball cards were collected, not for investments, but for the joy. You raced for the baseball diamond at every free moment to play until you were called home for supper—without an adult being anywhere in sight. A trip to a major league ballpark, if it happened, was magical. Double headers were plentiful. There were only eight teams in each baseball major league. A trade was a major deal. There were no free agents. There were no agents. There was no Astroturf. There was no designated hitter. It was speed and control not velocity and location. It was the lane not the paint. There were no World Series night games. You waited impatiently each Fall for the Converse Basketball Yearbook and every Spring for the Louisville Slugger Handbook. It was a great time to grow up in America. And your coach was your hero. Your coach was almost like a god. Your coach was always right, and your coach was always right there.

Bob Knight is a coach the way coaches used to be in an America that is not the way it used to be. I constantly tell my two sons that the world was different when I was a youth, and they say, "Yeah, well for one thing, it was flat." When Knight graduated from high school, Alaska and Hawaii were not U. S. states. When he graduated from college in 1962, Marilyn Monroe was still acting, Johnny Carson had yet to appear on the Tonight Show, the very first diet soda called Diet Rite appeared, and Cassius Clay's fiancé, Dee Dee Sharp, had a hit song called Mashed Potato Time. And consider what happened in 1971, the year Knight became Head Coach at Indiana University. It was the year of the Pentagon Papers and Attica. There were still cigarette commercials on TV, hot pants in the streets, "Joy to the World" and "Me and Bobby McGee" on the jukebox. *Look* magazine was on the newsstands and "The Last Picture Show" *was* at the picture show. And maybe you'd "like to buy the world a Coke" as the first major league baseball night World Series game was played. And the Cubs were in the 63rd year of their five-year plan.

In our youth, some youngsters read all twenty three of Clair Bee's Chip Hilton series. In Orrville, Ohio, Bob Knight did. Others, like me, read every one of John Tunis' youth sports sagas. From the age of ten, I have been a serious collector of sports books. During that time—for the sake of argument, let's call it thirty years—my favorite book style is the "eavesdropping" type where the subject talks in his own words without the "then he said" or "the air is so thick here you could cut it with a butter knife" waste of verbiage that makes it harder to get to the meat of the matter. Books like Lawrence Ritter's *The Glory of Their Times,* Donald Honig's *Baseball When the Grass was Real,* or any of my friend, Pete Golenbock's books like *Fenway or Wrigleyville.* Thus, I adopted that style when I started compiling oral histories of the Harry Carays of the world.

I'm a sports fan, first and foremost. This book is written solely for other sports fans. I really don't care what the publisher, editors or critics think. I'm only interested in the fans having an enjoyable read and getting their money's worth.

A little background: most readers of this book probably have never been to Bloomington, Indiana, attended a game at Assembly Hall or been near Bob Knight in person. With apologies to the Indiana faithful, the heathens should know: Bloomington, for much of the year, is Norman Rockwell-pretty; Assembly Hall, which looks like a glorified high school gym on TV, is a cavernous arena and Bob Knight is a large person. For many years, he was the tallest coach in division one sports.

We are not here to solve world problems. So have some laughs, learn some interesting facts, read some fascinating tales and get a better understanding of Coach Knight. There has already been a lot of ink written on a lot of dead trees about Bob Knight—nevertheless, I sincerely wish that you enjoy this book. Go now.

Rich Wolfe,
Scottsdale, Arizona

Introduction

The Future is History

The object isn't to be the youngest head coach. The object is to be the oldest head coach. Bob Knight is an enigma. He's the only active coach to win as many as three NCAA titles, yet he is perpetually dissatisfied and rarely able to savor his triumphs. He demands total discipline on the part of his players, yet he is himself prone to outbursts and indiscretions that tarnish his successes and keep him in constant trouble.

He's a tough guy who cries.

A man with an obsession for winning who points to his players' graduation rate as one of his proudest achievements.

A father figure who abuses and humiliates the young men he most loves.

A person who never forgives a slight and never forgets a friend.

He's one of the most written about, talked about, analyzed, and misunderstood men in American sports.

Knight's players talk about their college experience almost as if it was combat. Steve Alford, one of Knight's favorite players, was asked before the 1987 NCAA championship game what misconceptions the public might have about his coach. The quiet, devout Alford, who was selected by Knight for the 1984 U. S. Olympic Team while still a freshman, but who was also repeatedly thrown out of practice, demoted to the second unit, and publicly berated by his coach during his time at Indiana, replied, "I've survived for four years, and I've only got one more game left." A fellow Olympian, Jeff Turner, when

asked whether he could live with four years of Bob Knight, tactfully responded, “I have a lot of respect for Steve Alford.”

Knight has always taught his teams to play not just against their opponents, but against themselves, as he pushes them to reach the limit of their potential. “He wants to play that perfect basketball game,” said Alford. “He would love to win 100 to nothing.” Hard work, dedication, and the sacrifice of individual goals for the team are all part of Knight’s prescription for perfection. He also insists on his own absolute control—both mental and physical—of his teams and players. And he is willing to go to extraordinary lengths to maintain that control.

When Knight was coaching Army during the 1969 NIT against South Carolina, he told his point guard Mike Krzyzewski, “If you shoot, it’ll be the last thing you do on this earth.” Krzyzewski remembers that he found himself all alone with the ball, went up for the shot, hung there for a minute and passed it off.

In 1976, Knight benched Quinn Buckner, one of his most hard-nosed, disciplined, and dedicated players ever, to get a point across. After an Indiana loss in 1984, he ordered his players out of the locker room and back onto the court for practice. He once sat down an entire starting five—on national TV—because they weren’t disciplined enough. And he kicked his best freshman off the team in 1990, and then refused to let him transfer to the school of his choice.

He has never accepted any deviation from his instructions. Even when he coached one of the greatest collections of players in basketball history—the 1984 Olympic team—he made it clear it was his ball. Patrick Ewing sat for long stretches and when he played he was under strict orders to stay with his man rather than float underneath to block shots. Chris Mullin and Alvin Robertson didn’t get enough playing time to allow them to unleash their particular offensive and defensive talents. Even Michael Jordan was kept largely under wraps, averaging just 17 points per game.

Even more than the 1984 Olympic team, the 1976 Indiana Hoosiers were Bob Knight’s perfect team. Not just because of their record (they were the last major college team to finish undefeated), but because of their collective personality as well. Individually, they were excellent players (every member of the starting five went on to play in the NBA), but none of them had the ability to dominate a game by himself. Instead they dominated as a team. They were a group of supremely disciplined role players who knew their jobs and did them with single-mindedness and dedication. They did exactly what the coach ordered them to do.

In some ways, Knight is even harder on himself than he is on his players. He's so driven that he couldn't even take the time to enjoy the 1976 championship. Immediately after winning the tournament, he told the press, "I'm not paid to relax. I'll be on the plane tomorrow morning. Recruiting."

Despite his perfectionism, Knight does not always hold himself to the same high standards that he demands from team members. While he insists on total discipline from his players, he himself is known almost as much for his erratic behavior as for his victories. His temper, his indiscretion, and his lack of judgment are all as much a part of the public's perception of him as are his strategic brilliance and talent for getting the most out of his players.

Time and again his obscene language and violent temper have gotten him into trouble. He's been know to use physical force on team members, including one documented instance of throwing a ball in a player's face in practice and another of grabbing a player off the floor during a game and yanking him into his seat. These happened long before the Neil Reed incident.

He was arrested for assaulting an officer while serving as the U. S. Pan American Games coach in 1979 in Puerto Rico; witnesses said the incident was the policeman's fault, but Knight aggravated it by insulting local fans.

In 1980 he pointed a gun and fired a blank at a reporter. In 1981 he shoved an LSU fan into a trashcan after a contentious tournament game. The following season he cursed Big Ten commissioner Wayne Duke at midcourt while complaining about the officiating at conference games. In 1985, he threw a chair across the court during a game against Purdue in Bloomington. In 1987, he smashed a telephone on the scorer's table during a tournament game.

Sometimes there's even an element of self-parody in Knight's outbursts: once during an Indiana exhibition against a Soviet team he objected to a call by taking off his shoe and banging it on a table (a la the former Coach Nikita K. of the U of SSR). But in a much more serious incident, he pulled his team off the court in the middle of a game against the Soviets when he didn't like the officials' calls.

It's a shame that Knight draws so much negative attention to himself, because in so many ways his accomplishments are truly remarkable. The Orrville, Ohio, native, a substitute guard on Ohio State's 1960 NCAA champions, became the Army coach in 1965 at the age of 24. In six years at West Point, the Cadets made four NIT appearances while leading the nation in scoring defense three times. In 1971, he moved to Bloomington to become coach of Indiana.

At Indiana, he immediately implemented his coaching philosophy, scrapping the run-and-gun style that was prevalent in the Big Ten at the time and replacing it with an aggressive pressing defense that contested every shot, every pass, and nearly every move by the opposition, along with a precision motion offense that relied on picks, passing, and moving without the ball. In 1975, at the age of 34, he won his first national Coach of the Year award after leading the Hoosiers to a 31–1 record. The following year his undefeated team won the national championship. He has since won two more NCAA titles, in 1981 and 1987.

In 1984 Knight became the youngest coach in history to post 400 major college victories, and in 1989, at the age of 48, he became the second youngest ever to win 500 games. He has the best winning percentage and the most Big Ten conference wins of any coach ever. He's coached NIT, Pan American Games and Olympic champions, and has produced six Olympians in his own programs, including Olympic captains Mike Silliman of Army in 1968 and Quinn Buckner of Indiana in 1976.

At the age of 40, however, after winning his second NCAA title, Knight almost called it quits. There were no more hurdles to overcome, no more challenges to face. And CBS, which had just acquired the rights to televise the NCAA tournament, was offering him major money to handle the tournament coverage. But when Landon Turner, one of the stars of his 1981 championship team, was paralyzed in a car crash, he threw himself heart and soul into setting up a fund to care for Turner and help provide him with necessities of his new life. Knight realized that it wasn't just the money, and it wasn't just the winning that made him a coach—he turned down the CBS job.

He stands by his friends—his teachers as well as his students. After the U. S. Olympic victory in 1984, when team members tried to lift him onto their shoulders and celebrate, he waved them off and ordered them to first pick up an old man sitting courtside. The old man, Henry Iba, had been the coach of several winning U. S. Olympic teams, but his last experience in the international arena had been a bitter one. After Iba's 1972 team lost a disputed championship game to the Soviets, he was widely castigated for his archaic ideas, both in the press and among his coaching peers. Knight felt the victory was stolen from him, that the criticism was unwarranted, and that Iba deserved better. So he ordered his players to make Iba's last Olympic experience a memorable one. The old man was lifted onto their shoulders in celebration.

Knight is a brilliant strategist and is unsurpassed in his attention to detail. Give him time to prepare and his strategic adjustments will generally take his opponents out of their game. He's also a teacher in the best sense of

the word: a man who's able to impart his fundamental knowledge of the game to others. Numerous current head coaches started out as his assistants—no other coach in modern times even comes close to Knight as a teacher of basketball.

In recent years, Knight has shown himself to be capable of adjusting his basic strategies as the game changes and rules and recruiting practices evolve. The rule changes—particularly the institution of the 35-second clock and the 3-point shot—have made Knight's mainstay set-up offense less effective that it was in the past; he's responded by pushing the ball down court and taking advantage of fast-break opportunities and quick 3-pointers and by utilizing a three-guard offense to create match up problems for the opposition. He's also made his defenses harder to read, as he mixed up his man-to-man with a zone.

Knight's also changed his recruiting practices to maintain his competitive edge. The top schoolboys in Indiana no longer become automatic Hoosiers, and even if they did it might not be enough to ensure victory in today's game. As a result, he's begun making personnel moves he once rejected as unnecessary, even unethical. He started to follow his friend Jerry Tarkanian's example and use junior college transfers. (Two of his first jucos, Keith Smart and Dean Garrett, were instrumental in bringing the NCAA Championship back to Bloomington in 1987.) In addition, he's started to red-shirt players. (Red-shirting is a practice whereby a player sits out a year and gains an extra year of eligibility as a fifth-year senior. Coaches often red-shirt a player to bolster a future team when a current team is stocked with talented upperclassmen.)

The nineties began with Indiana being the first Big Ten team to make the NCAA Tournament with a losing record in league play and ended with an uproar and three-game suspension involving a former player, Neil Reed.

Then came the ultimate suspension. After 29 seasons, Indiana University President Myles Brand, fired Knight on September 10, 2000.

As Bob Knight reached the age of 60, he's still a tough guy, hard to understand at times and even harder to take at others. His temper still gets him in trouble. His inflexibility is still at times astonishing. But he's also the knight-errant of the coaching profession, a Don Quixote tilting at windmills.

Will he prove it again?

Will he get the chance?

Where?

The object isn't to be the youngest head coach. The object is to be the oldest head coach.

Bobby Hoosier: Sweeter than Sugar

Hilda Van Arsdale
Barry Donovan
Teresa Godwin Phelps
Bret Bearup
Greg Erickson
Dick Vitale

It's hard to cheer with a broken heart

Hilda Van Arsdale

Hilda was born on a farm near Banquo, Indiana in the southwest corner of Huntington County in 1910. After high school she went to college at St. Mary's of Notre Dame and was a student there when Knute Rockne was a student at Notre Dame. After college she moved to Indianapolis, where she met her husband, Ben, who passed in 1973. They had two children, Dick and Tom—twins who were Co-Mr. Basketball in the state of Indiana for 1961. The twins became second-team All Americans at Indiana University and later had long pro careers. Now they are successful businessmen in Phoenix, Arizona. Over the years, Hilda grew very close with Bob Knight, and particularly close with his second wife, Karen.

Hilda Van Arsdale

Ben and I were so proud of Tom and Dick and the success they've made of themselves. I first met Bob Knight in 1972. I was working at Manual High School when my husband and I decided one day we wanted to go to an IU game. I called the coaching office and talked to Dave Bliss, who later became a head coach at several other schools, and asked if we would be able to purchase two tickets. Coach Bliss assured us there would be no problem.

About fifteen minutes later the phone rang, and it was Coach Knight. When he came from Army, we had never heard of him; we didn't know who he was. This was only his second year there, but Coach Knight said, "Whenever you want to come to a game, and we hope that you'll come to every single IU game, rest assured that you'll have two tickets waiting for you at any time." When my Ben died the following year, I continued to go to the games and went to many of them with Dr. Rebecca Markel whom I had met at the Indiana games and who since has become a very, very close friend. Many times after the games, we're invited over to Bob's house. Bob Knight is the most thoughtful, kindest man I have ever met in my life. He has just a wonderful sense of humor. My fondest memories of being over at his house are with Isiah Thomas's mom where we swapped recipes and just had a gay old time.

Now Karen is a sweetheart. She's a very, very dear lady. She has the most beautiful big, brown eyes you've ever seen in your life and she has been absolutely wonderful to me. One time we went to a Notre Dame football game, and she kept wanting to buy me Cokes. I didn't want to drink any Cokes because I hate to use public restroom facilities. It was a very hot day and as we were leaving the stadium, I started to feel faint. I grabbed onto a rail and later collapsed on the ground. The Notre Dame security people were absolutely wonderful, and when I came to, I asked one of the paramedics if they knew my nephew, Dr. Mike Thomas in Elkhart, which he did. I ended up at the infirmary. Karen was with me all the way, and, lo and behold, here comes Dr. Larry Rink, the IU team physician who happened to be at the game that day. Karen and I have just done so many things together. She is just so sweet and so kind and I feel so bad about what happened.

But really in the last four or five years, nothing was the same at IU. I don't think Bob had any chance under the zero tolerance policy. I haven't talked to him since he was fired. I just feel so bad about it. Bob Knight has done so many wonderful things for that University. You have no idea. He has done so many things for Riley's Children's Hospital here in Indianapolis and for so many other charities.

I just think he is a wonderful, wonderful person. I remember working with Karen to surprise him for his fiftieth birthday party. Karen had me dress up like a hooker with all this "hooker" stuff on, and she hid me in the garage at the Knights' house. At the proper time I came in, and Bob just took one look at me and said, "Hilda!"

I just feel terrible. I'm gonna miss seeing him and miss him coaching the team and I'm gonna miss seeing him on the sidelines. I'm just sick about the whole matter.

Eighty-one percent of people who have seen at least two Police Academy movies think that Knight is innocent

Barry Donovan

Barry Donovan was a talented disc jockey in Lafayette, Indiana when he pulled an off-the-wall prank on Bob Knight several years ago. Donovan is a master at imitating voices and had a lot of fun needling famous people. If you could hear how close his voice is to Sly Stallone, you might be able to appreciate the following story better, but rest assured his voice is almost a duplicate of Stallone's.

Courtesy of Indiana Pacers

Barry Donovan

I had pulled something like this before pretending to be Reagan. I got Sam Donaldson to bite into it. "Well, Sam, this is Ronnie, how are you?" "Fine, Mr. President." Then about half way through it, he got onto it and said, "I don't know who you are, but you do a damn good Ronnie."

I can't remember the date we did it. Knight was pretty teed off about it. He eventually decided that yeah it was pretty funny. We kept trying to get hold of Coach Knight and every time we'd call he was unavailable or whatever and we kept saying we were with the Stallone's Publicists. This was a morning radio show up in Lafayette. We were doing a show prep and we were off the air while making these calls. We were gonna call and see if we could get Coach Knight to bite on the fact that Sylvester Stallone wanted to do a movie with him—to see if we could convince him of it. We called for a couple of months. We finally found out he was on a fishing trip and was coming in that morning. We had learned that after coming back from fishing trips, coach is in pretty good moods.

So we called and convinced secretaries that we were with Sly Stallone's Publicists. She wanted to talk to Stallone first so I disguised my voice and said (in almost-perfect Stallone dialect) "How ya doin? This is Sylvester." So she goes, "Coach, it's him; it really is him!"

Coach took the call and he was convinced. We talked about picking Stallone up—how I would get down to Bloomington if I landed there. Told him

I wanted to do a movie. I was still doing the phony Stallone voice—"Bobby, I'm really a big fan of yours. I'm going to need some help on this basketball movie. I don't know much about basketball." He said, "You're a man after my own heart. I've got too many God damn people around here who think they know too much about basketball." "So, you wouldn't mind helping me on this?" "Nah, nah, if you want me to be a consultant on it, I'll do whatever you want me to do."

I said, "Where is Indiana University? Is that in Indianapolis?" He said, "No, no, no, south of Indianapolis in Bloomington." "How do I get there?" "If you're coming in here, I'll send somebody up there to pick you up. I'll have somebody pick you up and drive you down here to us."

So we were arranging all that and we went on and I said, "Would you want to be in the movie?" He said, "I'll do whatever you want me to do—you tell me what you want. I'm a big fan of your movies—I think they've got a lot of good messages in them."

I asked him if he wanted to do a love scene. He said, "Oh no, I'm not gonna do any love scene—my secretary says I shouldn't do that. No, I'm not gonna do any love scenes." Then I said, "I'm kinda short you know—about 5'7" or so. Would you mind walking in a trench here or something so we'll look like we're the same height?" "I'll do whatever you want me to do; you just arrange this and you tell me what you want and I'll do whatever you want."

Other people were in the room with me and were laughing their asses off so I had to struggle to keep a straight face. So he went along with everything, and at the very end I tell him that it's a scam.

He really lit into me. Some of the things he said were not even biologically possible. Afterwards, we talked to him for about half an hour convincing him people would see a different side of him—they'd see he could take a joke as well as dish it out; he could take it. He said, "You know what; it's pretty damn funny. I've got to admit it's pretty damn funny. You can go ahead and run it, but don't ever pull any shit like this on me again."

We ran it in morning "drive." In our promos, we mentioned that we had a secret phone conversation we had taped. That we got a tape from IU with Sylvester Stallone and Bobby Knight talking about a movie so there was a really big buzz around town. "Oh, Bobby Knight's doing a movie with Sylvester Stallone and everything." I don't know—well Gene Keady heard it

The name of Stallone's dog in Rocky was Butkus, after Dick Butkus.

and called me and said he was laughing so hard he had to pull off to the side of the road. Then later Bobby's people called up and said they got all kinds of calls about it and Coach said "Don't run that damn thing anymore." I offered to send him a copy and he said he didn't want one. He just laughed about it and said, "You guys got me." That must have been about 1984–85. There was a big rivalry between Purdue and IU so I just thought I'd try it.

The only fallout we had with the Knight scam was sponsors who wanted to put it on a CD and sell it. We said, "Oh no, we can't do that. Coach doesn't want that done. We'd just be taking it too far." Other radio stations (just about every Big Ten school) called and requested it. I just said, "No, better not." You can carry things like that too far. *Sports Illustrated* did a story on it. They did a little blurb on it, and talked about Coach Knight being a good sport and that kind of stuff. At the end they kind of scared me though. They go, but did Barry Donovan get Sylvester Stallone's permission? I go "Great, thanks for that." Like Sylvester Stallone would never see a *Sports Illustrated*, you know.

WAZY in Lafayette was the radio station. We had been pulling this sort of thing. I am actually an IU grad—went to IU law school and my Dad's a HUGE Bobby Knight fan, but I was more of a Gene Keady fan and so I just kind of thought it would be fun to pull that off. I did get Gene Keady later though. I got him as an old woman who was a real big fan of his. An old woman "You know who this is, Gene?" "Gene, I love you." She was this real old lady and I got him to leave the phone. "Well, I just want one thing, Gene, if you could just give me a kiss on the phone?" "I can't do that, Ma'am." "Well, just a little peck on the cheek, Gene." He goes, "Well, all right." It was kinda fun just to put people of prominence in awkward positions like that.

I also got Al Michaels, Dan Dierdorf and Frank Gifford one time—the first time they ever did Monday Night Football in Indianapolis. They were pretty funny. I had Frank Gifford as Punkin' Head of Monrovia Punkin' Festival, and he would say "Well I'd be proud to be Mr. Pumpkin for your festival, but I don't think I can be there." I said, "Well Mr. Gifford, this is the mayor of Monrovia and as the mayor I'd be proud to present you with a giant punkin'." Frank Gifford is just a very nice guy so he said, "Well I'll tell you. I'm gonna be there at the Hoosier Dome," and he arranged for me to present it to him. He said I'd be proud to be Mr. Pumpkin." I said, "Oh no, you can't say pumpkin, you gotta say punkin'. "Okay, punkin', I'd be proud." He was funny.

Cody and Cassidy Gifford are uncle and aunt to Frank Gifford's grandchildren.

Dan Dierdorf was funny. It was Halloween the first time they did Monday Night Football at the Hoosier Dome and made him agree to wear a costume of some kind. We went through various costumes; he had to wear like a Batman costume. Al Michaels would have to wear like the penguin or something like that. Dan just laughed his ass off; he thought it was funny as hell. I think he would have done it.

So, Bobby Knight was really a great sport. A lot of guys wouldn't be able to laugh at themselves, but he really did; he thought it was funny as hell. After he calmed down, after he realized it wasn't Sylvester, he laughed his ass off. He said, "I'll tell you what. That's pretty damn good. That's one of the better ones I've ever had pulled on me. That's pretty damn good." "I'm an alum of IU so I'm not gonna put you in a bad light or anything like that. You're a hell of a basketball coach, but a lot of people don't know you've got a hell of a sense of humor." He goes, "That was a good one—a really good one. Were the secretaries in on it?" I go, "No, they really didn't know." He goes, "You just saved their jobs." He just laughed.

We had talked to him for about half an hour trying to get his permission to play the tape on the air. "Coach, come on, ('cause we had to have his permission to play it)." He said, "Why should I give you permission to do that?" "Coach, people don't know that side of you; they don't know you have that great sense of humor that you have the ability to be very funny and stuff." I knew from his lectures that people had said he's got a tremendous sense of humor. He really does. I think some of the stuff he says he thinks is funny and other people are just offended by it.

I think he's kind of dry in his delivery. Because he's such an intimidating figure, he doesn't lend himself to be like a Will Rogers-friendly type. He's just a very awesome, large individual. They go, "Is he trying to be funny or what's he doing—oh my God!" I think they don't get the joke sometimes; then when they sit back and look at it, they go "He's just being funny." A prime example is when he had that bull whip, I'm sure he thought that was just being funny and was a good way to laugh that whole thing off, but because of his perception with people, and you know perception is everything in the market place. I think people just kinda looked at it like "this guy who's very intimidating was making light of the fact of slavery" and that never entered his mind in any form or fashion."

There is absolutely no way that Bob Knight is a racist, quite the opposite . . . and he does have a great sense of humor.

Bob Knight was the first Army coach to recruit blacks.

You can always tell a Notre Dame man, but you can't tell him much

Teresa Godwin Phelps

Teresa was married for many years to Digger Phelps, the former Notre Dame coach. She is a member of the law school faculty at Notre Dame and is currently in the middle of a year's sabbatical enjoying the dunes of Lake Michigan. She has authored a book called The Coach's Wife, *a unique perspective of big-time college basketball through her eyes. In the following story, she alludes to how she almost lost her husband in a plane crash. Notre Dame canceled the flight at the last minute and sadly the University of Evansville used the plane the same night and the plane crashed killing all 29 on board.*

The night our flight was canceled, I remember my husband getting upset saying we've got to get down there. We've got to do this. I said well, consider the alternative. If the plane shouldn't be going, we shouldn't be going. I think Notre Dame just made a decision that the weather was too bad and they would just bus it. Then the plane was used by the Evansville team. It was so tragic.

Personally I have known Bob Knight for probably 25 years. We came to Indiana about the same time. As a person, one on one, I like Bobby very, very much. He's very nice, smart, funny man. What I read about the way he behaves he shocks me sometimes, but I've never seen anything like that up close. My former husband knew him better than I did. He coached at Army, West Point, when we were at Fordham. I think we actually played each other that year. We crossed paths here and there. But one very good thing about Bobby is he is an extremely loyal person. If you're his friend, you remain his friend forever. I'm sure that's one of those things with his players, the ones who played for him and liked him, experience, why there is so much loyalty to Bobby is probably because he is very loyal to people who are his friends. There are many things about Bobby that are admirable. My personal experience with Bobby has been positive, across the board positive.

Right before my book came out, Bobby told me he would do a blurb for the back of the book. I didn't have it from him, and my publisher was on me to get it and I was trying to get it. I would call down to Indiana. With a guy like Bobby Knight, you go through a phalanx of people to talk to him. You get transferred six times. I would tell them, "Look, I'm a personal friend; I've got an important question to ask him and I just couldn't get through to him." So

finally I faxed him or FEDEX-ed him, 'personal and confidential' and just said, "What does it take to talk to you? I've been calling and calling and no one will let me talk to you. I'm so frustrated. I need this blurb." The next day I was at my eye doctor. The funny thing about it is my eye doctor is a huge Indiana fan. He's got Indiana stuff all over the office. I'm there in one of their little dark rooms and his receptionist comes in and says "there's a phone call for Mrs. Phelps and it's Coach Knight." Everyone in the place is just "WHAT?" This is like a legend called the place. So Coach Knight was upset when he got my message that I was having so much trouble getting in touch with him. So he had called my secretary and had made my secretary tell him where I was. For some reason I told her where I was and he had tracked me down at the eye doctor and called me there and apologized because I hadn't been able to reach him. I am now the most important person in the world in my doctor's eye because Bobby Knight had called me. They thought it was a prank and actually they didn't believe it. Everyone was standing around me at the receptionist's desk while I was talking and it was clear that I was talking to Bobby Knight. Then I got the blurb.

I understand the incredible pressure on somebody like Bobby. There's also an awful lot of ego stress that goes on. People think you're wonderful—think you're God, etc. And that's certainly the situation at Indiana. No one was keeping him humble. He had a lot of power. And athletes in general are like that, they never grow up—people who are in athletics. They play games their whole life. Many of them are very immature. Because they act in a manner that is so sophisticated in whatever they are doing—basketball, baseball, whatever, we expect that their character and their personality and their intelligence is the same as their physical ability—as their savvy in a game, and it's not. I remember our players. We would get someone with so much polish at eighteen or nineteen years old on the basketball court who acted like he was going on fourteen off the court. And people were surprised. I said, "He's a kid; he's acting like a kid." They're surprised because they have so much smoothness in their game. But athletes in general are protected from reality, and people who are in sports are very protected from reality. What they do is a game. And it's a game that's way overvalued by our culture. We attach incredible importance to touchdowns and things like that.

Teflon Bobby Knight, one of the most complicated men I've ever known. On the one hand, there's the private Bobby—generous, softhearted, a good listener, my friend. On the other hand, there's the public Bobby, whose outrageous acts I need not reopen here. I know he's really the private person, the man with whom I would trust nearly anything. I wish he'd let the

public in on that guy. But, then again, why should he? Bobby gets away with anything. No one, *no one* else would have lasted as long as he has behaving the way he sometimes does. His public acts just wash right off.

Notre Dame has beaten more number-1 ranked basketball teams than any other school. Nine times they have defeated the number-1 team.

While a small school of about 7,000, no university has sent more players to the NFL and only three colleges have had more NBA alumni. Notre Dame also ranks fourth in the number of major league baseball players.

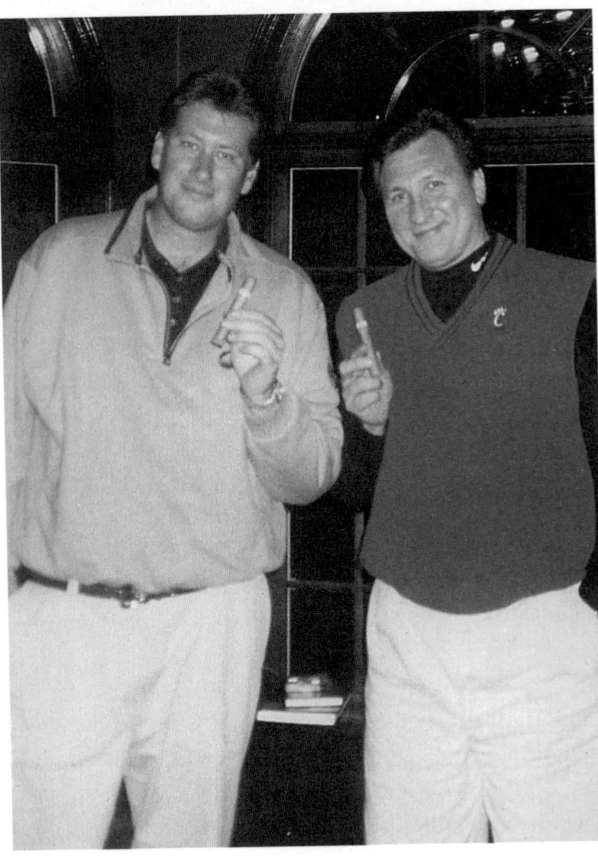

Bret Bearup and Bob Huggins see page 27.

I like Bobby Knight, hell, I love everyone, you're next

Bret Bearup

Bret Bearup fits the description of a "Gentle Giant," almost seven feet tall and weighing near three hundred pounds, his boyish face usually has a quizzical and wry look to it. Bearup was a McDonald's High School All American on Long Island and was one of the bluest blue chips his senior year in high school.

The great Bearup story of his high school years is being recruited by Jim Valvano. Long before Jim Valvano won the 1983 National Title at North Carolina State, he was the coach at little Iona College at New Rochelle, New York. One time, as Bearup was walking off the floor after another stellar high school performance, this enthusiastic dark-haired guy came bouncing up and said, "Hi Bret, I'm Jim Valvano, Iona college." Bearup stopped, looked him straight in the eye and said, "Wow, you look awfully young to own a college."

Courtesy of University of Kentucky

Bret Bearup

After being pursued by just about every major college program other than Indiana, Bearup cast his lot with the University of Kentucky and Coach Joe B. Hall. Later, when Hall was forced out at the University of Kentucky and became head of a large bank in Lexington, Bearup said, "That bank will soon become the easiest bank in the state of Kentucky to rob." Everyone looked at Bret and said, "Why would you say that?" Bearup said, "Because Joe B. Hall will never let the guards shoot."

After joining a prestigious Louisville law firm out of college, Bearup now lives in Atlanta, Georgia where he is one of the top financial advisors to professional athletes in the country. His company, ProTrust handles all the financial investments for Shaquille O'Neal, Kevin Garnett and other top-flight athletes. As a young lawyer in Louisville, Bearup became embroiled in a minor controversy involving an Indiana University outstanding freshman player named Lawrence Funderburke who wanted to transfer during the middle of his freshman year.

> *The only person to score back-to-back, fifty-point games in the history of Long Island High School basketball is Jim Brown, the NFL legend.*

Bobby Hoosier: Sweeter Than Sugar

In the book, *Raw Recruits*—I was very flattered to read Knight's quote: "Bearup's wasting away on that bench in Kentucky; I'd love to have him here." I was very flattered when he said that. I've always been a Bobby Knight fan. Even when I was in high school. First, he wins. Secondly, he turns out great kids. You take a look at the kids who graduate from IU, their graduation rate is simply astonishing for a big time college basketball program. It's really not just that they graduated, they go on to achievement. I think the Indiana basketball program in that particular regard is a bright shining star. I just don't know if it can be duplicated elsewhere again. . . . An achievement incredible in its scope—given what I see out there these days, it's unbelievable.

You know I didn't really know Coach Knight that well; he didn't even recruit me. I don't know why he seemed to like me so much. I did seem to always have good games against Indiana.

I met Funderburke when I was in law school at UK. He came down for a UK game and came by and introduced himself. I didn't know who Lawrence was; he was a sophomore in high school in Ohio. This guy who brought him down there was a UK alum who had been bringing kids to one UK game a year. He's involved in AAU, amateur basketball, there. He'd call me and I'd agree to go to lunch with him. Funderburke turned out to be a great player and great kid.

At Indiana, he got in touch with me when he decided to transfer. He showed up in Louisville and told me I was the only lawyer he knew. Knight wasn't letting him out of his letter of intent, could I help? So, first of all, I asked my law firm if I could work on the case pro bono and they said yes. I was a first year lawyer. Funderburke was from Columbus. He's at IU and he's unhappy. He wants to transfer, and Knight won't let him out of his letter of intent.

I called Knight. The first few conversations I had with Knight were fine—definitely certain places that Knight wanted Lawrence to go, but Lawrence really wasn't into that. There were two places that he absolutely would not release Lawrence to—Louisville and Kentucky. I think he suspected Scooter McCray, a Louisville Assistant Coach, had come up there to IU to recruit Lawrence. So Lawrence went to St. Catherines, a junior college in Kentucky, one semester to finish up one year at that school.

Lawrence had gone home to Columbus to see his mom and sister. Apparently, one time when he went up there he ran into Randy Ayers, the Ohio State coach. I got a fax from Knight that had copied some anonymous letter that somebody had sent him saying that my supervising partner in the law firm, Jim Milliman, was a big Louisville fan, and he would watch out for

Louisville. It was an inter-conference transfer so Lawrence wasn't eligible for a scholarship but he was an Ohio resident who would be accepted into Ohio State and wouldn't cost too damn much money to go there back in those days. I don't know how Knight felt about him going to Ohio State—he never would return my phone calls after that.

Lawrence is religious almost to the point of fanaticism. I remember a couple of years ago, Lawrence called and told me he wanted all his investments liquidated because the day of the coming of the Lord was at hand. So I said, "Okay, when you meet Jesus, you want to be liquid—is that what you're saying?" He was like "Man, come on, this is no joking matter." I was like "I'm just trying to understand the reason behind your wanting to do this."

I really enjoyed playing against Knight. He's obviously larger than life. I remember being out on the floor keeping an eye on the sideline watching him pace up and down, listening to him yell and such. Especially when I had twelve points in the first half, listening to Knight scream at Uwe Blab when I was doing that.

UK-IU a huge rivalry—gargantuan—I know when I played there, we really prepared for that game. And I remember, one of Coach Hall's big things was that Indiana set moving picks. He didn't think referees ever called them so we actually practiced knocking down the picker. If a guy was moving when he tried to set a pick for us we were to just run right the hell over him. It was incredible, two days before the Indiana game we were beating the shit out of each other, knocking each other to the floor. Sometimes the referee would call it, but Joe B., from the minute we walked on the floor, would say, "Hey listen, I told my guys that Indiana sets so many damn moving picks, if they move them, knock them over." When the refs did call a moving pick on Indiana, Knight wouldn't be too damn happy.

In 1981, the year they won the national championship, the way we beat them in Bloomington. I remember the way we beat them was Derrick Hord got a steal and put us up by two. Isiah Thomas, they had the ball, ran a play to lob to Ray Tolbert, a perfect lob and Ray Tolbert was so far from the rim that he just lost his balance a little bit and couldn't put it in the hole, missing on a slam-dunk ball. We got the ball and we won 68–66, I believe. Anyway we went back in the locker room and we thought Coach Hall was having a heart attack. There were guys around him over there and he was like bent over. Before he started that, he said, "I just want you to know I've never been prouder of a team. That was one of the best wins of my life" He was pasty white and they had a doctor in there, had him laying down. We really had a big scare.

I wouldn't have any problem letting my kid play basketball under Coach Knight.

I often reminisce about the good old day

Greg Erickson

When Bob Knight went absolutely ballistic during a post-game NCAA press conference in Boise, Idaho after the final game of Indiana's 1995 season, young Greg Erickson, a student at Boise State found himself in the middle of a brouhaha. Knight's rantings and ravings at that press conference have been replayed many times on ESPN over the years, but here is a behind-the-scenes look through Greg Erickson's eyes. Greg is a graduate of Boise State University, class of 1996, and is involved with his family's business, the publication Contract Employment Weekly.

Courtesy of Greg Erickson

Greg Erickson

Basically, my image of Bobby Knight, growing up, being a sports fan, was what I had seen on TV—the tirades, the chairs thrown, the balls kicked and heard stories about him. My Dad was never a very big fan of Coach Knight just because all he knew was what he had seen on TV.

My junior year in college at Boise State, I was a scholarshipped athlete, and the university uses scholarship athletes for event hosts. For the NCAA Regionals that year in 1995, I was chosen as one of the hosts. I was assigned to host Indiana for their game with Missouri. Basically, my duties were to get players and coaches from the locker room out to the court before the game, back and forth at halftime again, and then after the game, I would follow the team back to the locker room. Then after ten minutes, the coach and two or three players were to report to the press conferences. This was the final game. Indiana lost. They were not real happy about going to the press conference. They needed some time. They were in their locker room being quiet. I waited outside for the ten minutes, and I expected the coach and a couple of players to come out and head off to the press conferences. Ten-twelve minutes passed. No coaches. Someone from the press room came running up to me. I knocked on the door and went into the locker room and told them that the press conference people were asking for them and that they were late.

It's a mandatory NCAA rule that the coach has to represent the school in this press conference, win or lose. Obviously, because they had lost this game, they were not real happy about doing it. I remember going into the locker room, and it was just silent—very quiet. I remember how small I felt. I remember that very well, because I'm just small guy and these guys were all big basketball players. They were mostly sitting around, with a couple standing, and it was just eerily silent in there. I told Coach Knight that they were asking for him at the press conference. He told me to go tell them he would be there in a few minutes. I believe he told me to ask if the other team could go on first. The losing team was scheduled to go up on the podium first to answer questions.

I remember running down the long hallway, and around these corners, and into the back gym where these press conferences were being held. I ran in there and Rance Pugmire, the Moderator, was up on stage. He was sitting in the middle of a long press conference table, elevated. I remember the big blue NCAA banners hanging down behind. I walked in front of the table so I was quite a ways down below the table. I remember reaching my hands up and getting Rance Pugmire's attention, and I told him that Coach Knight would be a little bit late. I turn around and start to walk off and the coach from Missouri and a couple of their players were kind of waiting in the wings for this press conference.

As I was walking out, I heard some commotion in the background. The moderator had said that Coach Knight was not going to be there. So the Missouri coach and players came up on stage, and they had just started their portion of the press conference. Then Coach Knight came in. I don't know if anything was said again or not, but Coach Knight came up and was told by somebody in the hallway that the moderator had made a comment that he was not going to show up for the press conference. He went up on stage and really let Rance Pugmire have it—really let him have it. I know there were some choice profanities thrown in here and there, and Pugmire just sat there and took it. Everybody in the whole place heard him. It was not something that was kept quiet. At that time, I definitely was not worried that I had screwed up because I did what I was told to do. Coach Knight had told me to tell them—not ask them—that he would be there in a few minutes. He never told me he wasn't going to show up.

So I'm waiting offstage and I'm hearing this go on. I don't remember if it started instantly as a real loud tirade or if it started off as something quiet. But I do remember, at one point, Coach Knight was standing up and looking

down at Pugmire waving his finger and was not happy. Obviously, he had just lost a game that ended his season and was not happy about that.

Then Coach Knight came down into the hallway, and he had his hand on my shoulder, and he didn't know me at all except for the fact that I had hosted him that night. He was just standing there waiting with me. The Indiana players, the two that would have come in with him, kind of scrapped the whole press conference when this thing happened. Coach was waiting with an older gentleman who was not associated with the basketball team. He was dressed in street clothes and was a friend of Coach Knight. We waited in that hallway and when Mr. Pugmire finally came down off stage, Coach Knight was still standing there with his hand on my shoulder. I was, basically, standing right between these two guys just a little off to the side, and one of the things that really surprised me about Coach Knight was how big he is. I had no idea he was such a tall man. Here I am standing next to this guy who is a legend for yelling at people. He's got his hand on my shoulder yelling at Pugmire again, and I'm just standing there, being quiet—I'm not gonna go anywhere while he's got his big hand on my shoulder. This went on for a few more minutes. When it did end, Mr. Pugmire turned around and walked one way and Coach Knight turned and walked the other way.

Then Coach Knight asked me to take him out of a back door of the Boise State University pavilion where they play. He said, "I don't want to see anybody." We walked out the back door. He put a hat on; it was a kind of chilly night. Coach Knight, the older gentleman, and I walked across the intramural field and through campus. It was late at night at this point, and it was dark and cold. There was not a word said. I knew that I was walking him toward his hotel because he had asked me when we left "which way?" I told him I would walk with him until I was sure he knew the way. So we walked toward his hotel—probably a half mile—and we got close enough to his hotel where I was gonna turn around and go back to my car and head home. Not a word was said until the very end. He asked me for my address, and I wrote it down for him.

I actually expected nothing, but I figured if he was going to send something, it would be some sort of form letter. He apologized repeatedly to me for having to go through that press conference scene, and he just said he was very sorry. Not even a week had passed and in the mail came a package from Indiana University which had a letter that was mostly just a form letter that his secretary had typed—nothing personal, but he wrote a few lines at the bottom in handwriting. He wrote that he was sorry and thanked me for

helping out that night. There was also a t-shirt in the package, and I wore that t-shirt under my shoulder pads the entire next season. Every game day, I wore that t-shirt.

I don't know why nothing was said as we walked from the arena toward his hotel. It was just a time of reflection that night, I guess. For him it was the end of his season. He was disappointed in his loss; he's extremely passionate about what he does.

I know that my impression of Coach Knight really changed. I found him to be an extremely personable man. He was so nice to me the whole time. I really liked him a lot. For him to take the time to even write a couple of lines and send them to me really made me respect the person more. There are things he has done that are not acceptable in sports. I've grown up my whole life in sports. Actually I've played soccer all over the world. I ended up playing college football. I know all about coaches. For a coach to have so many players say so many good things about him, I know the man has got to be a great basketball coach. Most of his players like him.

My wife's step-dad knows the story, and he's another avid anti-Bobby Knight guy. I've really had it out with him a couple of times—in good fun. He bugs me about it every now and then—when Knight got fired he brought it up for sure.

I don't know if my dad has a different opinion of Coach Knight now; he still thinks Coach has a loud mouth, is an obnoxious punk, but my dad's a small guy, too, and would never say that to his face. But I do think he understands a little bit more that there's more to this guy than just the tirades that you see on ESPN. That's definitely one of the things that I took away that night. There's a whole lot more to Coach Knight than just what people see.

In the land of the blind, the one-eyed man is king, baby

Dick Vitale

Dick Vitale

My first taste of the General was when I was just about winding up my stint as a high school coach. Knight was the head coach at Army, and he was working at a summer basketball camp at the New York Military Academy near West Point. It was a warm summer day, and the gym door was open. I heard the balls bouncing. And then—I couldn't believe it—I heard this voice. "DEFENSE. This is about DEFENSE," the voice came blasting out the door and careened through the trees outside. "I'm going to teach you to TAKE the CHARGE. And you're going to learn some GUTS."

There were several bleeps in there. Bleep, bleep. You bleeping bleeps, Bobby is the captain and king of the All-Bleep team. But I'll leave those out. Just as I got inside, all of a sudden Knight blew the whistle and sent two kids to opposite ends of the gym. One of the kids was this little chubby guy who looked like he had never played the game in his life. His mother had written the check for two hundred dollars or whatever and said here, go have a good time. He had the black socks and the underwear hanging down below his basketball shorts. The guy at the other end looked quick and athletic, a player.

"I'm going to roll this ball to midcourt," Knight bellowed. "When I roll the ball, you guys re going to take off and see who can get the ball, UNDERSTAND? Whoever gets the ball is on offense. The other guy is on defense and has to protect the BASKET. GOT IT? It's not real DIFFICULT. Now, when the guy with the ball drives to the basket, the other guy gets in his way. He doesn't let him score. No. He takes the charge. I want to see him TAKE THE CHARGE."

With that, Knight rolled the ball out there. Well, the chubby kid was about a half-hour late getting to midcourt. The other kid blew by him and went in for the lay-up. Immediately Knight blew the whistle, sprinted out on the floor and was in the chubby kid's face. "I want you to do me a FAVOR, kid," he screamed. "I want you to apply to the NAVAL Academy and put me

down as your number-one recommendation. Bobby Knight recommends ME. Because I want to play against you every day of the week!"

That was my first experience with Knight up close. I told that story, at the Naismith Award banquet where Knight got the award as Coach of the Year for 1987. After he spoke, Knight pulled me aside. "That wasn't even the worst," he said. "At John Havlicek's camp I had a drill where I'd tell everyone we were going to learn how hard they could hustle. I lined them up all around the court, and when I blew the whistle I wanted everyone to spring into the center jump circle. There must have been 300 kids going full speed, crashing into each other, banging heads, piling on top of each other. John looked at me like I was crazy-like I wanted him to get sued or something. I got rid of that drill quick."

I started watching Knight's teams at West Point; you talk about over-achieving! He had kids like Billy Shutsky; Rollie Massimino had coached Shutsky at Hillside High School. He was tough, physical, a battler with great shot selection. Knight made him tougher. Shutsky would scratch your eyes out for a loose ball. Oh, how teams hated to play Knight's Army clubs. All the biggies would come into the NIT, play Army, and go home with all their little L's intact-limbs, baby.

And the Army brass! They loved those wins but they must have hated the part of the Knight experience when he'd rage up and down the bench at Madison Square Garden shaking his fists at generals and getting in the faces of his own administration. If a guy was an officer and sat on Knight's bench at Army, that guy had better be up rooting and roaring like it was any other war or Knight would be after his butt.

They tell the story about the time Army lost a big game and one of the scrambled-egg officers at West Point came into the locker room afterward congratulating all the players for their "effort."

"Effort?" Knight screamed. "EFFORT? What the #$%@# is that? These guys are going to be fighting a war! They're going to be second lieutenants with their $#!%ing lives at stake! If all they give is effort, you might as well get the body bags ready NOW! What the hell are you talking about, effort! We go for victory here. We got our asses kicked tonight. We LOST. You can take your effort and SHOVE IT!"

Hamburger king Dave Thomas's daughter, Wendy, for whom his franchise is named, used to baby-sit John Havlicek's kids.

• • •

When Knight coached at Army, the New York press referred to him as "Bobby T" because of the Technical fouls he received.

Bloomington, Indiana had to be on the list of the top environments in the game. Bloomington meant the red sweater, the volcano, the explosion. It might mean flying chairs or a game called on account of darkness: a darkness of mood. It means the General, Robert Montgomery Knight. Indiana on the basketball court is like John McEnroe on the tennis court; when's the thing gonna blow? Going to an Indiana practice, baby . . . you talk about motivators. If I wanted one guy alongside those 50-by-94-foot lines for one special game, I'd want the General. His practice is like a clinic, and when he starts attacking, when he jumps on his best players all the time, eats them up alive, lets out all his profanities and hostility but above all gets them ready to win, well, he's just a sight to see.

Hey, baby, love him or hate him, you better believe he is a giant in the world of college basketball.

The General was bigger than anyone in the state of Indiana, including the governor. The guy is a giant, and he's divided the fans there into opposite camps. Some love him and some loathe him. You don't find many people who are ambivalent about him.

I always thought it was one of the special moments in college hoops when Knight came strutting onto the floor at Assembly Hall in Bloomington before a game with his red sweater on. You knew hoops hysteria was about to take place in Hoosierland.

If I had to win one game, I'd want Knight on my side. All things being equal, give him a week in the gym to prepare, and he'll usually win because of his understanding of the game and his ability to get the maximum out of his players. He has the track record to prove that.

You talk about powerful. I traveled with Knight to see Damon Bailey when he was a high school star in Bedford, Indiana, which is about 30 miles south of Bloomington. We went down there, and I couldn't believe it. The place was packed with people who all came out to watch Damon.

When we walked in, I said, "Bob, I can't believe all these people came out for me."

He burst out laughing.

As soon as Knight entered the gym, they gave him a standing ovation. I thought I was walking in there with a king. Basketball is so big in that state and Knight commands that type of loyalty.

I just hope people remember him as one of the legends of the college game, a guy who has drawn from the likes of Pete Newell and the late Hank Iba, instead of a guy who has been involved in a lot of incidents.

Obviously, I don't agree with everything he's done over the years, just as I'm sure he doesn't agree with everything I've done. We've had our dis-

agreements. For example, The General and yours truly had a skirmish during the shooting of the movie *Blue Chips*. I haven't said much about it, but let me tell you what happened. I walked into a room and saw Knight, who was sitting down. I snuck up behind him and threw a bear hug around him and screamed, "Do you want to fight, baby?!"" I really caught him off-guard. Little did I know he wasn't having the best of afternoons. He instinctively swung back his left arm and I went to the deck. He didn't hit me with a punch, it was a jab with his arm to get me off his back. And believe me, I got off his back

We've laughed about it on a number of occasions. In fact, he later told me he wanted to give me a lesson on how to protect my left side. He told me, "When you're blind in your left eye, you don't sneak up on somebody like that and expose your left side."

That's what the guy is all about. He has an outburst, and then it's simply forgotten. It's history, baby. Tuck it away. The bottom line is, this guy has tremendous loyalty to those who are loyal to him. He'll go to the mountaintop for his friends.

He's been involved in a lot of controversies over the years, but if you look at the total picture, he's got a lot more positives than negatives. We have a tendency to look at Knight as a mean-spirited, tough, my-way-or-the-highway guy, but if you get to know him you discover he does a lot of beautiful things behind the scenes—like reaching out to youngsters in a hospital who may need a helping hand, or helping his ex-players. When Landon Turner, one of his stars, was paralyzed in a 1981 car accident, no one did more to raise funds for his rehabilitation and treatment.

I've seen letters in his office from guys he coached at West Point who went over to Desert Storm as officers in the Army. They were heartwarming. "Coach, all the things you've taught me about discipline, about life, I'm applying them in the real world. Please, coach, watch out for my family if something happens to me." I wanted to put them on the air. They were so moving. But the General said, "No way."

"Dick," he said, "I really don't need any publicity. These are just beautiful people who I love dearly."

Knight has established a reading program in the state for elementary school kids and a drug awareness program. He contacted all the NBA stars—Michael Jordan, Charles Barkley and all those guys—to come do two minutes apiece for a video on the importance of staying away from drugs and alcohol. He made it available to all the schools in Indiana.

Unfortunately, some people don't get a chance to see that side of his personality.

Any time he blows up, tongues start wagging. The media jumped all over him in the 1992 NCAA Tournament when he playfully whipped some of his players in response to accusations he was too tough on them. His players took it in stride, but when the wires moved a picture of him whipping Calbert Cheaney, one of his black players, some people took offense.

Another Knight outburst occurred after Indiana lost to Missouri, 65–60, in the first round of the 1995 NCAA Tournament in Boise. Knight had been on his best behavior throughout his brief stay, but he ripped into Rance Pugmire, the moderator of the post game interviews, after Pugmire had been incorrectly informed that Knight wouldn't be coming to the news conference and announced it to the media.

Knight's actions obviously were inexcusable, but it was set up by some miscommunication among the NCAA representatives running the post game news conference. The NCAA later came down big on him, fining him $30,000. He responded in vintage fashion, with a statement that jabbed the members of the NCAA's committee that imposed the fine by pointing out that most of them had worked at schools that had been guilty of NCAA rules violations.

Knight's just an explosive, competitive person. He lets it blow in one outburst, then sits down and says, "Why, why did I do it?"

I've had the pleasure of sitting down with Knight on several occasions for a one-on-one for ESPN. Let me tell you something, he's an absolutely intriguing personality. He's so bright on so many issues that he amazes me. When he sits down to converse, he has you listening to every word. I told him point blank, you have to be disappointed with some of the things you've done in the past. He simply said, "Obviously there are some things I wish I didn't do, but that's true for everybody."

One of the great ironies of college athletics is that coaches want their players to react in a disciplined manner during games and practices, but all too often they have difficulty controlling themselves.

Hey, I was as guilty as anyone. I was absolutely wacky on the sidelines. I was up from the moment the game started to the moment the game ended,

In 1989, Calbert Cheaney became the first left-handed starter in Bob Knight's 19 years at Indiana.

• • •

ESPN debuted September 7, 1979. ESPN2 debuted October 1, 1993. ESPN magazine made its first appearance on March 11, 1998.

screaming, cajoling, trying to get the maximum out of my players—and yes, the zebras, too. I was fortunate because college basketball wasn't covered then like it is today, otherwise I probably would have come in for some criticism.

Sometimes, the pressure can even catch up to the great ones. Knight is the Big Ten's all-time winningest coach. But he didn't have one of his better teams in the 1994–95 season. He had a legitimate star in 6–9 forward Alan Henderson, who was a first-round draft pick of the Atlanta Hawks, but the Hoosiers were young. They started three freshmen at times. The state of Indiana is known for producing shooters like Steve Alford and Larry Bird and Rick Mount, but Knight didn't have one, and that led to a lot of erratic moments.

Indiana won 19 games, but Knight became so disillusioned at one point that he actually talked about leaving the game after a crazy victory at Northwestern in which the Hoosiers lost an early 19-point lead but regrouped and won by 21.

Knight wondered afterward if the game had passed him by. He reiterated the same sentiments to me later in the year. "What am I doing?" he said, "The '90s have become baggy shorts, black sneakers, black socks, chains and earrings. It's become three-point shooting, the 35-second clock. Everything I don't believe in is part of the game. Maybe I'm getting too old, and I should get out."

Knight later admitted he wasn't going anywhere. He'll just try to beat the system. When it comes to the end, I really believe The General will head for the fishing pond and never look back. Until then, he'll keep doing it the Robert Montgomery Knight way—playing solid defense, getting a high-percentage shot and playing with intensity.

I say this with all due respect to the 1976 Indiana team that finished 32–0. That was the last team to finish undefeated and the best team I've ever seen assembled in terms of everybody complementing each other and understanding his role. They epitomized the word T-E-A-M in every respect. Quinn Buckner knew how to distribute the ball and defend. Scott May, the National Player of the Year, knew how to score and rebound. He averaged 23.5 points and nearly eight rebounds. Bobby Wilkerson was a great defender. Kent Benson could score and rebound.

In March of 1954, the Hawks and the Lakers played a regulation game using a twelve-foot high basket. The very next night the same two teams played a double header.

Forward Tom Abernethy was a perfect complement to the other four, a solid defender and rebounder who could hit open shots. All five starters played at least five years in the NBA. And they had the luxury of being coached by Bob Knight, who came up with great game plans.

Knight coached Indiana to 36 straight wins in the Big Ten in 1975 and 1976. We'll probably never see that again in a major conference. That's like Joe DiMaggio's 56-game hitting streak. I honestly believe that group would have won the 1975 national title if Scott May hadn't broken his arm just before the tournament. May came back for the Kentucky game in the regional finals, but he was extremely limited during a 92–90 loss.

Knight hasn't changed much, of course. One season I was subject of a similar outburst one night after I told him I thought his junior forward, Ricky Calloway, who had helped win Indiana a national championship the year before, had played a good game.

"What do you know about it?" he started in. "You don't know anything about the game. Calloway didn't do #$%@. Just like (Steve) Eyl, Check out Eyl (a senior forward who had been starting). Three big games. He plays sixty-eight minutes and gets zip. Zero for sixty-eight. You gonna tell me about Eyl, too? Calloway and Eyl, they'll sit their asses next to me on the bench because they can't play!"

"Bobby, you're too tough on these guys." I said.

Whoops.

"What do you know about tough, Vitale?" Knight said. "That's why I've won all my life. That's why I keep winning. Because I'm tough and these @#$%#'s need discipline."

Sure enough, the benching of Calloway and Eyl turned around Indiana's season. Knight went on and on that day about his treatment of players. I'll say this-and I've said it on the air: There's two guys who stand alone in the history of motivation in sports. Vince Lombardi was one. The General is the other. The people in Chicago talk about Mike Ditka when he was with the Bears, but Ditka has miles and miles to go before the catches up to my guy Knight.

My guy. Hah. I didn't think he was my guy another time one year when he put on that intimidation act against me. Sometimes it's Knight's way of teasing, to get loud and nasty and in your face. Intimidation City. At a practice the day before his game with Northwestern in Evanston we were sitting

In 1957, North Carolina went unbeaten. But their last two games both went three overtimes.

there talking, having a regular human-being type of conversation-he had thanked me for sending flowers for his mother, who had passed away that week-when he walked to the other end of the floor where his team was in their shootaround.

My ESPN producer wanted to get some information on Northwestern, to find out what Knight thought of the Wildcats, so I walked down to ask him. He was sitting on a table talking to a Chicago TV guy at the time.

"Hey Bobby, what about Northwestern?" I said.

"What about #$#@ NORTHWESTERN?" he screamed. "I'm not telling you about Northwestern. Can't you see I'm busy with this guy? Can't you see I'm doing something? What do you have to interfere for?" He was getting louder and louder and cursing, naturally. I just turned away but then the Italian temper in me surfaced. I've got a little volcano in me too, you know. I whirled around and let Knight have it.

"Let's get one thing straight right now, Bobby," I said, "I'm not one of your $%$#@ players. I've had enough of your act. I'm not one of your players. I'm just here trying to do a job." We were nose to nose. Then I went stalking off the court.

But here came Knight. "I'm not going to stand around and massage your $%$#@ ego like I have to do all these other guys," he said, "I was only playing with you. I was kidding. And then you take it like that."

"How am I supposed to know you were kidding?" I said.

Five minutes later we were laughing and shaking hands and hugging, having a blast. He also said he had just finished telling some other media people that he thought I was an okay guy and that he appreciated some of the things I had said about him.

"Hey, I never know when you're serious and when you're not," I told Knight. "I have my dignity too, in front of all these people."

The payoff is that the TV guy from Chicago was taping this whole episode and showed his audience the entire incident to its completion.

I think Knight and I have a relationship now where we can either kid around or really get on one another and show mutual respect either way. Take the three-overtime game Indiana played up at Wisconsin in '87. For a long time the Big Ten had been complaining that the league wasn't on TV enough. That's why they contracted for our Big Mondays package as the late game

Arnold Schwarzenegger graduated from the University of Wisconsin–Madison in 1979.

after the Big East. So now we had Indiana with Steve Alford, Keith Smart and company against second-division Wisconsin. What should have been a blow-out instead became a real knuckle-muncher and went three OT's before Indiana pulled it out on what I thought was a shaky call down the stretch.

I don't want to take anything away from the Hoosiers, but J. J. Webber of Wisconsin and the rest of his teammates played their hearts out and should have won the game. For the effort-uh-oh, there's that word again-and energy the Badgers gave, the folks in Madison should have put on a parade for the team, that's how great the intensity was for fifty-five minutes. To show you what the school thought of the game, Wisconsin presented the senior players with a tape of the marathon contest at their year-end banquet-even though it was a loss!

Anyway, after Indiana came away with the W, Knight devoted most of his press conference to going absolutely nuts about the lateness of the game and how TV was ruling basketball and how they shouldn't have to start games this late just so the Big Ten can get on TV. He ripped TV. He buried ESPN. "I don't need this (TV) for recruiting. I don't need this for attention," Knight said. "My team won't get back to Bloomington until the middle of the night. My kids have to get up for class tomorrow. Where's the priorities here?" On and on he went.

But I got the last word. Following the season Knight was being honored as Coach of the Year at the Naismith banquet in Atlanta. I was a speaker as well. Everybody there seemed to be worried about who would introduce Knight, so I volunteered.

After I told a few stories on him, I related Knight's harangue against TV and against the late starting times that night following the Wisconsin game. "Now I know you're a genius, Bobby," I said. "You've got the pride, the knowledge, the discipline. You get the kids graduated. You stand for all the good things in the game. You've won three national championships. Count 'em. 1976, 1981, 1987. You're brilliant. The greatest . . . But did anybody tell you that if you had done your job with the national champions that night in Madison, Wisconsin, instead of getting your sweet ass outcoached, the game would have ended an hour earlier?"

Another time, I was talking to Bob Knight's son, Patrick, when he was a freshman at Indiana and playing on the team. I asked, "Is your dad allowed to give you a car?" "Is he allowed to give you any cash? Or, is that a recruiting violation?" Patrick answered, in all seriousness, "My dad took my car away from me." It turns out that Patrick missed a class and got nailed. The General won't let anyone slide—not even his own son.

Another time we were televising a Purdue—Indiana game, and Knight came strolling in. The first words out of his mouth were, "Man, I'm tired of these 9:40 tip-off times. When is somebody gonna take an interest in the kids and care about them?" He went on and on. "Maybe we should move to Ted Turner's station and go up against the Big East on Monday night and kick their butt," he said. I tried to remind the General, as I always do, that life is adjusting—life isn't always smooth. "You got to teach players to be able to deal with adversity, baby." "Come on Robert, you always preach that."

Then we started talking about the NCAA convention. Knight was really upset about it. He said he didn't like the idea of reducing scholarships and he didn't want to hear about walk-ons. "I don't need any walk-on players," he said, "everybody in the University thinks they can play. These guys walk on, then they start moaning and groaning thinking they should get a scholarship. It 'causes more morale problems than ever." But Knight didn't stop there. "They talk about cleaning up academics," he said, "but they voted down legislation that would have forced schools to graduate fifty percent of their seniors to maintain Division One status. Hell, that rule would have been such a positive move. It would have made guys go out and recruit student athletes who have a chance to graduate."

This was at the time when Damon Bailey was playing for Indiana. Damon happened to walk over, and I said, "Hi Damon." Knight exploded, "Now why would you say hello to Damon?" he said, "Why don't you go over there and say hello to my son Patrick? And go over and say hello to Matt Nover. Why do you have to say hello to Damon?" I said, "Give me a break, will you please."

I introduced my associate producer Tom McNeely to Knight and asked Bob if he followed boxing. He said, "Nope." I said, "Well, his father fought Floyd Patterson." "So what?" Knight said. Typical Bobby Knight, you know. He laid the intimidating eyes on McNeely, who is about six feet one inch, two hundred twenty pounds, former football player, but McNeely shrunk to about five feet one, one thirty five. Incredible.

Then Gene Keady came in and asked Knight for some advice about coaching the Pan Am team which Keady was about to do that year. First thing Knight said was, "You gotta hire a guy to handle all the little details so you can just oversee the trials. Make sure you invite the players you want and forget about the seniors. There's no way the agents are gonna let the seniors of the world play so you have to know that."

Knight was getting ready to leave that particular day when all of the a sudden the word "tennis" popped up in a conversation. "I hear you play a lot

of tennis." He said to me, "Well, let's hook up." He immediately went to his pocket and threw a wad of cash on the ground—a wad of singles. "Put it up," he said. I couldn't believe it. I mean, the guy's a multimillionaire. He's got all kinds of cash, and he throws down these one-dollar bills. So I threw mine down, too, man, I had some twenties. I really did. I didn't have too many; I can guarantee you that. I'm not a betting man. I'll play him for a nice little dinner though. I definitely will. "Don't you be attacking my bad eye, though," I said, "Come on now, I know I can beat you, I just know it. Look at that gut hanging out there. I'll run you right and I'll run you left. I've never seen you play and I know I can get a "W" over you, baby."

A few weeks later, I arrived at my hotel in Bloomington. I received a phone call from Knight. "You #$%** son-of-a-gun," he said, "Where's your racket? Come on, bring it down. Come on. You told me last week in the Purdue game that you'd whip my butt, that you'd pummel me in tennis. Well, I'm at the Tennis Center right now, and I'm ready for you." I told him I didn't bring a racket but that didn't stop him. "I don't want to hear that nonsense," he says, "I've got any size you want, any kind of racket here at the Tennis Center. And don't tell me you haven't got any shoes 'cause I've got any size you want. Get your butt down here." If I'd said yes, he probably would have made me wear adidas sneakers. I'm a Nike guy, baby. Fortunately, I got out of it by telling him I was tired. Knight was all fired up. You think I'm gonna play him now. He would have blitzed me.

It was two hours before game time, and we were just sitting there having fun. We started talking about baseball. Knight's a baseball nut, and he was surprised to find out I was, too. "You know what," I said, "maybe I should do some baseball." He said, "Hell, maybe you'd do a hell of a lot better in that sport, 'cause you certainly screwed basketball up."

Bobby loves guys like Ted Williams. We were talking about great hitters and I think I shocked him when I said, "Williams? Let me tell you about Williams, Billy Goodman, Dom DiMaggio, Vern Stephens, Bobby Doerr, Mel Parnell." What else do you want to know about the Red Sox team in the fifties?" Knight shook his head. "I'll have to admit it," he said, "Now name me the starting second baseman for the Phillies Whiz Kids in 1950." "That's easy," I said, "Mike Goliat."

After a while I could see he was getting a little tense. "Boy," I said, "you really look like you're feeling it now all of a sudden." "Yeah," he said, "my

adidas is named after its founder, Adi Dassler.

stomach is churning. I feel this way almost every game. The expectations, every time we play, people come to beat us. It's like Notre Dame football. People play at another level, and you're always worried if you can sustain it and keep it rolling."

But now it's over with the General at IU. It'll never be the same. . . .

The man was a genius. And he IS a genius. And that's the sad part. He's so talented. He's such an unbelievable, knowledgeable guy about so many other things—other than basketball. Yet he couldn't control his temper. It's amazing how he should have known better than to put a hand on that youngster—whether that youngster provoked him or not. The bottom line is, it was "zero tolerance," and unfortunately that was the culmination of so many other incidents.

I'm saddened by it because I've been a big, big Bob Knight fan, and I hope and pray that he can bounce back, and he can go on and become the winningest coach of all time. But it's a sad day. A sad day for basketball. And for those like myself who learned so much from him in my early years as a coach.

Hoops—There It Is

Charles Barkley
Tony McAndrews

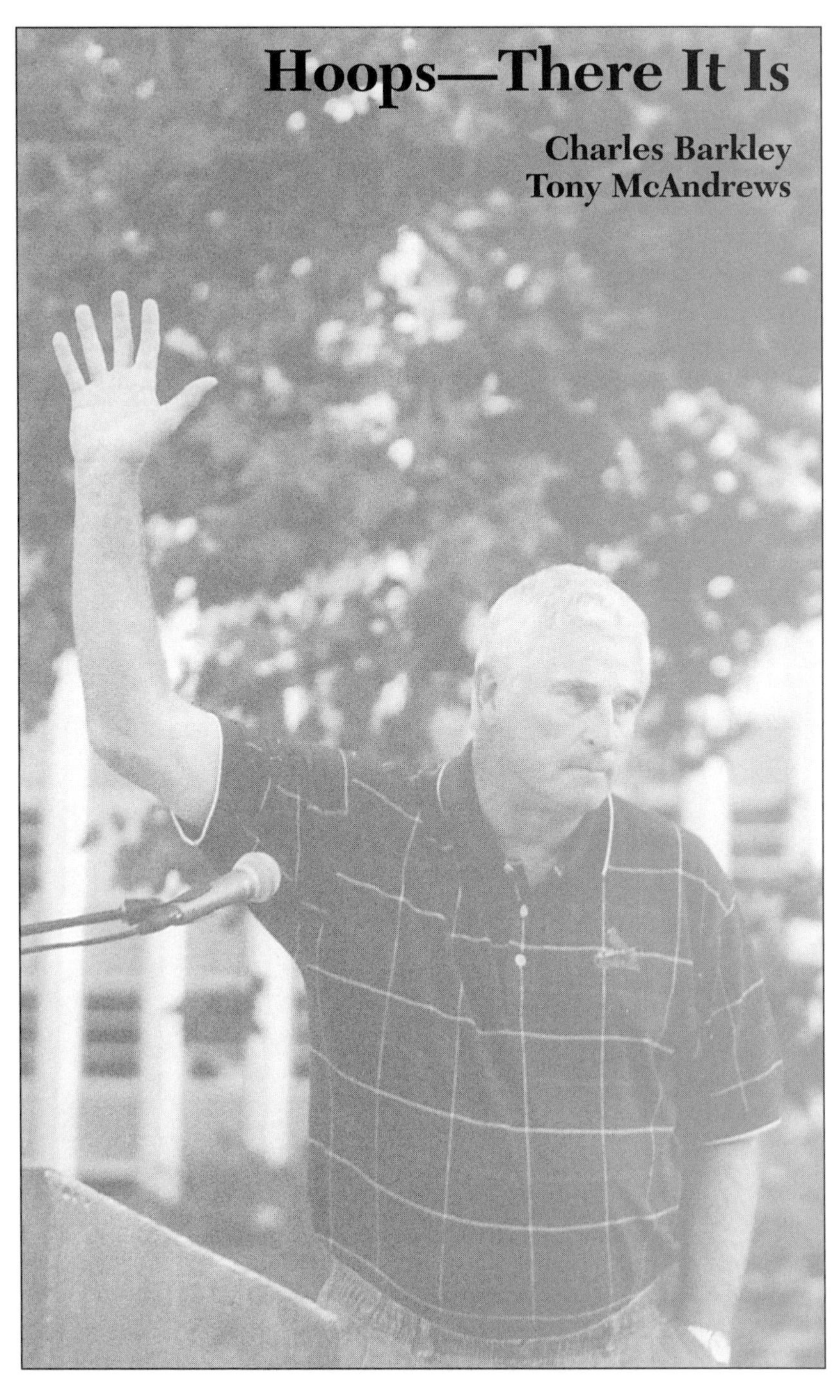

Charles, we called the clinic about your case, they said that you're over your shyness

Charles Barkley

Barkley was virtually unknown to most basketball fans when he was selected to try out for the 1984 Olympic team. He had just finished his junior year at Auburn which was never seen on national TV.

Barkley was the leading scorer on 1992's original Dream Team . . . a team that never called a time out.

Barkley was also the NBA's MVP in 1993.

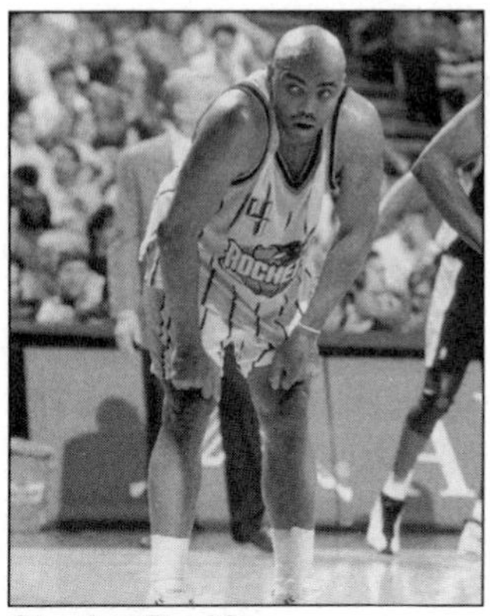

Charles Barkley

It all began when I reached into the mailbox that morning in the spring of 1984 and grabbed the telegram that had found its way down to Leeds, Alabama. I already knew what message was waiting for me inside the envelope: I was being invited to try out for the United States Olympic basketball team.

Knight was the team's head coach, and he was going to make certain that we were going to romp—no matter which countries ignored the boycott by the Soviet Union and eventually showed up.

I should've been pretty excited about getting the chance to represent my country on such a team. It was undoubtedly going to be composed of some of the very best players from the very best programs in college basketball, guys I'd been watching on television and reading about during my three seasons at Auburn.

Rah-rah patriotism has never been my thing. But I wasn't excited. Not one damn bit. But I'm not stupid. I knew better than to tell anyone that I didn't want to spend my summer sweating for Old Glory because the Trials were really my big chance, my opportunity to prepare myself for professional basketball, for which I hoped I was going to get paid big money. I knew that if I was going to cash in on my basketball skills, I would have to go to the Trials and show people that I was ready for the NBA. I hadn't announced my inten-

tion to leave school, but in my mind I was gone. And the Trials were going to be my springboard.

I went to the trials intending to change everyone's mind about Charles Barkley. I was going to, as Muhammad Ali used to say, "shock the world." That's what excited me most about the Olympic Trials—that, and the prospect of making money. I went to Bloomington with only one goal in mind: to play well enough to convince all the NBA scouts that I should be one of the first few players picked in the 1984 college draft. U!S!A!? Please. Give somebody else the gold medal; I just wanted the gold.

During the weeks before I left Leeds for the Indiana University campus, I began to have second thoughts. I worried if I would be able to make a favorable impression, given my image as an overweight curiosity. I didn't know if anyone would take me seriously, or if they would continue to focus on my weight rather than my game. There was only one thing I could do to ensure that my size wouldn't become an issue: lose weight. I placed a call to Coach Knight about ten days before the Trials were to begin to ask him how much he wanted me to weigh at the Trials. If he had wanted me to lose ten pounds, I would have lost ten pounds. If he had wanted me to lose twenty pounds, I would have lost twenty pounds. Thirty pounds? I would have thought about it.

I left a message with Coach Knight's secretary, but he never returned my call. Fine. "Fuck him," I thought. I weighed in at the Trials at about 280 pounds, 284 to be exact. And I felt damn good about it, too. My weight didn't bother me nearly as much as it seemed to bother everyone else at the Trials, particularly Coach Knight. But I didn't give a damn what he, or anybody else, thought about it.

During the first week of Trials, I finally asked Coach Knight why he didn't return my telephone call. "I would've wanted you to report at 215 pounds, but I didn't think you could make it so I didn't call you back," he said. Maybe he was right.

At the trials, I was usually Knight's straight man, the butt of his sometimes-biting jokes to reporters, who lapped it all up like thirsty dogs. One day he said, "Asking Charles Barkley to get down to 215 would be like asking Raquel Welch to undergo plastic surgery." He wasn't talking about face-lifts or tummy-tucks either. When someone told me later what he had said, they expected me to blow up and trash Knight. But actually I thought it was a great line. I laughed.

Someone later asked Knight if he had ever coached a player as heavy as I was.

Knight smiled, "Not for long."

The other hot topic in Bloomington, besides my weight, was my relationship with Coach Knight. It was billed as the most explosive and controversial coach in the country versus the most explosive and controversial player in the country. People thought we would be at each other's throat before the end of the first week. But Knight kept his distance, not just from me but from all of the players. He fed his hard-ass image by looming over us from atop a tower in the gym while the assistant coaches ran the seventy-two players who had been invited to the Trials through drills and scrimmages.

We called Knight "crazy man," but not to his face, because from the very beginning of the Trials he had every one of us completely intimidated. Even me.

Knight hardly said a word from up there on his throne, and even though you knew he couldn't watch every player at all times, you felt like he was watching *your* every move at all times. Now that's intimidation.

When he gathered us together in the middle of the gym and spoke to us before and after each of the sessions, everybody grew quiet. When he yelled during workouts, everything stopped. The sound of squeaking sneakers and balls bouncing on the court suddenly went silent and no one dared move. You could almost hear seventy-two hearts pounding in fear. I thought it was funny, but I wasn't crazy enough to make anything of it or even laugh anywhere within earshot of Coach Knight. Or at least, I usually had more sense than to upstage Knight.

During our huddle one day, I started making fun of his shoes. They were some of the ugliest things I'd ever seen—some old wing tips—and I told him so. "Hey, Coach, where'd you get those granddaddy shoes?"

Everyone cracked up—except you know who.

"Listen, you fat pig!" he screamed. "The privates shouldn't make fun of the generals!"

I was somewhat luckier than a lot of the players at the Trials because my roommate turned out to be my best informant. He was Steve Alford, who had just finished his freshman season—I mean *survived* his freshman season—under Knight. When I first heard that we were rooming together, I thought it was someone's idea of a very sick joke, or at least a psychological experi-

When Alford was a senior in high school in 1983 in New Castle, Indiana, his high school team averaged more people in attendance per game than the Indiana Pacers.

ment. Putting a little white kid from the Midwest together with a big black kid from the South, what could be more entertaining? What could be crazier? You never know how a kid will be after playing for somebody like Knight, and to be truthful, I expected the worst: a stuffy, uptight jerk who would be critical of everything I did because he was Mr. Perfect. I was ready to chew him up and have him for breakfast, lunch, dinner, and midnight snack. Instead, I was pleasantly surprised.

Steve and I were a perfect match. He was a great guy, a lot of fun, friendly, down-to-earth, everything nice that you can say about a person. He also had a great family; they made me feel welcomed and comfortable in Bloomington, which was no easy task, and he helped me get a better understanding of Coach Knight, which some people thought would be damn near impossible.

"He's just intense," is how Steve described Coach Knight.

"Yeah, right," I said. "Thanks a lot. Is there anybody on earth who didn't know that already?"

"Okay," Steve said, "He's the hardest-coach in America to play for." Wonderful.

"Coach Knight," he concluded, "demands you to be perfect."

That was quickly apparent to every player at the Trials, which explains why probably the best group of college players ever assembled for an Olympic Trials remained so insecure. Some of the best players in the country looked like bumbling idiots during the drills and scrimmages because we all knew that at any time we could get our asses kicked by any of the other players on the floor. That's how much talent was there.

We were a pretty tight-knit bunch. We spent a lot of nights talking about something we all had in common: pressure. Away from the court, away from basketball, and especially away from Coach Knight, very few of us took life too seriously because we all had experienced the stress of having to play for our lives every day for our respective teams, and every day at the Trials. So when the coaches put away the whistles, all we wanted to do was have fun.

For those of us who didn't come from any of the traditional basketball conferences, such as the Big East, ACC, and Big Ten, the trials were a time for introductions. I'd seen a lot of the players at the Trials on television during the season, but in Bloomington, I saw a lot of them in a whole new light.

Michael Jordan became my biggest opponent at the Trials. Not on the floor; he was smart enough to keep his skinny body out of my way. But we went head-to-head every night in a card game called Tonk. To this day, I think Michael still owes me money. None of us knew much about Michael's game

before he got to the Trials. He hadn't been an explosive player at North Carolina, thanks to Dean Smith's superstar-prevent offense, and like the rest of us; he wasn't in a class by himself at Bloomington. He was solid, competitive and smart. But none of us said, "He'll be a superstar."

Deep inside I was excited to meet a lot of these players, but I wasn't in awe of anyone. Instead, most of the guys were in awe of me because I was stronger and quicker than anybody else in the gym. When I got out on the break during the scrimmages, I could feel the field house humming in anticipation. Would I pass it? Or would I jam? Either way, I didn't care who got in my way because they would pay with pain. I did spare one player, though. When 6'6", 210-pound Mark Halsel of Northwestern stepped in my path, I didn't run him down like I normally would have, by planting one knee into his ribs. Instead, when I saw him step in front of me like he was going to take a charge, I placed my left hand on his face, then boosted myself toward the basket and jammed with my right hand. The place went wild.

It didn't take long for most players to figure out that trying to impress Coach Knight by taking a charge against me wasn't worth the price: possible loss of life. I've always tried to kill guys who get in my way on a breakaway play. They'll sometimes get the call the first time they try it, like receiving a Purple Heart. But there's hardly ever a second time. It's called physical intimidation and it's one of the most important aspects of my game.

I was spared much of Knight's wrath during the Trials, but only because I was kickin' everybody's ass. I was rolling. I played as well as anyone there, better than most. I was running the floor like a guard. I was jamming like a monster, and I was making Magic-like passes to Michael on the break. I was the hit of the Trials. Reporters, NBA scouts, and the fans in the stands at the scrimmages were speculating about the damage I was going to do to the foreign teams under international rules, which allow more contact than American rules. It's practically mugging.

Yeah, it would've been my kind of game, but every moment of the Trials I had just one thing on my mind: money. I wanted to take care of my family, to buy my mother and grandmother a house and cars and take care of my two brothers. I owed them that, and as the Trials ended at the end of April, my only thought was that I wanted to give it to them as soon as possible.

Michael Jordan wore number 9 in the '84 Olympics. All player numbers were between 1—10. In the NBA he wore numbers 23, 45 and 12. The latter occurred in Orlando one night when his uniform was stolen.

After watching a couple of scrimmages at the Trials, Mark Heisler of the *Los Angeles Times* wrote that my "worth in the draft must be going up $250,000 a day." But there was actually more than money to consider.

I announced that I was leaving Auburn on April 28, 1984, less than two weeks before the best twenty players from the Trials returned to Bloomington for a four-day minicamp. I was there, of course, having survived cuts to fifty-four players, thirty-six, twenty-four, then finally the lucky twenty. But I was there in body only.

Coach Knight was always vocal about the players being punctual for all of our meetings. Knight was late for one of our nightly meetings. He kept us waiting for about fifteen minutes. When he finally walked through the door, I jumped up and started shouting, "Hey, where the hell have you been?" Well, Knight just went off. "Let me tell you something, Charles, you fat son-of-a-bitch, there's only one chief in this army and that's me. Your fat ass won't be around here much longer." That's when I knew I didn't have a chance of being an Olympian even though I had done well at the trials. But you know how that goes, they chose whoever they want to be on the team. After that night, I knew Coach Knight didn't want Charles Barkley.

Reporters weren't allowed at the minicamp. If they had been, they would have known that I wasn't even close to the same player that I had been at the Trials. I was just hanging out and having fun, secure that I had accomplished what I wanted to do: shock the world and move up in draft. That had been my major objective. Mission accomplished.

By the time the day arrived when Knight was going to make his cut down to sixteen players, I already knew my fate. I was actually happy to get out of there because for several days Knight had been criticizing my skills, almost like he was trying to devalue me for the draft. Obviously, I didn't appreciate it. He said all I wanted to do was post up, and that I didn't have good ball handling and shooting skills. He said he didn't want a 6'4" guy on his team who would do nothing but post up all the time. He wanted me to score from the outside, but said that I couldn't.

"You've got to be versatile," he told me.

"That's not my game," I said. "I'm an inside player."

When he called me into his office to tell me that I had been cut—along with three other players: John Stockton of Gonzaga, Maurice Martin, who

The last few picks in the first round of the NBA draft today would be fourth round picks in the 1960s.

played at St. Joseph's University in Philadelphia, and Terry Porter of tiny Wisconsin-Stevens Point, all future NBA players—I was stunned by what happened: I saw genuine hurt in Knight's face. Suddenly, the hard-ass became a softie. I thought he'd be glad to get rid of me, but he was truly upset. I think it hurt him to cut all of us, and it was an emotional moment for him. It really affected him. I believe Bobby Knight is more compassionate than he would like anyone to believe.

That's when I finally gained respect for Knight because I realized that we were very much alike. We both do crazy things and say things that we sometimes later regret. But neither one of us will ever bullshit anyone either, and that's the only kind of person I can respect.

Coach Knight wished me luck, but I knew that luck had nothing to do with the NBA draft. I came to the Olympic Trials to make my own luck, and I was convinced that I wasn't going to be drafted any later than fifth, maybe sixth. One way or another, I was gone from the college scene, and I haven't regretted it for one single moment.

The Hoosier Classic was a whup-up sandwich—hold the mercy

Tony McAndrews

Tony McAndrews is a native of Lost Nation, Iowa, a graduate of St. Ambrose College, and Head Basketball Coach at Nova College, an NAIA school in southern Florida. McAndrews was an assistant to Lute Olson at Iowa for many years before taking the Head Coaching Job at Colorado State University from 1980–1987. He then returned to be Lute's assistant at the University of Arizona before settling into the job at Nova.

Courtesy of Nova University

Tony McAndrews

When I was at Iowa, Indiana University was probably the easiest team to prepare for because you knew what they were going to do. They weren't real complicated but they were just so sound and fundamentally tough, both on offense and defense. They never gave you any easy baskets. You had to work for everything. They constantly fought through screens. They screened out. They played tough defense. You never got an easy basket. Then they just grind you on offense; they pass and screen, and pass and screen, and cut, so nothing was ever easy. I observed their play against us and other people, and they always started out at one level at the beginning of the game, and at the end of the game they are playing at a higher level. We, as coaches, like to think that's somewhat normal, but it's really not. In fact, the norm is the reverse—there's a great deal of slippage. But I respected his teams so much and in the year they had Benson, Buckner and Wilkerson, May and Green and that bunch that they were just so good. They went 32–0.

In 1939, the Heisman Trophy winner was Nile Kinnick of Iowa. He is the only Heisman Trophy winner to have his university's football stadium named after him. In 1934, Nile Kinnick was Bob Feller's catcher on an American Legion baseball team.

I remember when we were going to play them at Iowa, we were going to use a Bob Spear version of ball-zone defense. Bob Spear was a very good coach who used to be at Air Force, and Dean Smith worked under him for a while. It was the type of defense where you have one guy in the middle, and a point, two wings and a tail. Four guys really revolve around the middleman so it was somewhat of a match up but it looked like a 1–3–1, and combination of all above and very simple. I remember we thought that was going to be something that might really bother them. I also recall the score being 11–0, we took a time out, and got back into a man defense.

Bob Knight is a great coach. He's very smart. He's given great ideas and established great trends in basketball. To me, it's just really disappointing to have him go out the way he did and do some of the kind of crazy things that he did. But it all goes back to, at some point in time, of somebody not putting their foot down and letting him get away with it. Then he maybe thought it was cute, I don't know, but obviously it challenged him to see what he could get away with and obviously it caught up with him.

He does such a psych job. When I was at Colorado State, we'd go there to Assembly Hall, and you're dressing, and two of the managers, they have about ten, bring in the programs and make sure that everybody gets one. It was my first year as head Coach at Colorado State and we weren't very good. We did get rather excited before some games which was not a great combination. Our guys started reading the program—reading how IU had never lost a game in the Hoosier Classic. And here we are the next lunch tray, so to speak, in the buffet. My guys, I thought I'd have to have a gun to get them out of the locker room. And we played like that for a while—we were rather tight and didn't play well. But we did play well the next night and beat SMU which was coached by Dave Bliss, Knight's former assistant. But it is an intimidating situation. They were very good, and we were playing at their place and the Legend—Bobby Knight—is coaching.

Like when Iowa, or another Big Ten team, goes into Assembly Hall, you go in and start stretching, home-area media is there—they came with you. Then Bobby Knight happens to walk through about then while we were stretching and says something to the press to further establish his tradition with the press. Our guys go, "Oh, that's Coach Knight!" So he kinda plays games with everybody from the very beginning. It's a tough place to play. I recall one time after we won a game there, at breakfast the next morning we had two players with broken arms, Vince Brookins and William Mayfield, our starting forward and number three forward. Just rough Big Ten play, obviously no calls.

Before my first season here in Florida, I had gotten this tape on Coach Knight, a talk he had prior to Purdue, and so I brought my team in at the first part of the season. I told my team, "Well I went to a coaching clinic this summer, and I got some pointers on how to prepare my team and talk to my team at half time. So this is what I'm going to try to follow—an approach to dealing with you guys at half time if we're not playing up to par." So I got this tape out. I told my guys: "this is a half-time speech I made at Iowa during a game against Purdue just so you guys will know what to expect from me this season." (McAndrews plays the Knight tape.) "And then I'm leaving and you fucking guys will run until you can't eat supper. Now I am tired of this shit. I'm sick and fucking tired of an 8–10 record. I'm fucking tired of losing to Purdue. I'm not here to fuck around this week. Now you may be, but I'm not. Now I am gonna fucking guarantee you that if we don't play up there Monday night, you aren't gonna believe the next four fucking days. Now I am not here to get my ass beat on Monday. Now you better understand that right now. This is absolute fucking bullshit. Now I'll fucking run your ass right into the ground. I mean I'll fucking run you, you'll think last night was a fucking picnic. I had to sit around for a fucking year with an 8–10 record in this fucking league and I mean you will not put me in that fucking position again, or you will Goddamn pay for it like you can't fucking believe." They all started looking at each other like, "Wow, what did we get into?" A couple of guys knew the voice so needless to say, they were pleased to see that they had Coach Mac there, but Knight has had a great career and a lot of ups and downs and great players. I know one thing. I'm not a betting man but if I ever bet on a game, I would bet on a team coached by Coach Knight, playing an opponent that had beat him previously.

I never had any one-on-one with him. When we were at that Classic, I think we got beat by twenty or something, and I know it was the next night after we had beaten SMU, Knight said, "Tony, you guys run some good stuff." I don't know if he was joking and referring to how well we ran our offense against them because it wasn't very good, but we did do some good things the next night. He's been gracious, but he's always been a distant kind of guy. Unless you're his kind of guy and played for him or coached for him, and me being with Lute—he was not very fond of Lute—so he was not going to be too warm to me regardless.

Kyle Macy of Purdue holds the Big Ten record for most points in a game by a freshman. Macy, from Peru, Indiana, later transferred to Kentucky.

I don't know why he didn't like Lute. I think maybe it was just a Big Ten thing. When he got in the Big Ten, Lute did very well—his image and everything. He did everything so well, and his image—he was not a cusser, a ranter, and a raver—was so different than Coach Knight, and yet very successful.

You're nice guys as long as he can beat you. But a lot of guys are like that. Maybe Bobby's a little bit more so. But a lot of guys are like that; you're a real nice guy while they're beating you but then when you beat them, all of a sudden, either you think you're egotistical, or you think you're better than somebody else, or you cheated, or you're recruiting illegally, or whatever. It's never the fact that maybe the guy's just turned the program around and is doing a good job.

I Think, Therefore IU

Larry Bird
Dick Van Arsdale
Tom Ackerman
Greg Elkin
Eric Ruden
Todd Starowitz

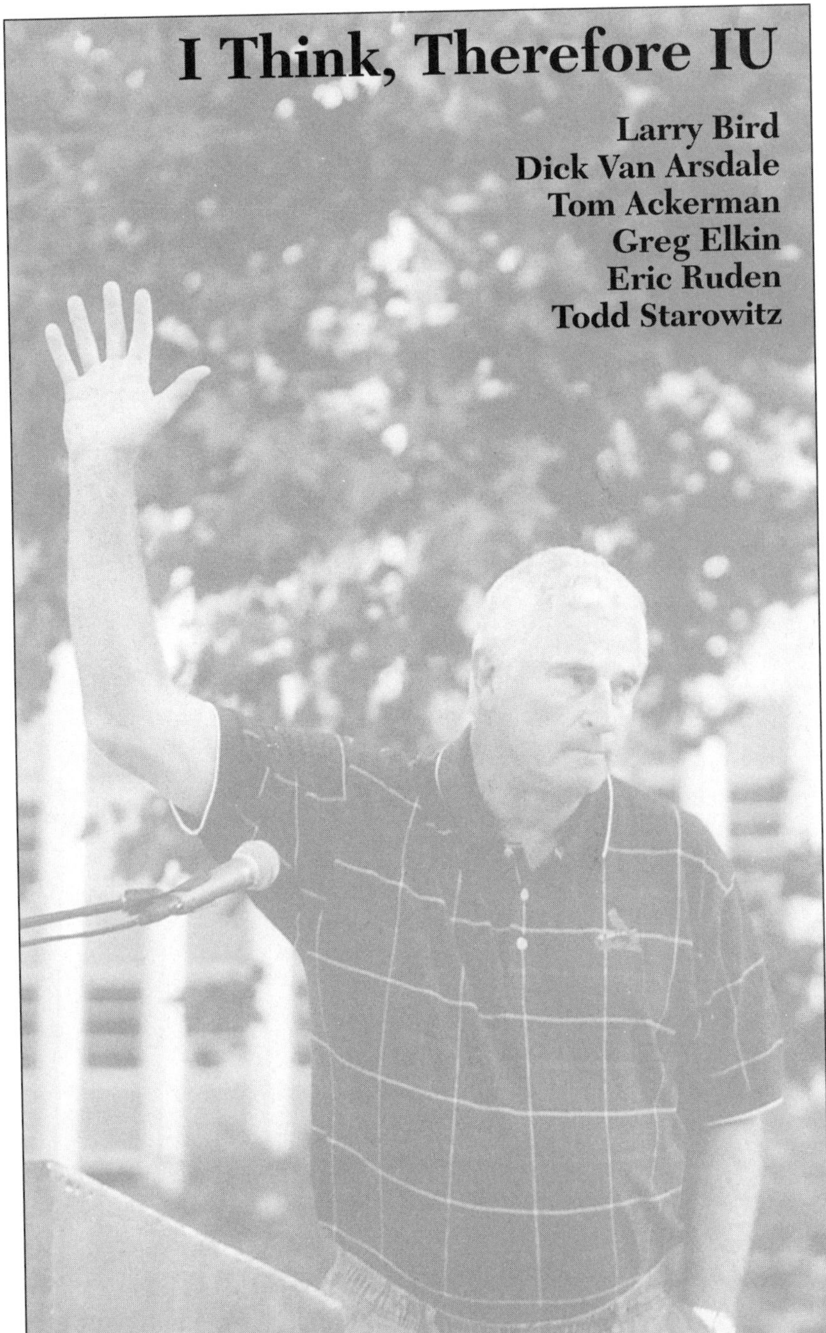

Courtesy of Larry Hawkins. Photo by Max Gibson

Larry Bird on his first day at Indiana University with Coach Knight in September 1974.

A Bird in the hand for 24 days . . . can make your hand messy

Larry Bird

Larry Bird is the most famous athlete ever to attend high school in Indiana if you don't count Wayne Gretzky who went to Broad Ripple High School (David Letterman's alma mater) in Indianapolis when he played hockey for the WHA's Indianapolis Racers.

Bird retired in the spring of 2000 after coaching the Indiana Pacers for three years, but he's not the only NBA Head Coach from French Lick, Indiana. Jerry Reynolds coached the Sacramento Kings in the early 1990s. Once, during the middle of a game, Reynolds had a heart attack. He fell to the floor and was writhing about in pain, the referee, thinking that Reynolds was "showing him up" gave him a technical foul.

Larry Bird

Knight recruited Bird to IU in the fall of 1974 . . . but Bird didn't last a month. He didn't leave because of a falling out with Knight—as had been widely reported but for the reasons he outlines below.

I didn't exactly have a worldview. I knew about Indiana University, of course. Bobby Knight had been there about two or three years by that time and people in the state were excited about IU. But I wasn't a fan of college basketball. I knew next to nothing about it.

So I was about as small town a kid as you could get and when the scouts started coming in hard, I reacted the way you might expect. I'd say to each of them "Hey, I don't want to visit your school." Finally I decided I would just pick one school and stay with it—if only to keep those recruiters off my back.

I did visit Kentucky. Joe B. Hall had come to see me play once and I didn't have a very good game. I got about twenty-five points and fifteen rebounds, but he said I was too slow and probably couldn't get off my shot against bigger guys. But for some reason, the Bird family went down there anyway on an official visit.

The things that Coach Hall had said bothered me. Here was a big-time coach who said I couldn't play for him. That helped motivate me to go to IU because I knew we would be playing Kentucky.

I went to IU and to Indiana State and I was planning a trip to Florida—because I had never been there and I was curious about *that*—but I never did get down there. Purdue recruited me hard—*real hard*. The problem with Purdue was they had Wayne Walls and Walter Jordan, both forwards, coming in and there was no sense in going up there for a visit.

The man who recruited me the hardest was Denny Crum at Louisville. He was doing everything he could to get me to come down there and look at the school. Finally he said, "I'll tell you what. If I could beat you in a game of Horse, would you come for a visit?" I said, "Sure." I had no problem with that. Coach Crum thought he was still a pretty decent player, but it was my court and I wasn't *too* worried. I started taking him real deep, out in three-point territory. I put him away in about eight shots.

He went over to Coach Holland (high school) and said, "Can this kid shoot this good from the outside?" And Holland says, "Well, you just saw him. You want to shoot some more?" Crum said, "No, I've seen enough." Coach Crum was just dying to get me to come down there, but I never did go.

Bobby Knight came to a lot of games. Mom wanted me to go to Indiana University. Coach Jones and their high school coach had gone to IU. My dad liked IU, but he also liked Indiana State. The truth is he liked every school that came up. No matter which college you'd mention, he'd say, "Good place, Larry, good place." I think he just wanted to make sure that I did go to college somewhere, so he supported them all. In the end, it came down to IU. It seemed as if *everybody* wanted me to go to IU and they really made the decision for me. In a way, I just went along with what they felt was best for me. My mom was happy, my dad was happy and Coach Jones was happy.

Since I didn't really know much about college basketball or Indiana University or even Bobby Knight, for that matter, I started reading up on the school before I went up there.

I got excited about playing for Bobby Knight. I love that man. I admire him so much for what he has accomplished. I was really looking forward to playing for him.

He had asked me to get up there during the summer and get settled, which I did. I was reluctant to leave home right away, but he had asked me to come up, so I did it. I didn't have any problems at first.

The 1979 Final Four between Larry Bird's Indiana State Sycamores and Magic Johnson's Michigan State Spartans is still the highest rated Final Four ever.

Things went well in the beginning. Jim Wisman and I were shooting around on a court one day when Scotty May came over and introduced himself. Then Bobby Wilkerson came over. Jim and I played those two guys, two-on-two, and when it was over I said, "Oh no. There's no way I'll ever make *this* team." Scotty was making every shot. Those guys looked unbelievable to me. But we continued to play over there two or three nights a week. Kent Benson and somebody else would choose up the team. Scotty never did.

Kent Benson can be a nice guy, but, point-blank, he treated me terribly. He treated us freshmen as if we were idiots. That's why to this day I never treat rookies badly. I always try to take them under my wing.

Benson came down one day while I was shooting and just took my ball and went to the other end to shoot. He'd say, "You freshmen don't deserve a ball." Of course, Wisman and I would be the first two out there and Benson would come along and pull this stuff just about every day.

When they chose sides, we'd never play. Wisman and Wayne Radford and myself were the ones who always sat out. When someone did take a break, Radford would be the one they'd pick to go in. I never got to play. Benson had no idea what I could do. Finally Scotty May spoke up a little and I got to play, but Benson continued to treat me like a jerk, like I was nothing.

You'd see Bobby Wilkerson and some of the others around campus and they'd say hello and make you feel good. I couldn't believe the way Benson was acting. But I'm not saying that he was the reason I finally left. It wasn't just him—it was the school itself.

But ever since then, I've wanted the Celtics to beat Benson's team whenever we play. I got a big kick in 1985 when Kevin McHale set the Celtics' scoring record of fifty-six points in a game where Kent Benson was guarding him. Benson got so frustrated in the third period that he picked up two quick T's and then got ejected!

My problems really began when classes started; I wasn't much of a scholar to begin with, although I had gotten a good enough grade-point average to get into college. But I certainly wasn't ready for a school the size of Indiana University.

The school was way too big for me. There were too many students. One

Kent Benson didn't make a free throw during his first fourteen college games.

• • •

The Boston Celtics eight-peated.

classroom could have held half of West Baden—or so it seemed to me. Thirty-three thousand students was not my idea of a school—it was more like a whole country to me. It was too far to go to your classes. I'd be thinking, "Which building do I go to next?" I walked around for two days, trying to figure out where I was going.

I knew I was really going to have to hit the books hard. In my senior year of high school, I started paying better attention in class. I felt it would not be a problem for me at IU If I listened, took notes and kept my head in it. But I'd go to a class and there would be three hundred people. I was intimidated by the size and it got so I just couldn't handle it. I felt awkward asking questions in front of all those people and I could see that it was going to be hard for me to take advantage of the educational opportunities there.

Things weren't much better socially. I had no money—and I mean *no* money. I arrived there with $75. Where was I supposed to get money? I had virtually no clothes. Knight had me room with a guy from Quincy, Illinois, Jim Wisman, who was a very worldly seventeen-year-old kid—just the opposite of me. Jim may not have been wealthy, but he was solid middle-class. I came in with my few clothes and he just filled up the rest of the closet. He had a full wardrobe, while all I had was five or six pair of jeans, a couple of slacks, a few shirts, some T-shirts and my tennis shoes. I didn't have a sport coat or even a pair of dress shoes. Wisman said I could wear anything of his that I wanted at any time and I ended up wearing all his clothes. He also gave me money when I needed it. But I couldn't go on that way for long. I said to myself, "How can I keep wearing Jim Wisman's clothes and accepting Jim Wisman's money?"

It didn't take too long for me to decide that I was in the wrong place. I figured I'd go back home, work for a year and try it someplace else. IU just didn't feel right to me.

Bobby Knight has said subsequently that he has learned a lot over the years about how to treat kids. Recently he said that his thinking back then was since he had never catered to a Scott May or a Kent Benson or a Quinn Buckner, why should he have catered to a Larry Bird? Of course, the bottom line is that he had a great team—seven guys from the 1974–75 Indiana team would go on to spend time in the NBA—and he sure didn't need me.

But I do think Coach Knight knew he had a kid who could play. I say that because of what he's said since then and because of one little incident.

We were all down in the gym playing one day and this was one time when I actually got into the game. Knight had been out of town and now he

was back in Bloomington. Anyway, we're out there playing and I am moving without the ball—I'm moving, I'm cutting, I'm rebounding and I'm doing everything.

I make a nice backdoor cut and get open and Jim Crews—he's now the coach at Evansville—misses me. Suddenly you hear a voice. *His* voice. Nobody knew Coach Knight was back in town, but he sure was and he sure didn't like what he just saw. He stopped that game. He came down and started yelling at the top of his lungs. I can just tell you it wasn't *me* he was screaming at.

We'll never know what would have happened if I had played on that IU team that year, but it would have been interesting if I had been around. That team lost just one game, but it was to Kentucky in the Mideast Regional and it knocked them out of the NCAA Tournament. They went on to win the whole thing the following season. IU is a great school with a great sports program and I'm' sure that if I only could have hung in there, things would have worked out fine.

I really believe in my mind that if I had kept my head in my schoolwork and did everything Coach Knight had asked and if someone had gotten hurt, I would have moved right into the starting five. It turned out that Scott May did break his wrist or something and although he did play in that Kentucky loss he wasn't himself. And IU only lost by two. I never even made it to the official beginning of practice on October 15. When the time came, I just packed up, which didn't take me long. I didn't even tell Coach Knight. I just left.

I walked out to Highway 37 and hitchhiked. I figured I could catch a ride from someone heading back in my direction. A man picked me up in a truck and left me off in Mitchell and eventually I got home.

Typical of my nature, I hadn't told anyone at home how unhappy I was, so they were surprised when I showed up. Their reaction wasn't good at all.

Everybody was disappointed. My family was upset and the townspeople were shocked. It was considered a great honor to play for Indiana University. At first, people kept hoping I had just made a rash decision and they could talk me into going back. I believe I came home on a Friday. On Sunday, somebody in the house said, "I'll take you back up there if you want to go." I said no. Once I make my mind up, I make it up.

That was the first extremely important decision I had ever made for myself and I was sticking to it. I knew everybody would be angry with me when I made it and that there would be a lot of pressure on me when I got back, but I didn't care.

Mom was so mad at me that she barely talked to me for a month. I went back to living at Granny's and Mom would walk into that house and not say a word to me. Mark, my brother, was playing at Oakland City College at the time and I rode down with a friend to see a game. When we got there, Mom and Dad were already there. Dad started talking to me, but Mom wouldn't say a word.

She was convinced I was ruining my whole life by rejecting Indiana University. "You disappoint me," she'd say when she finally spoke. Mom would tell people, "He's never going back to college." She just didn't understand what the problem was. Mom really took it hard. "What's he going to turn out to be? A bum?" I figured. "Well, if I do, I do." That was my response. A lot of people around town took it hard. But I didn't like it at IU. It's like when people complain about their jobs. If you don't like it, why do it?

Sometimes you just don't feel that you have a choice. The only reason I quit IU was because I didn't feel comfortable there. I just couldn't motivate myself to get the job done. I wanted to work a year and I didn't want to go directly to another school.

I wanted to make some money and then decide about my future. I totally believed I was doing the right thing. I didn't have even a vague notion of becoming a professional basketball player at this point, so I didn't feel that I was jeopardizing any career opportunities. I didn't have any thoughts about turning pro until late in my college career. I just knew it was going to help—both mentally and financially—to sit out that year.

The symbol for Gemini is twins; some people say that Geminis have dual personalities, but I don't think that's true, and neither do I

Dick Van Arsdale

Before Damon Bailey, there was Tom Van Arsdale. Before Steve Alford, there was Dick Van Arsdale. The twins were co-Mr. Basketball in 1961 in Indiana.

After an All-American career at IU, Dick spent most of his pro career with the Phoenix Suns. His number was the first ever retired by the Suns.

He is currently a senior vice-president for the Suns. He and wife Barb have two grown children: Jill and Jason.

Dick Van Arsdale

My Mom, Hilda, is like a second Mom to Knight. Hilda, back in Greenwood, Indiana, will be ninety soon. Karen, Bobby's wife, comes up and takes her out to dinner. Last winter, I went on a scouting trip to the Midwest. I see Cincinnati play; I go over to Ohio State and see Minnesota. Last game on my trip I see IU at Michigan State so I go up there and I get in and it's cold—typical Midwestern day. It's snowing and I don't like it. But I finally got hold of Knight where he was staying. He said, "Come on over and have breakfast with me." He said, "You're not gonna do s_ _ _ today. Come on, go to practice with us." So I get on the bus to ride over with them. I don't usually like to talk to him about basketball much. We usually wind up talking about fishing.

We get to the arena at East Lansing, you walk in through the tunnel. The team walks out on the court. Just the two of us are standing in the tunnel talking about whatever. Some young guy walks up, and he's an assistant at Michigan State now, and he used to do video stuff for Bobby at IU. He comes up and sticks out his hand and says, "Hey Coach, how you doing?" I could just look at Knight and know what was coming. He didn't shake the kid's hand.

He looked at him and then kinda looked away. If he doesn't like you, he'll kinda look at you and look away. He said, "I hear you have been passing some bad stories around about me, and I don't effin' appreciate it. As far as I'm concerned you get the eff out of here. I don't ever want to see you again." I've seen him do something like that before. The kid says, "Well, Coach, I'm sorry." He said, "No, get the eff out of here." The kid walked away, red from ear to ear. Bob says, "You know—I gotta let somebody know what I think."

Coach absolutely can't stand two-faced people. You always know where you stand with him. Unfortunately, he is constantly fighting untrue things: misquotes, embellished stories or statements out of context.

About three years ago, about fifteen of us, including Knight, went to Russia fishing, both his sons went, some of his cronies. Tom and I both went. We were there for a week. I fished for salmon—fly fished—seven days hard and didn't catch a darn fish. We get to Russia and miss the salmon run. The guy who set up the trip must have pulled the wool over our eyes. The Russian guide says "What the heck you boys doing here now?" You missed the salmon run." We tried to keep Knight in the background so he wouldn't blow up. He wanted to kill a couple of people. You learn a lot about people when you go fishing with them. Mike Gallagher, a friend of mine, went on the trip, too. He was just learning how to fish and wanted to go so we had room for one more guy and took him with us. Mosquitoes were eating us up and we're out there smoking a cigar and drinking a beer. There's a cat sitting on the levee. Gallagher just takes his dork out and starts peeing on the cat. All week Gallagher tried to kill that cat.

I was gone from Indiana six years before Knight showed up. Nine years before, in 1962,Tom and I went to the last game his class played at Ohio State. Lucas and Havlicek. Mom & Dad drove us to see that final game; we were seniors in high school. Knight didn't play very much. We knew who all those guys were. We followed them. That's the game Jerry Lucas outrebounded the entire Indiana team.

The first time I really met him was when I saw Army play in the Garden in New York. I remember seeing him kick a chair there. When he became the coach at Indiana, he was really good about including players who had played there—called and let them know he wanted them to still have an interest in the school. We just kinda got to know him that way. He kind of adopted Mom or vice versa and I don't know it just went on from there. We have the love of fishing so we've been fishing a lot of times together. Just kind of a friendship developed. I think the world of the guy. I'd be the first to say, and I think all

of his friends would say, I don't approve of everything he does. But, shoot, over all he's a great guy. I stay in pretty good shape. When you go fishing with him—we had to walk a long way in the brushes in the tundra to go to these different rivers. That son of a gun is right with you and you've got to work to keep up with him. He's strong.

Yo, Tommy, give me my ball retriever, I just had it regripped

Tom Ackerman

At the tender age of 25, Tom Ackerman is on a fast-career track. At KMOX Radio—"The Cradle of Sports Announcers:"—in his native St. Louis, he has his own sports show. Because of his background of producing and directing successful programs at WIUS, the Indiana Student Station, and other shows at KMOX, many media experts expect him to continue his rapid rise. He is the weekend host of Budweiser's Sports Open Line, the longest running sports talk show in America. The tall and talented Ackerman had an unusual insight into Coach Knight as his caddy, his pupil, and covering IU basketball for the student station.

Courtesy Tom Ackerman

Caddy Tom Ackerman with Bob Knight.

The first time I met Bobby Knight was through a friend of my dad's who was a senior PGA tour player, Larry Ziegler. Ziegler said, "Hey I'm gonna play with Knight. Why don't you come along?" I was in essence caddying for him—I was about 14. I'm thinking to myself, "Man, this is the coolest thing ever." The first thing I said to Coach Knight was "So are you ready for the basketball season?" He turned and looked at me and said, "I don't know when you're ever ready for the basketball season. Right now, I'm thinking about this next shot." It wasn't like a mean comment or anything. He just kind of said it with a smile and put his arm around me.

Out on the golf course that day, one of the things I remember—that flash of temper. He just has the temper and he has admitted to it. He hit a

shot that went off to the left into the woods a little bit. He goes, "You know what, Tommy?" and he looked at me and kinda smiled and said, "I wish I could take every club I own and break it." I looked at him. I didn't think he was gonna do anything—we all say that. Before I know it, I look over there and he just has the shaft in his hand. He had broken it on the tire on the cart. It was like a natural wood. And he goes, "Oh," and he looks down. I remember the next thing I knew he was holding the club in his hand and comes over to the women who were with us and he said, "I'm sorry about that; did I startle you?" One of them said, "Yeah." He put his arm around her and said, "I'm sorry about that." I thought it was a funny moment. He just kinda snapped, and bang.

I remember him asking me "Where do you want to go to college?" I wasn't really sure yet, I was just fifteen and I'm thinking I want to go to the University of Missouri, I want to go to Miami of Ohio, I've been interested in SMU down in Dallas, University of Miami, Florida. I kinda stopped and he said, "What about Indiana?" I said, "I don't know; I never really thought about Indiana that much." He was like, "Well, you should." I'm like yeah. He said, "Yeah, it's great. Obviously it's one of the great schools; you'll love it." I said, "Well I haven't visited or anything like that." He said, "Well how about I set you up with somebody there; they can show you around and get you acquainted with the campus." It was really neat.

It wasn't too much longer that I did tour the campus. I called the person and ended up becoming great friends with the person, Elizabeth "Buzz" Kurpius, Academic Advisor, very nice lady. Coach Knight couldn't have introduced me to a nicer person. It was just a really nice thing on his part. He set it up. He called her and said, "Hey I met this kid. He's gonna call you." It was just really a nice feeling. I toured the Indiana campus and ended up going there, mainly because Coach Knight introduced me to this incredible lady, Buzz Kurpius. I loved the campus. I loved all the schools I applied to but Indiana in particular had a strong sports program, school spirit, and a good telecommunications school. It was just an overall terrific place to be. I wanted to be there. It's what you think of when you're little—the fraternities, all the activities, the spirit, it has it all. I applied to IU and got accepted.

When I started as a freshman, I wanted to get a radio show there, and WIUS accepted me to do a late night show, and I ended up doing sports. I did play-by-play of the basketball games for the college station and attended

Do you confuse Miami of Ohio and Miami of Florida? Miami of Ohio was a school before Florida was a state.

the press conferences. That's where I started to see Coach Knight in his element. I respected him as a coach but was always impressed because you always knew when he was in the room—when Bob Knight walked into the room. He commanded respect just by being there and just knew he was there. I really enjoyed listening to him and he was a guy who you had to think about what you were asking. He really challenged you as a reporter, and that's something I respect. I had always seen the TV videos of him cursing out all the reporters. I never witnessed that in Bloomington, and I'm being honest.

I can never remember him screaming at a reporter. He might have said to one "that's not a very good question to ask." Or he might say "what you really need to do is read this book that I read by Hans Christian Andersen." I remember him saying that to a student reporter one time. "There's a great book by Hans Christian Andersen I would like you to read." He would change the subject, and was cool and calm about everything, but I never saw him scream at anybody.

I've seen him at a game obviously yell at officials, and I've seen him yell at his players. The practices were closed at IU but if there was any practice where I was allowed to go or to Midnight Madness practice, I went. He treated his players with discipline. I never saw him yell at reporters, and I never felt intimidated at a press conference. He was always very straightforward. He always opened his press conferences with about a one or two minute spiel on what he thought the game was like, and what he expected and what he thought a couple of players did and what he expected so, basically, don't ask him a question about what he just said.

I ended up taking his class, which was called "Coaching of Basketball." I met him a couple of days later. My favorite story is the beginning of class. This was essential; you always knew Knight was in the room, the authority figure. The first day of class: We were sitting there waiting for class to begin and Norm Ellenberger walks in, the assistant now with the Chicago Bulls. He walks in and says "Hey, name's Ellenberger and I'll be teaching this class for the first couple of weeks. Coach Knight is in Canada on a fishing trip so I'm gonna be teaching you all the offense and a little bit about Indiana basketball. Coach Knight is gonna join us later in the semester." We're all sitting there taking our notes as Coach Ellenberger starts drawing on the chalkboard.

Probably ten minutes into class we hear, "I'll take it from here, Coach."

Bob Knight once had Woody Hayes as one of his instructors in a class at Ohio State.

And it's Bob Knight. He had just gotten through saying the guy was out of town. People turn around and the first thing he says is, "Everybody get your hats off. There are women in the room. You don't wear a hat in my class." He said, "I have eighty to a hundred kids. I'd say one-third are girls; I think most of the rest are boys. You can never be sure on a college campus." He gets to the front of the class and hasn't even looked at anyone yet. He gets to the front of the class, wheels around, hats are off—no one is wearing a hat. He says, "You can get an A in this class. Hell, I don't care if all 85 of you get an A." I just remember this so well. "That's fine—all 85 of you can get A's. But if you skip my class once you have a C, no questions asked. You skip it twice, I'll fail you." And then he goes, "don't give me any of that cute stuff about signing in your friends on the attendance sheet 'cause I'll find both of you and fail both of you." "Now, as for the class. . . ." And he starts describing the class, and people start taking their hands and gripping the sides of their desk. We finally relax a little bit.

Basically, Coach Knight taught leadership, getting a job, dealing with co-workers, I guess he really didn't talk about basketball. That was Coach Ellenberger's job to talk about the offense and we ran drills on the basketball floor. Then we would go on the floor later and run drills with Norm Ellenberger. But Coach Knight's job was to lecture that lasted about 45 minutes each day we had class. We had to be on time. Nobody was ever late. God forbid you walk in ten minutes late on Bob Knight's class, you know. His lectures didn't have anything to do with basketball. He spoke about his experiences and about people he respects a lot. He had an entire day on D. Wayne Lucas, the trainer, talking about how he gets up at four in the morning and goes to bed at midnight—the work ethic and getting after it every day. He had an entire day on Bill Parcells and Tony LaRussa talking about their work ethic and how he respects them and how they work with their players, how they instill discipline with their teams. It was very interesting. It was more about the coaching profession I would say—about being a coach, being a leader than learning how IU plays basketball. It was very little about the game of basketball. It was all about motivation. I'm absolutely glad I took the course; it was my favorite course—the one I'll always remember. I was never late—always made sure I was there on time. You don't want to miss that one. I probably paid attention more in that class than any other class I had. It was basically a lecture, then we would go through basketball drills. We were essentially graded on attendance, and a book we put together at the end of the semester—our class notes organized in a nice way, and what we learned, and parts of the offense. It was a very thorough book that we put together—about a 25 or 30-page

book. I'm sure he looked at them, there's no doubt in my mind he personally graded each one.

There's no question that people signed up because it was Bob Knight's class. And sure there were some people in there who were interested in being a basketball coach some day, but the reason that I think 98 per cent of the people were in there was because Bob Knight was teaching the class. Who's to blame them? This is a guy who is paid thousands of dollars by corporations to speak. This guy gives motivational speeches. Here you are having him in a class twice a week. Here he is talking to you. It was a nice opportunity to be up close and personal. On the last day of class, he walked in and said, "Okay, this is your opportunity to ask me any questions, so shoot, ask me anything you want." So people were just asking him questions—he would answer them if he wanted to. He would answer, if appropriate. It was very interesting.

One day I said "Hey Coach, remember me?" That seemed very unprofessional but when I caught him after class in the hallway I reintroduced myself and he said, "Well, Tommy, how are you, it's great to see you." He remembered me and the whole thing. He asked, "How's your Dad doing?" He remembered meeting my Dad and said he was a great guy. We all had lunch that day at the golf course and my Dad insisted he would pay for it. My Dad passed away before I got to Indiana, so I told this to Coach Knight. He put his arm around me, said, "I'm really sorry about that. If there's anything I can do, just give me a call. Are you comfortable here? Are you enjoying yourself? How are your grades? How's this?" It was just a really nice thing.

I'm not saying I spent a lot of time with him or went to his office or anything like that. My sister goes there now; she's a senior. She works in the athletic department. She's an assistant for Buzz.

Knight has done some things that are negative that stood out. But the national media looks for the negative in anything he does. You will see leading off the highlight show, they will show Bob Knight screaming at a player. If you ever see a feature on Knight, they'll show him grabbing a player by the jersey or screaming at his assistants or yelling at an official. You never, never see a shot of him smiling, or patting a player after a great play, or clapping his hands, hardly ever.

He visited hospitals. I know that he helped area businesses. He helped area activities—university activities, area charities, without any sort of fanfare. You never had IU with camera crews following him around. He did that on his own and he was fine with that. If you're gonna go out and cover him in a negative light, he doesn't really care. He didn't really bother either way. That's why he never responded to a lot of that stuff. At least in my opinion.

His job was to have the best basketball team he could possibly have. Number one: to make sure that his players, the ones who played for him, had the best college experience they could have, that they graduated, they were educated, that was his priority and to make sure the university flourished under him. I don't think he really cared that the nation was painting a bad picture of him. His whole thing is if you know about Indiana basketball, if you know what's going on within our program, that's fine. If not, I don't think he really has a lot of time for you.

Neil Reed was a year behind me at IU. Reed was a scrappy player and an excellent shooter way before any of this uproar ever happened. This was way before he was voted off the team. But you always had these rumors about the fact that he and Coach Knight differed on a lot of things in practice. Some of the players were a little bit upset with the fact that he didn't spend a lot of time in the weight room working on his individual conditioning and that sometimes in practice he had his own agenda—that he was somewhat rebellious and wanted to do it his own way. When you play at Indiana, the name is on the front of the jersey, that's just the way it is. You're playing for Coach Knight. That is Bob Knight's team. That is not "I'm Neil Reed, and I'm playing basketball." That's Bob Knight's team. It's a team game. You know that when you're recruited there. You know that when you're going there. I think they're the only college basketball team without names on the back of the jerseys. You never heard there was any sort of physical abuse or anything like that but you heard that Reed was not exactly a hundred per cent respected by some of his teammates for some of his actions. I'm not saying that he wasn't a scrappy player; the fans really did enjoy him while he was there. I think it took a lot of people by surprise that things turned out like they did—that he left, but I think that you had always heard and this was never confirmed—that the players weren't totally enthralled with the fact that he strayed from that team concept. I think that bothered some people and eventually led to his being removed from the team by his own teammates.

It sounds to me like the team didn't want the guy on the team anymore. I guess I don't know how many times they came to him and asked him to be more of a teammate. Reed was always nice to me. I met him after class one time; he was very nice. I asked him if he would come on my radio show if I ever call him, would he want to do it. He said, "Yeah." He was very nice and from everything I had heard he was a nice guy. I was a sports reporter all four years there. I did play by play for basketball, I did a show at WIUS, and I was a stringer for USA Today for their on-line service, USA Today Online. I saw the job opportunity on the Internet. They sent out a mass email from List-

Serve to a bunch of students. It said USA Today is looking for stringers for all Division One colleges, and I wrote the guy and called him and said I work for WIUS and do play-by-play. I go to all the press conferences; I know a lot about the program. I could do that for football and basketball for you, and I got it. I think normally they give it to one of the interns in the athletic department. I got paid $75 a week and that's not bad for a college student to write. I would prepare game notes or preview notes about five times a week.

Bob Knight's favorite drink is half Coke, half lemonade. Isn't that the strangest thing you've ever heard? We sat down at lunch and he said, "Can I get a half-Coke, half-lemonade?" I thought, "That's odd." The waitress kinda looked at us, and he goes, "I just want a glass half Coke and half lemonade, and she said okay, I think she brought back a half glass of lemonade and a can of Coke or something like that and he did it himself. I think he drinks that all the time. He's just a colorful character.

Bob Knight has had an extremely positive influence on my life, and I appreciate it.

The Boy Wonder had the boys wondering

Gregg Elkin

Gregg was assistant media relations director at Indiana University for nine years and now serves in a similar capacity for the NBA's Dallas Mavericks.

Elkin was raised in St. Charles, Ill., graduated from Arizona State and began his career at the University of Iowa.

Gregg Elkin

We always had to bus to Illinois to play. Every year for the last five or six years, there's a restaurant, the Beef House, Covington, Indiana, on I-74 right before the Illinois border, where the Indiana team always stopped and ate dinner. One year we were gonna leave and the coach wasn't on the bus. We took off. I think he was with Bob Hammel, the sportswriter. They drove because somebody had written Knight a letter about an elderly lady who was in the hospital and was a big IU fan and they stopped and saw that lady at the hospital and met us at the restaurant, then got on the bus with us and went to Champaign after were finished eating. That's the kind of thing he does all the time. He went from Bloomington, saw the lady, then caught up with us at the Beef House.

In my job you you get to know all the parents. Neil Reed's Dad, Terry, was a parent I really got to know. He constantly called me when Neil played well, didn't play well, whatever. It got to the point, I remember one day I went home. A repairman was coming to our house so I went home to let him

Former Illinois coach, Lon Krueger, was drafted by the Houston Astros in 1970. In 1974 he signed with the St. Louis Cardinals and pitched one year in their farm system. He was drafted by the Atlanta Hawks. He was invited to the Dallas Cowboys Rookie Training Camp in both 1974 and '75. He played European Pro Basketball in 1975 and he went to the Detroit Pistons camp the following year.

in. Terry got the number on my desk at work. I'm at home. The only person who knows I'm home is the secretary in the office. I'm just waiting for the repairman to show up. The phone rings; it's Terry. He's bitching about coach 'cause Neil didn't play well the day before. "Coach doesn't know how to use him, blah, blah, blah, etc." So that would go on; he'd call at 11:30 at night, he'd call after I'd gone to bed; he'd call on weekends. Terry was not at IU then; this was a family whose hope and dreams were built on that kid playing in the NBA. That kid never had a chance to play in this league 'cause of his size and athletic ability—a good college player—not a great college player but was just fine playing in college and was having a nice college career but that's where it was gonna end.

Let me give you an example of how the family worked and thought. We played in the preseason NIT in 1996. We are playing Duke in the final. Neil starts the game and is playing okay; coach takes him out just like he would normally—to give him a rest and puts Michael Lewis, a freshman, into the game. Lewis and Guyton start playing really well and we start pulling away from Duke. One thing leads to another, and Neil probably only plays eight or ten minutes in that whole game. It was just one of those things. Knight took him out at the normal time when he would take him out and put a couple of guys back in and all of a sudden we started pulling away. To some players that rarely happens to, but that happens an awful lot of times even if you're the best player on the team. And also that night Andrae Patterson has 39 points, a bunch of rebounds, wins MVP of the tournament and Neil and Andrae were roommates. So we go back in the locker room there at Madison Square Garden real excited, we beat Duke, won this tournament again and it's kinda like—we'd had a bad year the previous season—we're back, we're 4–0, we're gonna be ranked pretty high now and had played really well. And look over at the corner of the locker room. There's Reed sitting in the corner, with a hooded sweatshirt on, with the hood pulled over his head, kinda all balled up in the corner. Get on the bus, he's the same way—just sitting there looking out the window with the hood pulled down. Everybody was excited, we had won by about fifteen, really beat them bad, won the finals, everybody was happy. Patterson was in his junior year, and had been kinda up and down so people thought Andrae's gonna start playing really well. What a great place to do it in. Everybody's there. People could talk all they want about the Hawaii tournament, this was THE Thanksgiving tournament. Everybody watches

Bob Knight's first year at Indiana was also the first year Indiana received an NIT bid.

those games. So Reed's upset because: 1) he didn't play as much as he wanted to, and 2) he didn't win the MVP of the tournament.

A couple of weeks later, we have our tournament at home. Reed wins MVP of the tournament. I tabulated the votes and gave them to our public address announcer. At the time there's only two people who know who's on the all-tournament team and who the MVP is. I see Reed's sister, and I say, "Hey, your brother got MVP." This is before they'd announced it. She goes, "Well, it doesn't count now; should have got it two weeks ago." That's a true story.

Knight only averaged 1.1 technicals per year in his career at Indiana. In 32 years, he's only gotten about 40 technical fouls in all that time.

The public address announcer for the Houston Astros (Colt 45s) during their first season in 1962 was Dan Rather. The PA announcer for the Brooklyn Dodgers in 1937 was John Forsythe, the actor.

Assembly Hall—the land of ahs

Eric Ruden

Eric is the Sports Information Director at The U. S. Naval Academy. He got his start back in the mid-80s in the IU Athletic Department.

Courtesy of U.S. Naval Academy

Eric Ruden

I left IU in late February of 1990 and started with the White Sox in early March. I had been a life-long White Sox fan, growing up in Joliet, and still am. This was a great opportunity. I can remember after being contacted by the White Sox and had interviewed there and had, of course, told Kit Klingelhoffer, my boss, but hadn't said anything to Coach Knight about it. And after I accepted the job, when I told Coach Knight, he said, "Jesus Christ, Eric you should have asked me for help. I could have negotiated you a better deal than you probably got," but I left on great terms.

Some of these blooper video tapes that have been going around for several years of some of Coach Knight's press conferences or outtakes from some of his TV shows and in one of them they show this clip of the last press

conference that I ever moderated for him. It was a win over Iowa. I would frequently, if I felt the press conference had gone on for a fair amount of time and some of the questions were getting a little bit off the mark, and I knew that Coach had something to get to. I would say "Final question for Coach Knight." Wouldn't do it every time, but occasionally would. Well, this particular day, after about fifteen minutes of questions about the game and what have you, there was a question, which I felt was not really in line with what we were talking about. I said, "That'll be our final question for Coach Knight today." He looked over at me and said, "Eric, goddamn, it's my press conference. I'll decide whether it's the final question or not. What's going to happen to you when you go up there with the White Sox? I'll tell you what's gonna happen. One of those players will take a bat and shove it up your ass and all you're gonna have is two front teeth sticking out of it." Here again, as people see that, and every year I get a call from a couple of people saying, "I saw this tape and you're on it and oh, my goodness, and blah, blah, blah. Knight really ripped you." Well I didn't take it that way, didn't see it that way at all. Again, it was his way of saying, kind of in front of everyone, good luck with the Sox and so long and we'll miss you. So it's a different perception. Everyone has a different perception. I certainly didn't take any offense to that at all. After finishing the season with the Sox, then in January of '91 losing my job there and word got back to Coach Knight, I'd say within 24 to 48 hours, that I no longer had my job with the Sox. I got a letter from him days later, what impressed me is that it was right in the middle of the 1991 basketball season, and they were right in the heat of a Big Ten race and everything that's going on that he took the time to write me, offered me his assistance in anything he could do. He later had a couple of people call me and offer me jobs just to attempt to help me out.

Shortly thereafter, Indiana was playing Northwestern at Evanston. I went over that morning of the game to watch the shoot-around. I was familiar with several of the players because I had only been gone less than a year. I talked to them, talked to Coach a little bit, and sat down and Moose Skowron, the former White Sox and Yankee slugger came over, and I knew Moose because he would come down to Bloomington once a year and spend some time with Coach Knight and do some fishing and what have you. They had become friends, I believe through Roger Maris, whom Coach thought a lot of. Moose came over. He was working for a trucking company at the time, and immediately offered me a job with this company and wanted to help me

Indiana University ranks twelfth in winning percentage in Big Ten football history . . . behind the University of Chicago.

out, and I knew that Coach had put him up to that. I obviously wanted to stay in athletics and public relations so I didn't take him up on the offer, but I appreciated it nonetheless.

During one of my early years at IU, I had been working with the basketball program and it was in the overlap part of the calendar year when football and basketball were going on at the same time. At that time the IU football program was going pretty well. Bill Mallory had the team going to bowl games quite frequently in the late 80s. So there was a lot of attention surrounding the football program. So we were in November and both seasons were going on, and I came down to the practice on this particular day. I came down to the floor and sat down at the scorers' table. Coach Knight came over and said, "What are you here for?" I said, "I came to watch practice." "I don't believe you're here to watch practice. You must have some interview request or something you want me to do. That's the only reason you come down here." I said, "No, I came to see how the team is doing." I sat there for about fifteen minutes longer. He had walked away. I watched some of the practice. Next day the same thing transpired. So finally, on the third consecutive day, Coach again saw me at practice, asked what I was doing, then questioned why, and said, "You're not interested in basketball, you're just here to do your job and ask me about a particular media request." I just got up and walked out and went back to my desk. About fifteen minutes later, one of the student managers came into the office and said Coach Knight wants to see you. I went down to the court and he came over and he said, "Eric, if you want to hang around with the big boys, you better learn how to take shit because I'm the best at giving it out." Then he put his arm around me and kinda slapped me on the back of the head and had a big grin on his face. I probably had the best feeling in the world because at that time I felt that he'd accepted me as one of the guys per se. And I was a 23-year-old assistant SID, handling the media relations for the men's basketball program. But for someone of his stature to do that really made me feel good. And as I've told some other people that story through the years, people who don't know Coach Knight, or haven't followed the program, say, "Oh my goodness, he hit you. That's physical assault. That's harassment. Why didn't you call the police?" And I just chuckle, and say, "don't you understand, that's the nicest thing he could have done to make me feel like I was part of the program.

Connie Chung had scheduled to do an interview because she was going to do a special on stress, and how different people in different professions handle stress, and Coach Knight was one of the individuals she wanted to talk to. So they had set up a session down on the floor at Assembly Hall and proceeded to do the interview. At one point, Coach referred to an old comment

that he had heard back in the old days. I believe he even attributed it to his father—that if rape is inevitable, relax and enjoy it. The minute he said it, he said, "Oh, geez, stop the tape. That's not gonna come across the way I intended it to." Connie Chung said, "Yeah, that's a good point." And she turned to the producer and asked him to write down the tape numbers and he did. Then she said, "We'll make sure that's not in the show, right?" And the producer nodded and they went on with the rest of the interview. Then a couple of months later, about a week before the special aired, all of a sudden CBS was promoting and publicizing the show that was coming up, the special that Connie Chung was doing on stress management. The lead comment in the news release and the lead piece of video for the promo was Bob Knight says "If rape is inevitable, relax and enjoy it." Coach Knight had totally had been betrayed by Connie Chung and the producer who had done the interview. Bobby Knight was very upset about it.

Connie Chung did the same thing to Newt Gingrich's mother a few years later.

I would say that the end probably doesn't justify the means. I think the fact that they are parting ways, speaking of the IU administration and Coach Knight, it is probably the best for both parties. I mean, as Coach has cited, it has become very difficult over the past few years to work with that administration. I think that's probably a good thing for both, but the way it happened and the way it's played out—it's a tragedy. It's very disheartening to see this happen and so from my standpoint, a thousand miles away, not being inside right now and not knowing what went on, I just wish that there would have been a better way. Could it have been handled differently and in a better way to avoid this mess that we have on our hands right now?

People always say that perception is a big part of reality and my thinking in this case a lot of people have watched the interview with Jeremy Schaap. Coach never raised his voice, he never raised his hand, he never threatened anyone. Yet the next day, on talk shows across America, people who are not fans of Coach Knight talked about how he "bullied" Jeremy Schaap and threatened him and intimidated him. And even at one point, the "two" shot of Jeremy Schaap even showed him flinch back a little bit when Coach Knight bit his lip so I don't think he did anything to force that reaction but yet it certainly seemed that Jeremy Schaap seemed intimidated.

I don't know anything about the background behind setting that thing up but at some point, Knight had to say "Yes I'd like you to come in and I'd like the opportunity to tell my side of the story." So, if you're gonna give him that, at least let him say his piece.

Take this job and love it

Todd Starowitz

Todd Starowitz is in his third year as Football Media Relations Director at Indiana, named to that position in July,1997. He is a 1993 graduate of Indiana with a degree in Journalism and Political Science. He served as a public relations assistant with the Philadelphia Eagles and Indianapolis Colts. How did a high school student in Canandaigua, New York end up going to college in Bloomington, Indiana?

I was in high school in up-state New York when I read *Season on the Brink*, a book that Coach doesn't have great feelings about. I would never talk with him personally about the book, but I know from what I've read that he wasn't overly pleased with it. I think sometimes in that situation, if you're the person who's being written about and critiqued, and even if you're spoken about positively, it can make one feel awkward. After reading the book, I dropped Coach Knight a note, because it said in the book that he personally responds to requests and letters so I wanted to get something back from Coach Knight to find out if he does. At the time, Indiana was playing some 2–3 zone, ironically, and they played the 2–3 against Notre Dame and David Rivers and I wanted to know if it was a match-up or just a straight 2–3. He wrote back to me and said, "No it was just a straight 2–3." Since I had read that in the book, I wasn't shocked to hear from him, but I was pleased that he wrote me. I still have that letter, and because of that, I looked into Indiana as a school. It has a wonderful journalism school—just a great University, and that's how I ended up at Indiana. I got off the phone with him about an hour ago actually. He's just been wonderful to work for.

I don't understand just how much of what Coach Knight does is—to send a message, and second of all, truly for effect. It was such a quiet year last year actually; there really weren't any incidents at all. Even the stuff that came up this spring was from two-three years ago. But the one that made the most news was the post game press conference after the Iowa contest with Alford, and Coach made two trips into the interview room and got on a writer a little bit and he walked out. And he looked at Pat, his son, and smiled and said, "How was that?" He does that. The day he walked in the media room and shook hands with all the media the day afterward because they made such a big deal about Steve not shaking Coach's hand after the Big Ten meetings. He invited most of his assistants in there to watch the press conference

because he was just gonna play a little bit. Jon Gruden, coach of the Oakland Raiders, grew up in Bloomington, and was pals with Tim Knight, Coach's son, and actually was a ball boy for the '76 team and just loves Coach Knight. He really spent a lot of time growing up around the program, and he's got some really neat stories.

Recently, the representative of Connie Chung's show called and requested an interview with Coach. I said, "You have got to be kidding. Do you not know the history. . . ?" The booking agent had no idea; she was embarrassed. It was pretty funny.

Ironically, at the very hour that President Brand was announcing Knight's firing, Gruden was leading his Raiders from a three-touchdown deficit to a victory over the Colts at the Hoosier Dome . . . Just a few blocks from where Brand's press conference was being held.

• • •

Connie Chung's late father-in-law, Shirley Povich, was a sports writer and Sports Editor with the Washington Post *for seventy-five years. Eisenhower and Nixon did not like the* Post *but subscribed because they loved Shirley Povich. He made the 1969 "Who's Who in American Women," whereupon Walter Cronkite sent a wire, "Miss Povich, will you marry me?"*

Why Does Bobby Say
We Suck When We Blow
Jim "Boomer" Bain
Rick Hartzell
Ted Valentine
Tom Rucker

Now here's Boomer with a four-word treatise

Jim Bain

Former Big Ten Referee. Now Supervisor of Officials, Missouri Valley Conference.

You want to talk about Bob Knight? Well, as my first Supervisor of Officials in the Big Ten said, "Ya can't quote silence."

No autopsy, no foul

Rick Hartzell

A native of the small town of Klemme, Iowa, Hartzell has earned enormous respect in the world of collegiate athletics. He has risen through the ranks from Head Baseball Coach at Coe College (where Bill Fitch and Marv Levy once coached) to Athletic Director at Bucknell and now holds a similar position at the University of Northern Iowa, his alma mater. He has been ranked as one of the top basketball referees in the ACC and Big Ten.

Courtesy of UNI Athletic Department

Rick Hartzell

Indiana opens the season a lot of times with the Russians. I guess Knight's had some trouble with the Russians, or whatever. This was about four or five years ago. When they line up for the gift exchange —Indiana's got these huge red Indiana travel bags and they're packed with shirts and shorts—you can just tell they've got all this stuff in them that they're going to give the Russians. They go through the gift exchange and the Russians give them one of these little pins about the size of a dime, you know— that's what they give these guys. Indiana is lugging these big bags out there. Then Knight comes back by us, and he turns around to all three of us and he holds this thing and says, "You know they've been screwing us for forty years, why did we expect it to change tonight?"

Last year I worked the Indiana/Purdue game. That's a heck of a rivalry and a hard game to work. Purdue had this kid named Brian Cardinal, a big kid who played, he wasn't dirty, he just played hard. About the middle of the second half somebody goes to the lane again, and it's just a little bit of contact and Knight came up beside me and said, "Rick, the last dozen times that we've come down this court on our end, Cardinal has just knocked the crap out of our kid, and I am just getting sick and tired of it. I don" know if I can take it; I might erupt." So we come down the next time and somebody goes across the middle and Cardinal whacks him and my partner calls it—calls a foul on Cardinal. I'm standing right there beside him and I just turn kinda a little bit and looked at him and said, "Coach, we're one for thirteen." He kinda hunches over and starts to grab his stomach a little bit and looked up at me and said, "You got me." There's a million times when stuff like that occurs with him and I think some—it isn't just me being extra witty or anything that's not the point.

I had Indiana and Purdue about four or five years ago and we had a situation all screwed up. He went wacko 'cause we had the wrong free throw shooter on the line for Purdue, and he was right. It was just one of those situations, and I had to go to him and hold onto him and say, "If you'll just calm down a second here and not go absolutely ballistic, I'll get this straightened out. But I can't stand here with you and keep you from going goofy on national television and have to throw you out and get this solved, too." I left once and when I came back, he was still goofy, and I got him stopped and settled down and got back and got the situation straightened out. Ever since then, I'd say that was trouble because he was gonna "go." But he waited 'til I got back; we got it straightened out. He was right; we were wrong; we knew we were wrong in the middle of it; we got it fixed. I felt like that was one of those things where you build instant credibility with the guy. You know, "he told me he was gonna fix it; he fixed it," and it wasn't like I was doing anybody a favor.

I worked the Indiana Holiday tournament in Market Square Arena about ten or twelve years ago—my first year in the Big Ten. There was a deal in that game where I had a really, really late whistle on a rebound. Sometimes, on a rebound play where somebody gets whacked, you wait a little bit to see what's gonna happen with the ball. If they get the ball back, you don't blow the whistle because there really isn't any advantage gained. I had one of those that was like two or three seconds late, and I called it. That was where it started—my being yelled at about how late it was. I just kinda looked at him calmly and said, "It was late, but it was right."

One of the things that really bothers Knight is when you're in the "trail position" refereeing you are generally right in front of the bench. A lot of the time, you're standing—and it's where you're supposed to be, your mark so to speak. He'll always tell you to slide down, move up, I can't see—you know it's constant. And I respect his problem because he's not a guy who coaches standing up a lot and he's sitting there. At Minnesota it's even worse 'cause he's sitting down below the court. One night there, we get a time out, and he said, "Rick, can you please move your fat ass down a little bit, because I can't see." I looked around at him and said, "Coach, I'd be glad to. You're partially right with your comment, but I'm gonna tell you this. If you were refereeing and if I were sitting there, you'd have to move all the way down to the end so I could see. " He loved that; he thought that was great. Stuff like that is priceless with him. It's a challenge. There're a couple of guys like that: Huggins, at Cincinnati, is one, he's one. It's a challenge to be able to say something back to them that isn't insulting, that's relatively intelligent that they kind of get a little bit—it disarms them a little bit. I enjoy that part of it more than anything else.

I've seen him lots of time off the court. Different guy—gentle, kind, sent my mother, when she was dying last winter, a picture and stuff after I'd written him a little note. I could never say anything negative.

My personal feeling on seeing Knight fired was being sad. I think college sports in general needs personalities, number one. And I think they need people who care about kids. And I think, down deep, he really cared about kids. But I'm sad because I think that at some level he doesn't get it. I think at some level he doesn't understand. It's kind of like the guy on the construction crew in New York City who whistles and ogles every woman who goes by. In 1930, it was okay. It isn't okay today. I don't think he completely gets it. But I'm sad because I know—I know for a fact—that down deep there's a real really-good guy there—really good, maybe better than most.

I miss him already. I've got an Indiana game this year. Somebody said the other day, "Do you have any Indiana games?" I said, "I don't care." I used to care. I used to care, but I don't care now. Not that it won't be exciting—and all that stuff, but it won't be the same. I think he's a good guy, and I really, really liked him, but you can't do some of the stuff he did—you just can't do it.

It's a travesty they haven't named a day for Knight, they named one for me

Ted Valentine

In one of Boby Knight's more famous outbursts about referees he called Ted Valentine "The Greatest Travesty" he has ever seen as a college coach. Valentine ejected Knight after he received three technical fouls in a February 1998 game with Illinois.

Valentine, with his great outlook on life, shrugged it off and continued to work on lowering his single-digit golf handicap near his West Virginia home.

This happened back when Knight was doing a NutraSweet (sweetener in a pink packet) commercial. One night I was going to Bloomington and I was working a game there, in fact the game was Ohio State, during Randy Ayers' last year there, at Indiana. We were in the course of the game. It was close, back and forth. Left-handed jump shooter, Brian Evans was hot, and we were in the game, and it was going along pretty good.

It was a time out. I had the ball and was bouncing it along the sidelines. Bobby gets up to me and says something to me, and I respond to him, "No, Coach, no." And he looked at me, and his exact words were, "Don't you ever fuckin' laugh or anything like that?" Those were his exact words he said to me, "Don't you ever fuckin' laugh? I'm trying to be kind to you." I reached in my back pocket (this is a true story, too.) and said, "Coach, if you're trying to show your sweeter side, then I'll show you my sweeter side." Then I reached in my back pocket and pulled out a blue pack of Equal and gave it to him. He looked at me and started laughing and said, "You know what? You've got a great sense of humor." And that's probably the last time I ever really had a joke with him. I had just happened to pick up a blue pack of Equal in a restaurant and put it in my coat and then I took it and put it in the back pocket of my referee pants. I always try to do things to get a laugh.

It was at the right time. He actually laughed. I couldn't believe he did.

I don't take the things he said to me personally. I understand it's in the heat of the battle when you say those type things. It's in the heat of the battle and it depends on how the team is playing. I understand that, and he didn't apologize, but an apology doesn't mean anything to me. I know Bob and if I ever looked at him face-to-face, he would probably say something—probably

something smart, but I would say something smart back, too, probably. Maybe one of these days he might say something and this is not in his makeup. This is not who he is and what he is about. I can see all through the stuff because I'm as tough as he is. I haven't been to IU in three years so I don't know how I'll feel about going there. Coach Knight is a great coach, and we used to have a lot of correspondence years ago. I used to write him little notes; most people don't know all the stuff I've seen. I've been in the Big Ten since 1985; I've worked in the Big Ten since I was 26 years old—maybe have been the youngest ever Big Ten referee. I can remember Coach Knight never had a bit of a problem. I'm a fisherman. I would say "Congratulations on winning your National Championship" when he beat Syracuse. That was before I made the NCAA tournament and all so I was watching it on TV. So I wrote him a card and he wrote me a nice little note, "Keep up the good work. Keep fishing. Yours in coaching, Bob Knight." Every time I wrote him a little note, he always sent me back a note. This was when I was younger—coming along or whatever.

It was around '85 or so when I worked my second Big Ten game when Montana State played at Indiana. Back then the Big Ten would put you on crews, and it was older refs' job to take care of me since I was a young kid. We were working Montana State one afternoon, and Bob Knight came out with a powder blue sweater like Montana State's colors—he wore their actual sweater. It was a light blue and had Montana State on the sweater. He was coaching his team, and this was my first time ever to be around him. He had Alford and that great team there and there was something going on. I was doing my best to referee the game but I was trying to stay away from him. Because when you watch TV you see all this stuff, and I'm going, "Well, I'm a young kid, and I don't know what I might do, or I may be a little bit intimidated of him or whatever." So I'm refereeing the game and we get this time out and they just changed the rule that year to where when the time out ended, you had to go get the team to get them out of the huddle. If you know Coach Knight, you know you don't go into his huddle. So I walked over toward them and clapped my hands and said, "Let's go white (they had their white uniforms on). He said, "They're coming, they're coming." So I waited a couple more seconds and I said, "Let's go White, let's go." And they haven't come out. Then the third time, I go back and say, "Let's go White." He said, "God damn it, I said they're coming." So now he turns, and I gotta inbound the ball right in front of his bench. So the team comes out, and I'm standing right beside him, and I'm gonna inbound the ball right near Joby Wright, his black assistant. Coach Knight says, "Just a second, just a second," and he goes

"Do you know you're supposed to not be up in my huddle?" I said, "No sir." Then he kept asking me a bunch of questions. He said, "Well, what were you doing in my huddle?" I said, "Well, sir, I was told by the NCAA I gotta start coming in and bringing you guys out." So every word I was using with him was with "sir." So he turned to me and said, "God damn it, you don't call me 'sir.' I said, "Well, sir, I gotta bring you out." He said "Wait a minute, God damn it." He turned, and he said, "You don't call me 'sir.' You call 'sir' to Lieutenants, Colonels and cocksuckers." He turned around to Joby Wright and pointed his finger at Joby Wright and said, "Joby, God damn it, I don't see him calling you 'sir.' "

I was thinking, "Jiminy Christmas, this guy here is a little bit off the wall." But it was great. I was a rookie, so it kinda like broke the ice a little bit. Here's a young kid, he's out here, and you don't know what this guy might do. Then all of a sudden he says something like that to you.

Those are probably the only two stories that I can ever remember about him. If you could mention me, say I got no animosity toward the guy. He's a good coach, and I'd be glad to tee up a golf ball and play golf with him. If I had to do it, and get in his face, that's just the way it would be. It's part of athletics. It's part of the territory. Believe me. I understand it.

He had some great players that some refs would warm up to. He had Damon Bailey who would always talk to you. In the eighties, he had the Sloan kid, whose dad coaches the Utah Jazz. He was a nice young kid; he would intermingle. Most of Coach Knight's players were pretty much close to the vest, and they never talk to officials. I think they respect them, and I think there was a thing where they didn't say anything about anything because he would do it for them. Most of his kids were good kids. Damon Bailey was probably one of my favorites there because he would smile. He was the All-American kid, I thought. He just played, and he would always pat you on the behind when you made a call for him or against him. He was a little bit different

When Steve Alford played, Alford was just—he just played. Keith Smart and Dean Garrett and those guys—they just played. You didn't get into conversations about a lot of stuff; they just played basketball. I don't know if it was the way Coach Knight structured them or what.

The Utah Jazz are the only NBA team never to participate in a draft lottery and the only NBA team never to have fined a player.

The reason Northwestern has two directions in its name is they don't know if they're coming or going

Tom Rucker

Tom Rucker of suburban Detroit has been one of Bob Knight's favorite targets for almost three decades as a Big 10 referee.

Tom Rucker

Bob has always been good to me. I was disappointed in the way his end came—I just thought it was gonna come eventually, but I was disappointed in the way it did come. He has done a lot of good for a lot of people. Believe it or not, he has been one of our biggest supporters. He's just supported us—me. Bob has his ways. I'm going to miss him. We had a little thing going. He wrote me a note, and said, "I know your time on the staff is coming to a close shortly (I'm going to retire in two years; I'm starting my twenty ninth year.), and when you do I want you to work your last game for me." Bob would be starting his thirtieth year this year so I started a year after he did. Next year, I'm thirty and out.

Coach Knight and I have been through a lot of battles together. I use the word battle, I don't look at him or any coach in an adversary way. It's just the situation I'm in and the situation he's in. He was almost an unknown when he first started. I never see him in the off-season. I can't think of any other coach I would compare with him. He gets more out of what he has than, I think, any other coach. I tell you one thing, any game I've been at Indiana, you always would see 25 to 35 former players behind that bench—all the time. There wasn't a game I would go to that you wouldn't see that because see Bob is one of the few coaches, I'm sure there are others, that once you finish playing with him, the game isn't over. He's with you—in terms of ways that he can help you. You know a lot of these kids, once their eligibility is up, you're long gone as far as the coach is concerned. Bob's not like that. He's very loyal and those kids that have stuck with him are loyal to him.

Bloomington: Where the Local Time is Always 1987
Don Pence
Greta York
Larry Hawkins
Louis Lemberger
Brian Spurlock
Stan Sutton

Knight gave IU the rings, IU gave him the finger

Don Pence

Don Pence is a throwback to the old days. A straightforward, hard-talking, hard-working businessman, he is one of the most successful General Motors dealers in the country. When not abiding for his passion for golf, he splits his time between Franklin and Danville, Indiana and his winter home in Florida. He has the largest collection of logo golf balls in the world.

I'll tell you I still stand like I always have. I like Bob Knight because he's run a clean program down there for twenty-nine years. You can just go around the Midwest, hell, even Purdue—they've had their problems, Northwestern, look at Minnesota—hell you can just keep on going if you want to. Look at all those teams. He's run a clean program. If players messed with dope, if they were totally out of line he would replace them, move them on, which he has done to several of them.

As a man, he is very, very intelligent, highly intelligent, probably more so than Myles Brand, if you want to be honest about it. You never know what goddamn crazy people will do. It's just like Knight said, the administration has changed. The old line, hell no, they wouldn't have fired him. They had more sense than that. The only reason—you know Knight could have gone to a lot of schools that didn't give a damn about things and had a program and been in trouble all the time. He didn't want to do that; he opted not to do that. Another thing, he kept the commercials pretty much out of the IU program. You didn't have all this Nike shoes shit and all that crap—you know that they feast on money. He didn't do that.

I've been going down there to games at Bloomington since Branch McCracken coached. It didn't have the same deal, see, he put the winning deal into the team. He injected it into the players and it went right on into the student body and the alumni. I think now that whoever they have, who knows? He's got this here deal where he gets a million point three but he's got to stay out of Indiana coaching and out of Kentucky. I don't know why they put that in there. I'd rather see him go down there and replace Tubby Thomas (sic) and just beat the piss out of IU every year.

I know that IU is making a mistake. Fans will miss him, and IU will miss him. He sold lots and lots of sporting garb; at their sports store, he sold thousands and thousands of dollars worth of stuff. And think of all the money he's poured directly into that library there—it's over five million, I know.

In 1976, I've was there sitting with the old Public Service Commissioner at the Philadelphia Bookbinders table right next to him. The Commissioner had gone to school at IU and he asked Coach Knight "What do you think you're gonna do Monday night, Coach?" He said, "Well, we'll just wait and see." Hell, he wasn't making no predictions. I was there in '76 and '81 and New Orleans in '87 and Minneapolis in '91. I used to have season tickets but as I got older, the trip got farther, and they started that nine o'clock at night tip-off shit. You're an hour from home when the game's over, three hours for the game starting at nine, and hell that's midnight. Then you've got another hour to get home at one or one thirty, and that's no fun. Knight was after them over that and said it wasn't fair for the players or the fans. I absolutely agreed with him on that—that wasn't fair to the players. Hell, they're students. All the administrators had on their mind was money and they're gonna miss that money. You gotta have a guy with a lot of go-go. The program down there will be a hell of a lot different.

It's the sports writers who are out to get him. Probably the coach who does come in a year from now will win about two and lose twenty. I am very upset about this. I'm not happy about it at all. They should let him go right on there and finish his career out there. Hell, he'll go coach somewhere, you don't need to worry about him.

This happened four or five days ago. The phone rang and my secretary said "Fred Garver," that's one of my lawyer friends, "wants to talk to you on line one." I'd just heard Knight give his little spiel down there about that "Mister" and all that crud. I punched line one, and said, "It's Mister Pence to you, you asshole." And you know what, Fred was on line two. I don't know who was on line one—I never heard nothing about it, but they sure hung up in a hurry. It's the damn truth. It happened to me not three days ago. So I think the best thing for me to do is just keep my damn mouth shut.

I sent one daughter through IU and she graduated. I sent Tom and he went one year down there. Five of my kids graduated from Ball State and one from IU. My daughter who graduated there doesn't like what's happened.

You just can't tell the difference from a lying ass kid, then the news comes out like "Knight lied about it again. Knight lied about it again." Well Knight didn't lie again. He never did nothing he ain't done a thousand times. I'll tell you what, if I was him, I'd take pride in that I got out of this mess. I'd

When Indiana won the National Title in 1976 in Philadelphia, it was the first time that two teams from the same conference would play for the national title. Michigan lost to IU 86–68.

go up there and look that Benner, Indiana Star News sports writer, up and ask the judge how much it was gonna cost me to hit that son of a bitch? If he said a hundred, I'd just give him five hundred and say, "I want to hit him five times." Hell, he's big enough to do it—6', 5".

They are certainly good down there at IU to terminate people. That deal they done down there with Lee Corso was the lowest life son of a bitching deal I ever seen in my life. That came out of IU twelve or fifteen years ago. They called the news media and told the media and Corso found it out over the news. He didn't even know it. That's no way to do anybody. Now they can say they're administrators, but they're son of a bitches to do something like that. I wouldn't ever fire anybody like that; hell, tell them up front. "We're gonna have to let you go," and that's it. Not make a big hullabaloo in the goddamn news media.

Did you hear the story about when Knight was recruiting "the baby boy Jesus," Damon Bailey, when Bailey was in the second grade down in southern Indiana around Shadswicke or Bedford?

One time several years ago Bobby Knight was scouting Damon Bailey when Damon was in the second grade near Heltonville, Indiana. His car broke down on the way back to Bloomington, and he was stuck on a lonely road.

An hour went by before the first car came by. It was a Cadillac El Dorado. The driver puts on the power brakes, puts down the power window and says to Knight, the hitchhiker, "Are you a sportswriter for the Indianapolis Star?" Knight is surprised and says, "Hell, no." The driver puts up the power window, speeds off, leaves Knight standing there in a cloud of dust.

Another hour goes by before a second car comes along. It was a beautiful, loaded Oldsmobile Aurora. The driver puts on the power brakes, puts down the power window and says to Knight, "Hey, are you a sportswriter for the Indianapolis News?" And Knight says, "Hell, no." The driver puts up the power window, takes off, leaving Knight standing there in a cloud of dust.

So Knight's thinking to himself, "Hell, I'm not getting a ride this way. If anybody else asks me a dumb-ass question like that, I'm gonna say 'yes.'" Well, about twenty minutes later, here comes a Mercedes 450SL convertible, beautiful gal driving the car. I mean the bishop would kick out a stained-glass window to get a closer look at her. She puts on the power brakes and says to

Former IU football coach Lee Corso and Burt Reynolds were roommates at Florida State in 1957.

the hitchhiker, "Hey, are you a sportswriter for the Indianapolis paper?" The hitchhiker, Bobby Knight, says, "Am I a sportswriter for the Indianapolis Star News? I'm the best sportswriter they have. In fact, I'm the best sportswriter in the whole state of Indiana if not the entire damn Midwest." The beautiful gal says, "Get in."

So Bobby Knight gets in the car. He takes a good look at her and she is beautiful—beautiful hair, low-cut top, Charlies out 'til Tuesday, miniskirt riding right up to her hips. He's thinking to himself, "Boy this is my lucky day. I've been hitchhiking on this road, and the very third car that came along picked me up. I'm really lucky." So they're driving along toward Bloomington, and the beautiful and sexy gal says, "Hey, you seem like a nice guy. Would you mind very much if, when we get to Bloomington, you came by my house to have a drink?" And Knight says, "Oh no, that would be fine, that would be great." This was when Knight was between marriages. He was looking down her top and he's looking up her skirt and Knight's thinking to himself, "My god, I've only been a sportswriter for the Indianapolis Star News for five minutes and already I want to fuck someone in Bloomington."

Now that's a true story, give or take a lie or two.

When I crossed over the river, the sign said: "Welcome to Indiana," it didn't say a damn thing about Purdue

Greta York

Greta York is a neat, older lady in Anderson, Indiana who loves Bobby Knight. Originally from Kentucky, she was interviewed both before and after Knight's firing.

Greta York

I've got a Bobby Knight ball. I've been corresponding with Bobby Knight for quite a while. I'm just crazy about Indiana basketball. Course when they started winning championships, you know, I never expected to get a letter back from him. And I've got a lot of pictures from him. I got my first letter back from him February 21, 1991.

"Dear Greta, Many thanks for taking the time to drop me a note. I greatly appreciate your thoughtfulness in doing so as well as the kind remarks you had to make. Once again, thank you for writing and best wishes. Sincerely yours, Bob Knight"

"April 1, 1991—Dear Greta, Thank you very much for taking the time to send me the picture of your niece. I greatly appreciate your thoughtfulness in doing so. Once again, thank you and best wishes."

"Picture—Best Wishes, Greta, Bob Knight"

Another one—Best Wishes, Greta, Bob Knight"

"Thank you very much for your note and sending me the calendar. I really appreciate your thoughtfulness in doing so. I have enclosed the team picture you requested. Thank you for being one of our best fans. Sincerely, Bob Knight"

"1992—Dear Greta, thank you very much for taking the time to send me the clipping. I greatly appreciate your thoughtfulness in doing so. Once again thank you and best wishes, Bob Knight, Sincerely yours, (And he sent me a picture in that one, signed Best Wishes, Bob Knight)"

"Dear Greta and friends, (I had told him I had a bunch of friends and

neighbors who would get together to watch the games.) Many thanks for taking the time to drop me a note. I greatly appreciate your thoughtfulness in doing so as well as the kind remarks you had to make. Once again thank you for writing and best wishes, Sincerely yours, Bob Knight"

I have gotten at least a dozen letters from him and many, many pictures. I am A HUGE Bobby Knight fan. Hell yes, my friends all believe me when I tell them I get letters and pictures from Bob Knight. Some of the pictures say 'Dear Greta and Roy,' my husband who passed away in May.

I get down to a few of the games and hope to meet him one of these days.

"It was awfully nice of you to take the time to drop me a note. I really appreciate your thoughtfulness. I have enclosed the picture you requested. Once again thank you for writing and for your interest in Indiana basketball. Sincerely yours, Bob Knight"

"Dear Greta, Many thanks for taking the time to drop me a note. I really appreciate your kind remarks you had to make. Once again thank you for writing and best wishes. Sincerely yours, And thank you very much for sending me the clippings. I greatly appreciate your thoughtfulness. Thank you and best wishes for a most enjoyable summer (that was June, 1996)."

I wasn't worried that Indiana would get rid of him.

"Thank you for taking the time to send me the card. (His birthday is in October). I greatly appreciate it. Once again thank you and best wishes. Sincerely, Bob Knight"

I wrote and told the president of the university to take me off the mailing list if Bob Knight left the university. I wrote him six times. He wrote back.

I was born in Kentucky but have been here since 1951. When I go back to Kentucky, I have to put mud over my license plates because I have IU plates. I didn't go to IU.

I was very upset with what's happened this spring at IU. If I'd had hold of Neil Reed, I'd have choked him. It didn't get him anyplace, so what can I say?

We used to go to Assembly Hall in groups like from General Motors here in Anderson, but my husband was sick so I haven't been much lately. I went down once when there wasn't a game, but they were in practice and Bob doesn't allow you to go in the gym when they are in practice, I found that out in a hurry.

I've probably got 25 IU shirts. I just love basketball and I love Bobby Knight for a coach 'cause I think he's done so much good for the state of Indiana. I probably couldn't have helped myself being a fan, but if they had fired

him, I probably would have gone down there and told them what I thought. Bobby Knight will leave the university on his terms not anybody else's.

His birthday is October 25, 1940, he's probably 60 this year so, see, he's got five years or more to coach. Look at Dean Smith at how long he coached. The guy who took his place—he just made it three years and he's out of there at North Carolina.

Hell no, I'm not a Purdue fan. You meant to say Purdon't didn't you, that's what I call it.

At a garage sale, they had some Purdue stuff. I said, "What happened to your IU stuff?" And this guy said, "Gene Keady came and bought it all." All my neighbors know I'm a big IU fan 'cause I got my flag up.

I do plan to go to more games this year. The IU team comes to Anderson every year and they play ball here 'cause there's 3 or 4 guys from Anderson that went there that were stars there so I go to the scrimmage games. I'd like to go down to say hello to Bob Knight, but they are all so jam-packed that I can't. I could walk in there with my Bobby Knight doll and I'll bet you I'd get through 'cause he only allowed 1,000 to be made. Now the bookends, he allowed 2500 to be made. The dolls of his were made in northern Indiana and cost $584.75 but $50 of that had to go to the library fund. Mine is #389. My bookends cost around $200 or $300 probably. The doll sits in my bedroom on the chest. It's got an extra pants on it that says what he said in the gym one year when the kids were doing their graduation speech, "When he died, he was gonna be buried upside down, so his critics could kiss his "you know what'."

By the way, how do you know when a Kentucky basketball player is married? When there's tobacco spit on both sides of the pickup.

(Greta was re-visited after Coach Knight was fired.)

I am so heartbroken. Myles Brand has gotten a letter from me every day since it happened. And they weren't very nice, and they get worse as they go. I was shocked—definitely shocked. I do not think he has been treated fairly.

Knight had an interview on television here last night, and he said that the last five years hadn't been the same because of the Athletic Director and the President. I think they're doing this because Myles Brand is trying to make a name for himself. So far, he's had his light post torn down and his mailbox torn down and four or five fires in his yard, so. . . .

Bobby Knight, Dan Issel and Dave Cowens have the same birthday—except Knight was born eight years earlier.

You wouldn't believe what's going on at Indiana. There's people driving up to Assembly Hall and throwing their shirts out. Everybody here in Anderson has taken their flags down. It will have an impact. This story will not go away for a long time. Brand is going to have to retire. He and his wife both have got security everywhere they go. His wife, as a matter of fact, went on TV to plead for people to please leave them alone.

When I write to Bobby Knight, I will tell him how sorry I am about all of it, and how soon all of my shirts and my flag and my stuff will come to Assembly Hall and be thrown out in the yard. I really am going to do that—that will be a truckload. I definitely am.

There was one lady who had a truck full of Indiana stuff, threw it down on the ground at Assembly Hall. Cars are lined up throwing stuff out at Assembly Hall.

I'm serious. It's broken my heart in two. I just can't hardly stand it. When I first heard it, it was like my blood just quit running for a minute. Wasn't it ironic that the kid who reported that wouldn't show the scratch marks, plus his stepfather wanted Bob Knight fired back in 1992? He is a radio personality and he's always been against Knight, and he's on the radio in Bloomington. All three of his children have been shipped out of state.

A lot of people love Bob Knight. He makes close to eleven million a year speaking and raising money for people, and cancer funds and going to hospitals.

And he's done so much for the Riley Hospital in Indianapolis for children who are very ill. He doesn't go around bragging about that; he just does it. Right here in Anderson, Indiana, Anderson Indians' coach Ron Hecklinski had to have a liver transplant; he was young. It was in our paper, and Bobby Knight called him up and asked him if he had the funds for this liver transplant. Knight just wanted to make sure. This Ron had the liver transplant and he did okay and is back to coaching. He said Bob Knight was the first person who called him to ask him if he had the funds for the transplant.

I'll use my van to take my things right down to Assembly Hall and dump them right in the yard. Since this has happened, I'm a Queen Bitch! My sister Rita says I was before—I'm the oldest of six kids. She lives in Dayton, Ohio and is a UK fan so we don't talk about basketball or we'd fight.

Tim Couch of the Cleveland Browns was the leading scorer in Kentucky high school basketball his junior year. When he was in the eighth grade, he averaged 16 points a game with the Hyden Varsity.

Ya can't get into heaven unless you're a Hoosier fan

Larry Hawkins

Larry Hawkins is the owner of That Sandwich Shop in Nashville, Indiana. Hawkins is an unabashed Indiana fan and has literally built a shrine to Knight within his restaurant. If you're driving to Bloomington, via the tourist mecca of Brown County, a stop in Nashville, Indiana is almost a must. If you're in Nashville, and you're near the Nashville Hotel and you happen to wander downstairs into a place called That Sandwich Shop, you'll think you entered the "Bob Knight Hall of Fame." The walls, ceilings and floors of this quaint restaurant are covered with Bob Knight and Indiana University memorabilia.

Courtesy of Larry Hawkins

Larry Hawkins

I sell basketballs—his autographed balls in my restaurant. Coach Knight signed fifteen balls for me four days before he got fired. I haven't talked to him since he got fired. Yeah, we've been good friends for a long time. The way it all started was, I came into this town and opened this restaurant in 1972. Coach started in 1971. Anyhow, about the first year I got going, I didn't watch IU too much. I was born in Kentucky, and I was a big Kentucky fan. So moving up here, I couldn't get any of the Louisville stations anymore. I got to watching Coach Knight and his ball team and then I just kept getting real interested. I just dropped Kentucky flat, and all of a sudden I became a big Bob Knight fan. I started picking up a memorabilia piece here and a piece there and pretty soon I just—I didn't have the stuff here in the restaurant for a few years, and all of a sudden my wife's getting mad at me because I've got this stuff laying all over the house. So I said, "I'll just take my IU stuff down and put it in the restaurant and take all my antiques off the wall" and ended up with a shrine here of Coach Knight.

Then Coach came over and started eating here, and he invited me to the games. My gosh, I sit down there—probably haven't missed a game in fifteen years—right behind him. I've taken him to some hunting spots over here and

some fishing spots, had some dinners with him and some luncheons for him, and we've just become good buddies. A few years ago, his son, Tim, we got together. So I started selling his Knight Sporting Wear and autographed basketballs and his autographed pictures.

The thing I'm most proud of in my collection would be a picture. At the final game of the season, Coach always had the seniors talk, and this was the last game his son, Pat, played. Coach Bob was speaking, "I guess everybody wants to know who my favorite Indiana ball player is. Well, I'll tell you right now, it's Patrick Knight." He goes over, and they're hugging each other. Coach has got real red teary eyes. That picture is of him hugging Pat, and then Pat and Coach both autographed it for me. That probably has more feeling than anything since I'm friends with him and friends with Pat.

People who haven't been in before will stop for a minute and look around. Purdue fans don't like it, and some of them will walk out. I've had people look around and say, "There's an awful lot of red and white in here. I don't know whether I'll be able to eat in here or not." Most people are in awe. Most people come in, sit down to eat and will look around. But you can tell the IU fans; they'll scrutinize every picture. They go look at every picture, and I go start talking to them, "You're a big IU fan aren't you?" "Oh my, yes, we are." So I get to talk to them.

Now that's what's nice about having my IU and my Bob Knight stuff is the fact that it's fun—your job's fun every day. I'm getting to do something I like best—talk IU basketball. I've been awful lucky. I've been blessed. Every day I get to come in to work and do what I enjoy doing—talking basketball. That's really great.

I have IU alumni come in here and say, "Why don't you have Dick and Tom Van Arsdale?" Like I said, I moved here in 1972 and didn't watch much IU basketball previous to that 'cause I couldn't get the TV station. So my collection really is from Bob Knight's era only. I've got every team picture in here that he's coached but none previous to '71.

But I've got one story. This pertains to his firing, and this is on an upbeat. This is not a downer. It's identical to what transpired in his firing. About three years ago—he always goes back to the corner to this round table and he eats. Of course, people are over there all the time asking for autographs, interrupting his meal. I'll bet he's been in here a hundred times maybe—but he's always been charming and pleasant. So two kids probably about the age of 10, 11, 12 years old, came over together and said, "Coach Knight, may we have your autograph?" He autographed two menus. He had a menu in each hand; the kids are sitting there waiting on these menus. He held both of them out.

The kids both grabbed them, and they are getting ready to take off running. Coach grabbed one of them by the arm and held his arm. I'm going, "My gosh, what's he going to do there?" He goes, "What do you say?" And the kids go, "Thank you." And they take off running. So what he was teaching there was manners. The same identical thing happened with that Harvey boy that he was fired for. When he came in, when those kids came by, all he wanted to do was teach them manners. That's what he did in here. Like I say, he's always teaching something, and he's teaching manners a lot. So what happened was the same thing that happened in my place so I can vouch for him on that. Back in the days past, we were raised like that. Nothing tears me up more with the kids nowadays—the times have changed so people say. I say, "I don't care what you say, manners don't change." You address your people by 'Mr.,' 'Mrs.,' 'yes maam,' 'no maam,' things like that. I'll always be like that. It just tears me up.

I was back in the alley behind here, ready to get into my car one day and was talking to this little girl who works down here at one of the shops. I talked to her a long time and after this incident happened, Bruce Williams, a friend of mine who has a shop next to me here, goes "Larry, do you remember what that little girl said? She dated that Harvey boy. Do you remember her telling you the reason she broke up with him because he didn't have any manners?" I said, "No, did she say that?" He said, "Yes, she broke up with him for that." This girl broke up with him because he didn't have any manners. So that backs up what I've been saying. He just wasn't taught manners by his mom or stepfather. Bob Knight was the most exciting coach around the whole world. He was just exciting, thrilling; I didn't miss a game. I sat right there. They were in awe when he would come into the stadium. They just loved the guy. But then he's got his enemies, too.

Whenever Bob Knight would introduce me to anybody, he'd always say, "Let me tell you about Larry's ham salad sandwich." This was back in the wintertime. We have specials of the day in the wintertime, and this particular day it was a ham salad sandwich platter. The cook realized we didn't have any ham so she made this 'ham salad' with bologna. You really couldn't tell the difference, so anyway Knight was sitting here with his assistant coaches, Dan Dakich, Norm Ellenberger, Ron Felling and I don't know which one noticed it, but one of them did. He calls me back and said, "Larry, have you got a pen?" I give him a pen and he goes around to the special signs that we had placed on all the tables and, he marks out the ham salad, then goes to the front window facing the street and takes out the sign that was in the window and marks the special out and writes in "Do not eat the ham salad." Then he

stood up, there weren't many people in here since it was winter, but he said, "Folks, don't eat the ham salad." But it was in a jovial mood—a friendly thing. He was kidding me.

A friend of mine, about three years ago, was taking Knight's class, Methods of Teaching and Coaching Basketball. A lot of stuff in the class was just about personnel and attitude and different attributes like that. All of it didn't have anything to do with coaching basketball. Anyway, on the very last day of class, they held the class in Assembly Hall instead of the usual classroom. All the class, probably two hundred are sitting in there. Knight is standing there in the middle of the floor and was talking to them about really what to look like when you go in to apply for a job—appearance wise—how you should look.

Bob Scott, a close friend of Bob's who taught him a lot about hunting, comes in the door. He had no idea, he saw Knight in the center, but these kids were to his blind side so he didn't know anyone was in the stands.

He's a tall slender guy, an earring, tattoos, a long ponytail and looks like a hippie from the 70s. He doesn't look like a Knight guy, but I tell you he's one of his closest confidants. He used to be in the firearms business and he is a very, very, very close—comes to the games a lot, friend of Coach Knight. Here Bob Scott comes in Assembly Hall to see Coach Bob. He walks in the door; Knight is facing the students in the stands telling them what they should look like when they go in to apply for a job. Here Bob opens the swinging door there in Assembly Hall. Coach Knight sees him, and says, "Come here, Bob." Knight goes over and puts his arm around Bob Scott, who is wearing a tight, white T-shirt which shows his tattoos and his long pony tail, and his earrings in his ear and Knight says, "Kids, now I've told you what to look like when you go to apply for a job. This is what you don't want to look like."

He is good friends with Joe Bonsall, the lead singer of the Oak Ridge Boys; knows them real well and goes to their shows all the time. They're playing here at our Big Country Theater at the Little Nashville Opry. I'm at work; we're staying open until eight that night. He calls me and the first show is about ready to start at six and the second one starts at nine-thirty. They're sold out. I know all those people out at the Opry, and I've been able to get tickets for him before so I was his best shot at getting him tickets. "Larry, I need four seats on the back row for the Oak Ridge Boys show, and I need four seats at The Seasons—a motel he likes to eat at—at seven-thirty. Do you think you can handle that?" I said, "Coach, I'll try." He wants to be close to the door so he can leave just before the show ends. I talked to the security

people, and they park his car in a place where he can leave before the show is over. I got the table at Seasons, and called the Opry and they had just had four cancellations on the back row. So I called him and shouted, "I did it—I didn't think I could do it that late." He says, "Okay, I appreciate it. Meet me at the Seasons and I'll pick the tickets up." It wasn't five minutes until the phone rang again, and it was Coach. "Do you think you could go out there and pick those tickets up for me?" I said, "Yes sir, I'll do that for you. I'll go pick them up and meet you and give them to you." Then after I get up there, he's not there, I wait a couple of minutes, here he comes, and I give them to him. He thanks me. I'm turn to walk away, and he grabs my arm, "Wait a minute, don't leave so fast. Do you think you can do me another favor?" I said, "Yes, sir." I'm going nuts. Would you go out there and tell Joe Bonsall that I would like for him to dedicate a song for me, "Dig a Little Deeper in the Well." I get in the car and am thinking I wish I had a pen to write this down so I won't forget the name of the song. But I get out there and find the road manager whom I know and tell him Coach Knight wants to hear the song. That's just the way he works. You have to be very fast and very quick.

When people enter my restaurant, all the reactions are about the same. They just stand in the doorway. When you first come down the stairs in the daytime and you turn left and come in my door, if it's sunshine there's a glare in my place because it's kind of dark in here anyway. Your eyes don't really focus for about thirty seconds and then all of a sudden when they can see all this stuff, they are just amazed. They've said for years, "How many years did it take you to collect this?" I tell him I had opened in 1972 and Coach Knight had come here in 1971, and I started then so that's been over 28 years. I've got about everything I think that's ever been put out on him—pictures. In 1984 Coach was interviewed in Playboy magazine, and I didn't have that article and had always wanted that. This is hard to believe, but last week a customer was paying his check and commented on my collection. I said there was an interview in an old Playboy magazine that I had never been able to get. He pulled out his business card and said, "You're dead serious, and you've been very nice to me; you'll have that article." I said, "What do you mean?" He said, "I'm Jeff Cohen, Vice-President for Playboy Enterprises International, from Chicago. " What year was it done?" When I told him, 1984, he told me I'd have that article. I offered him some money, but he said, "No, I don't want anything from you." He said, "I'm going over to pick up my son who is a student at IU, and we're going to see the football game. You can just treat him to a meal." I said, "Well, I'd have done that anyway." I thought

that was really a strange thing. And I was very pleased to get the magazine in the mail today.

I was closed during the Christmas season. Coach Knight called to say he was coming over. I told him I was closed, but he said he was coming anyway. That's just the way he is. So I called and had some food catered in. Jeremy and Dick Schaap, Knight came, and we were sitting here having lunch. We were sitting back here talking. Coach Knight is pretty close friends with Dick Schaap, Jeremy's dad, and you would think Jeremy would have tried to not be so mean to Coach Knight on the interview since his dad and Knight were such good buddies. Knight did tell him, "You're not as good as your Dad." That surprised me that Jeremy turned on him like that since they were such good friends.

I'm also good friends with his Mary Ann Davis, Knight's secretary over there, and she's getting relieved of her duties. They get stacks and stacks of mail daily still and she'll probably be sixty days working at home answering all this mail. Every letter that came in about Coach Knight, they answer—every one. You can ask anybody who has ever written him, he has always written a reply back. He's sent so many people books and pictures and autographed pictures, and press guides—things to dying cancer victims. Someone may call and say, "Coach, my aunt's dying." He's done it in here; he'll say, "What's her address?" He goes back to the office and arranges to send stuff to them. He does that all the time. He's so gracious over that. I just can't say enough good about him.

My collection is more popular now that it's ever been. People just want to come in and like when you go to a funeral, and the person is lying there in the casket, but the people are back there talking and remembering good things about him. That's the way my place feels right now. These people come in here just to sorta stay and talk about Coach Knight and all the good he's done. That's the way it makes me feel—a funeral type of thing. Everybody wants to look at the pictures of him and at the goodies—it's sort of a sad thing really.

I met him when he came in to have a hot dog—that was back in the '70s. I think at that time, I had only about three pictures of IU stuff on the wall. As he continued to come in, I got better acquainted with him. He hunts and fishes over here in this county; we have a lot of lakes and hills and there were a lot of people whose property he fished and hunted on so he was over here a lot. He just kept coming back in, and my collection kept growing and getting bigger. Pretty soon, it turned out to be a shrine on Coach Knight. You

see, I don't collect anything other than the stuff on him and his era. I don't go back prior to '71—it's all Knight and his players. I guess he sorta grew to liking that.

This kid came in here one day. This was on national news. He looks around and sees that I have a shrine to Knight. He says, "I want to tell you a story." He got in a contest—something to do with a bottle cap. I think this would have been in '81. It was a Coke contest where if you got a bottle cap with something on it, you could go to Philadelphia, all-expenses paid, to the Final Four. After realizing he had the winning bottle cap, he and his wife didn't have much money and had to decide if they should go, knowing it was still going to cost them some money after they got there. His wife said, "Let's go for it, let's go." They were heavy-duty IU fans. He worked for Pepsi and the contest was sponsored by the other company. They went on down to the game in Philadelphia, and afterward he got fired for this—for having entered the contest of their competitor. When he got home, about two weeks later, he answered the telephone, and it was Coach Knight. Apparently someone had shown Coach the article about the kid losing his job. Coach Knight said, "This is Coach Bob Knight. Anybody that loves IU basketball that much and will take a chance on losing his job, I want to do something for you. Come over here to my office and I'll find you a job." Can you believe that?

You don't have to print this but—He wouldn't kiss three people's ass, Christopher Simpson, Doninger and Brand, and that's why he's no longer there. That's basically it. He wouldn't do that. It's just like—two people said that one time—John Mellencamp the singer down here in Seymour, and Coach Knight says, "I'll kiss no man's ass." That's why he's no longer there, why he's out of a job. He's always gotten along with everybody else. These guys wanted to play the big role and wanted to show who's boss, and Knight wouldn't kiss their ass so he's out of a job.

If Coach Knight tells you something, you can take it to the bank because that's the way it is. The man does tell the truth. When he tells you something, it's gonna happen.

I invent Prozac and then he doesn't take it

Louis Lemberger

How many fans can ever say they've written a hard-cover book about their favorite college sports program? Louis Lemberger can. In 1990 he published a book called Where Basketball is King—or is it Knight? *Now a Hoosier for three decades, this transplanted New Yorker is a hard-core basketball junkie. Before his retirement from the Eli Lilly Company, he was regarded as the foremost expert on pharmacology in the United States.*

Courtesy of Louis Lemberger

Louis Lemberger

I was the first one to ever give Prozac and Lyprexia (to a human being), and the first one to give regularly labeled marijuana to a human being when I was at NIH. And as I say in the preview of my book, I'm a scientist who's published a lot in science journals, but never had to deal with publishers like I did with the book. The rejection is tremendous. I just went back to my high school reunion in New York and took a case, 32 books, and gave them out to people at the reunion—friends of mine. I'd write things in them—a nice personalized note in there. My daughter says I should put it on eBay now that Knight's finished. If you go to Amazon.com and put my name in, my two books are there. *The Physiologic Disposition of Drugs of Abuse*, which is a very technical book, an excellent book, and *Where Basketball is King—or is it Knight?*. I gave a copy to Ray Tolbert, a former IU player. I wrote, "Thanks for the Memories." He said, "Boy, Doc, you've been all over the place." I've found that, for me, it was something I enjoyed doing. I keep them in the house; I have about 1500 books left. My contract with Vantage was that after two years, they could sell the books for fifty cents apiece and give me a dime. I paid the shipping, and said "just send them to me." I got all the books back because the contract was over. If somebody comes and does repairs or something, instead of giving them a tip, I give them a book.

How did a fan write a book about Indiana University basketball? In 1971 I came to Indiana to join The Eli Lilly Company at IU Medical School. Years

later, I said, "Geez, you know, Knight came in '71, I came in '71. He came from West Point. I came from the Catskills. When I was growing up, the first coach's basketball camp was by Clair Bee in the Catskills at the Alamac Hotel. Clair Bee was one of Knight's idols. I said, "Hey, I'm a crazy fan," and I would travel all over and schedule lectures. So I was just gonna put all my IU memories down for myself. And I wrote the whole thing and friends of mine read it. They said, "It's good, you ought to get it published." So I sent it off to Macmillan and Random House and a couple of other places. If you don't have an agent, you don't get anything. *Season on the Brink* came out while I was writing it. First of all, I didn't know John Feinstein had an agent, but he's a sports writer so he had a reputation. So I put my book on the shelf for a while.

Respected people in Bloomington like Jeff Sagarin (Sagarin Computer Rankings) liked my manuscript and he's good friends with Bob Hammel who has written several IU books. Bob Hammel read my manuscript and liked it, but I couldn't get it published. So I had Vantage Press do it. It cost me ten thousand dollars and the first ten thousand that I made I kept. Then everything after that, I donated to the Bob Knight Library Endowment and Lilly matched it two for one. So all the royalties went to IU basically. It's very interesting. I sent Bob Knight a copy of the manuscript before I published it because I wanted his input. Then I sent him a copy of the book later when it was published. He said he didn't read it, but his wife Karen enjoyed it. I think it's an honest book. A friend of mine in the IU foundation introduced me and my wife to Knight when we presented Knight the check 'cause I wanted to give it to Knight personally. Knight said, "Well, anytime you want to come to practice" (you know, it's closed practices) so I used to go down there all the time after I retired. I went to three or four practices a year—there were a select group of people who could go. Visitors from other Universities, coaches and some others would be there.

I'm a member of the IU Varsity Club so I had met Coach before at functions but never in this sort of capacity. I would see him in the hallways and say 'hello'—things like that. When I went and saw him, we reminisced about the Catskills, about Clair Bee, about Army, about New York, and he took me to the Nike basketball camp where the high school kids come to in July and we went out to dinner. He travels in an entourage. You can't really become his friend. It's very difficult. He has very few people he's close to. I'm an acquaintance. We had a lovely day. I say hello to his son Timmy and to him but it's very hard to get close to him.

In Bob Knight's first year, 1971, he introduced the peppermint-striped warm-ups.

Jeff Sagarin and I were at a practice one time when Neil Reed got hit in the head by one of the ball players and was semi-unconscious on the floor, was there for a while, got up and rested on the sidelines and wanted to come back in and play. Knight patted him on the ass and said, "Now this is what an Indiana basketball player is all about." This is the same kid he kicked off the team. Obviously, Reed changed from his freshman and sophomore year to where he wanted to control the ball; he wanted to be the only star. That's my read on him. The whole thing was a setup, I'm sure, to get Knight out of there. Ron Felling and Terry Reed are good friends with one another. When Neil Reed got kicked off the team, I'm sure Ron Felling went and got the tape, and a week later, released it. That's what did Knight in, and, of course, CNN/Sports Illustrated started talking about it.

Coach Knight has had some major things happen in his life—one was the divorce and that counts for the '85 year and all where he had all that difficulty. He really recruited some real good kids that left—Jason Collier, but he may not have been that good. Any kid 7'2" who wants to be good and can't shoot with his left hand—that's one of the first things you learn. If you're gonna be around the basket you've got to be able to shoot with both hands. You can't shoot with your right hand from the left side; otherwise they'll block it. Collier left, and Reed got kicked off, Luke Recker left, but even with these kids, Coach couldn't win. The problem is, I think, that people found out how to beat him—you spread Indiana out—that's how you beat him. That defense is great when you're playing in tight to the basket, but when everybody learns, especially the Kansas team, you just spread them out, and you shoot three pointers from the outside, and you got big guys rebounding underneath. He never could figure out how to get around it. You take, for example, A. J. Guyton. He could have fantastic games and another game they'd hold him to three points because they just wear him out. When Steve Alford was playing, he had Brian Sloan and kids like that—role players who just set up screens, etc. They would screen off of him and Alford would work his tail and get free for the shot. IU's offense wasn't like that after a while.

I still like Knight. As I say in the book, if he did anything beyond what I reported up until '90, I would have to evaluate it. I didn't think the Reed incident was anything that doesn't happen to other players with other coaches, etc. When you go to practice, practice is hell—no question about it. Not just

Dick Harp of the University of Kansas is the only person to play in a Final Four game and coach in the Final Four game for the same school.

a Coach pushing kids around, but the players—the players are fighting with each other all the time. They're revved up. It's like combat. When you go driving under the basket, and somebody fouls you, you're not going to let them make the shot—you go to foul them. Practices are brutal. They're worse than the games. Why would someone make a big deal of this? There are things that Knight has done in the past years that I thought were bizarre. Making funny faces! The whipping thing I thought was an innocent thing—you know, the kid gave him the whip. He got to the point I think where he tried to talk away everything—the Sherron Wilkerson thing. But the point is, he's such an individual that has so much charisma. When you're with him, he's just full of charisma. Like on Senior Night with his boy, Pat—"My favorite all-time IU ball player." The things that he says like when he told the crowd to "kiss his ass." That, I don't like at all. I was there when he did that.

I think he should have been fired—not for the Reed incident, but if he threw a plant at Doninger's secretary, and I know Dottie Frapwell, the IU attorney that he supposedly cursed, one of his latest seventeen incidents or so, and she's a nice lady. I suspect he just threw her out of his office, "We're finished. Get the hell out of here." Something like that. This is his every-day language. You hear that language at the practices.

My daughter is devastated and will only root for Coach Knight in the future, not IU, her alma mater. As a family, we think very highly of Knight for what he's done for the University and all, but he just has a problem controlling his temper in situations where he could have. He could very easily have done that.

I certainly wouldn't have fired him on the incident with this Harvey kid, the student. First of all, that may very well have been a setup; this guy Mark Shaw has been a critic of Knight for years, but if IU had seventeen other things, and one of them was throwing Dottie Frapwell out of his office, I certainly would have fired him because if it's zero tolerance, it's zero tolerance. And for him to say he doesn't know what zero tolerance is is a fabrication. So you don't have to be a Rhodes scholar to know that zero tolerance means you keep your nose clean.

Indiana basketball will still be a part of our life, the football as well, but as a family, we're still devastated by it. I think Mike Davis will do a good job.

Bob Knight inaugurated Senior Day in 1973.

They shoot baskets, don't they?

Brian Spurlock

Brian Spurlock is a free-lance photographer who has covered Indiana Basketball since 1985. He has provided, over the years, photos for Indiana's basketball covers, Programs, Media Guides, Calendars and Trading Card Sets. He is a veteran on-court photographer. He has probably been closer to Coach Knight during the heat of the action than just about any other person.

Brian Spurlock

The one trademark that always seems to come up with Coach Knight is throwing the chair across the floor in a Purdue game. My friend, Steve Bush was one of a few photographers who captured the moment on film. Steve Bush, was a photographer for the Shelbyville News, a small newspaper in Indiana. Of course, friends and fans who have seen the photo have always asked Steve if they could buy a copy to keep for themselves. Several years had gone by since the chair-throwing incident, and Steve had quit covering the Indiana basketball games for the paper. Steve gets a phone call one day from Bob Knight's secretary asking him if he is the photographer who took the famous photo of Coach Knight throwing the chair. The first thought that comes to his mind is that Coach Knight might be upset at him for selling this photo to some of his friends. His secretary explains that she has been trying to locate him for years and tells him that Coach Knight wants to buy a few copies of this photo for himself. Steve agrees to sell the photos and also asks if he can get Coach Knight to autograph one of the photos that Steve can keep for himself. When the photo is returned with an autograph, there is a thank you letter personally signed by Coach Knight. In part of the letter Coach Knight writes "Can you actually believe that some dumb ass threw a chair across the floor?".

Coach Knight has always jokingly said that he threw the chair across the floor to an elderly lady who needed a chair to sit down on to watch the game. A few years after the chair incident had occurred, I am at an Indiana preseason luncheon at which Coach Knight was speaking. He opens the floor to

questions and comments from those attending. An elderly lady who appeared to be in her eighties stands up and says, "Coach, I just wanted to thank you for throwing that chair to me". Coach Knight and the audience just busted up laughing. To this day, there is cable that runs through the Indiana bench locking all the chairs together. Some preventative maintenance to keep chairs from ever being thrown again.

I was covering one of the Christmas tournaments that Indiana hosted every year at Market Square Arena. The hanging scoreboard over the floor went out. One of the referees goes over to the scorer's table to see if they can get that scoreboard clock functioning again. The referee then looks up at the very top of the seats of the arena where there is another clock stationed on that wall. Coach Knight walks over and says to the referee, "I don't know why you are looking way up there because you can't see that far."

I was hired as an extra to play a photographer in the movie, "Blue Chips." "Blue Chips" is a movie about illegal recruiting with Nick Nolte playing one of the coaches. In one of the ending scenes of the movie, Nike Nolte's team is playing number-one rated Indiana, and, of course, coach Knight is in the movie. The closing has Penny Hardaway throwing an alley oop pass to Shaquille O'Neal to slam in for the winning basket. The ending was taped twice, but the first one, which ended up being cut from the movie, was the following: As soon as Shaq made the basket, Shaq runs over to the Indiana bench and gets right in Coach Knight's face and starts taunting him. It was pretty obvious even though it was a movie that Coach Knight really did not like Shaq doing this. I just thought that it was pretty interesting that this was never shown in the movie.

Over the years, I have had the opportunity to photograph and be around some of the greatest athletes of my generation including Michael Jordan, Joe Montana, Muhammad Ali, Jack Nicklaus, Tiger Woods, A. J. Foyt, Larry Bird, Mark McGwire, Mickey Mantle, etc. In my opinion, Coach Knight has even more of a presence or aura around him than I ever sensed around any of these other famous athletes. Over the years I have passed Coach Knight numerous times in doorways, walking throughout Assembly Hall, etc., and he has always been extremely polite and soft spoken. I remember doing an assignment for *The Sporting News* in 1991 covering the NIKE summer camp in Indianapolis. Coach Knight is sitting with Coach K of Duke in the top row of the stands scouting the high school basketball players, and I am photographing them from a distance with a telephoto lens for almost five minutes. Before this time I had never spoken with Coach Knight. I am walking across the parking lot after I am done heading to my car, and out of nowhere

I feel someone giving me a hug from behind around my shoulders. It is Coach Knight, and he is being really friendly asking me how I am doing, etc. There is not a soul around anywhere, and it seemed like he just dropped out of the sky. My take is that he is courteous, polite, and friendly, and times that incidents have happened that he has been provoked. My father has written him a few times, and Coach Knight even invited him down to sit through one of their practices. I am telling you that this is not a normal thing for a coach to invite a fan he doesn't even know to a closed practice. Coach Knight has a very giving side that never seems to be brought out. I have seen him be nice to Ryan White, the child who died of AIDS. Unfortunately, many of the nice things that he does are never written about. In a lot of instances, the media have said or written something negative about Coach Knight, then does somebody really expect him to go out of his way to be nice to someone that just ripped him publicly? It almost becomes a vicious circle. Coach Knight does not accommodate their requests and then these media resent it and continue to write negative things.

My last take is that people who are outside of Indiana do not understand Coach Knight at all. All the negative instances are played over and over, and nobody dwells on any of the good things. This is the only thing people outside of Indiana see. I have come across Coach Knight numerous times and have observed him closer than the normal person ever gets to see him. I usually have to get to games hours before they start to set up strobes and other camera equipment and remote cameras in the catwalk. I have been up in the catwalk slot when the team and Coach Knight has come on to the floor for practice. All the times that I saw, Coach Knight hardly raised his voice. He was always instructing them on what he wanted them to do in the game. I was coming through one of the floor entrances last year with a cart piled up with four camera cases as Coach Knight and Pat Knight were coming through at the same time. I backed my cart up and told them to come through, and Coach Knight backed out of the doorway and insisted that I come through first. I am telling you that he couldn't have been any nicer or polite, but I also tried to be courteous also. Coach Knight may know my face, but I am not a friend or even an acquaintance of his. When I hear about the Kent Harvey incident, I am thinking of all the encounters that I have had with Coach Knight, and I am thinking that Kent Harvey must be a moron, an absolute moron to be disrespectful to Coach Knight. Then when you first see his stepfather just totally go off cussing and swearing in an earlier interview and saying that his son should have kicked the so and so out of Coach Knight, these people have no credibility with me whatsoever. The first thing his stepfather

does is go to ESPN to stir up trouble He can't be too smart to put his step kids in a position so that they are hated by most of the Indiana student body. Coach Knight probably knows all the NCAA regulations about as well as anybody. For him to go 29 years following all their regulations and running a clean program. I think he should definitely get the edge in who is really honest and telling the truth.

I cover on an average of 150 sporting events a year all across the United States. Coach Knight has always been one of my favorite people to photograph. Everything you get is so real and so genuine. Obviously there is never a dull moment. From my perspective, photographing Indiana basketball will never be the same.

My ups and downs with Coach Knight

Stan Sutton

Sutton is the Sports Editor of the Bloomington Times Herald.

One of my favorites is—we were up at the Marriott in Indianapolis. Indiana University was playing there in the holiday tournament. I think it's a four-floor hotel right in the business section; I'm on the third floor. There's an elevator in the back.

The door opens. It's coming down. Knight's on it, and one other assistant of his. I get on the elevator, "Hi Coach." I'm not one of his favorites at that time so he doesn't say much.

Then we go down one more floor—second floor. Door opens, Knight's about one foot from the door. There's a little tiny guy out there, about 5'4". Suddenly he's face-to-belt buckle with Bob Knight.

There's tons of room on this elevator. The little guy says, "Too full, I'll get on the next one." Knight says, "Jesus Christ, there's only three people on the thing." The guy didn't get on. He was just totally intimidated. That's kinda typical. The guy is so intimidating.

There was another deal, probably in the late eighties, before the Indiana Classic here in Bloomington, another holiday tournament. They always had this friend of Knight's who is a priest here get up and give this invocation. He welcomes everybody, Merry Christmas, and blah, blah, blah. Really it's a prayer. The guy is giving a prayer, and it gets too long. It really has gotten quite long. Knight takes three steps on the floor, motions his arm and says "Get out of there." The Invocation ends in mid sentence. It stopped and they started to play basketball.

Knight Missed His Friends 'Til His Aim Got Better

Kevin O'Malley
Dave Benner
Glen Banks
Chet Coppock
Tom Swanson
Frank Kush
Eddie White
Father Edmund Joyce, C.S.C.
Michael Gallagher

Brent, what the #%$*@# is this seven-second-delay button used for?

Kevin O'Malley

Kevin O'Malley grew up in Springfield, Massachusetts where his father was general manager of the San Francisco Giants' AA team. O'Malley got his start in sports as a batboy and groundskeeper for the Springfield Giants. O'Malley graduated Boston College and by a fortuitous accident got into sports with CBS Sports and rose to the highest levels at "Black Rock." He now is the honcho for Turner Sports in Atlanta.

Courtesy of Turner Sports

Kevin O'Malley

I can't take credit for hiring him because it was Knight's idea. In very early March of 1981, I was at CBS and we got the NCAA tournament rights for the future away from NBC. The following year, 1982, would be the first year to broadcast the tournament and we were gonna have to mount, very quickly, a regular season schedule for the '81–'82 season. The first thing I did was go out to visit a number of the tournament sites to make sure and meet all the NCAA people. When we had the negotiations we had met with Walter Byers and Wayne Duke and Dave Gavitt and some of those people, but I wanted to meet the other committee members and conference commissioners. I had been going to NCAA events for years; I went to their annual convention. I went to the Final Four beginning in 1974 and so I knew a number of these people. This would be the first time since the early sixties that CBS would be involved as a rights-holder with the NCAA so I wanted to go out and see these folks. So I went out to three of the first-round sites and a couple of the regional sites. I was at the regional site at Bloomington during the second weekend of the tournament. Indiana was hosting the regional. Boston College, which happened to be my alma mater and University of Alabama, Birmingham, and St. Joseph's of Pennsylvania were the other three teams.

I was sitting at the end of the press row and one of the writers who was sitting on the press row was a guy who might rather not be identified but he was friendly with Knight. He walked down on the semi-final night and gave

me a note from Bob. It basically said, "If you guys are going to seriously get into the basketball business, I might be interested in talking to you." I was stunned; I knew Indiana was headed for potentially its second national championship in five years which they ultimately did win that year. Secondly, I was very aware of Bob Knight's own awareness of his role in history as a coach. A man of such youth who would have a chance to win his second national championship. '81 was a time when Knight was really riding high so the idea he would give up coaching, which he would clearly have to do, never even occurred to me. I would never have approached him, thinking that he would laugh. It was very interesting to us because here we were the interlopers.

NBC had been doing college basketball for a number of years. I think it was generally perceived that they were doing a pretty good job with the NCAA tournament. We were the NBA carriers at the time and here we were coming along and suddenly taking over the big tournament—the biggest role in college basketball. For us to make a score like having a Bob Knight on our broadcast team would have been just a tremendous advantage particularly going out there to Madison Avenue and credibility with the schools and everything else. It would have been a front-page story. I sent a note back through the same writer to Bob Knight saying, "we would be very interested in talking to you but it would probably would be inappropriate before the end of this tournament." The last thing we wanted was the notion that we were out there tampering with a head coach who was still alive in the tournament and in fact was one of the favorites to win it. It was stacked in their favor and they were playing at home. I just suggested to him that whatever happens in Philadelphia at the Final Four, it was clear to me that Indiana was gonna win the regional. That we talk after that.

Literally, I guess within a week or so after Bob won the national tournament I did get in touch with him and flew out to Bloomington to see him and it was very, very interesting. It was clear to me right away that he was dead serious. Part of the reason this was going on, I think, was that both Nancy Knight and Pete Newell were really concerned about Bobby because he has always been a little tightly wound, to say the least. I do think that the coaching lifestyle that he had adopted; he was just so uptight all the time. Nancy was his wife and Pete was his best friend and they were very concerned about him. They encouraged him to pursue this and it may very well have been a conversation between Pete and Bobby that was the genesis of this whole idea. So that's the first week in April. By about June first, we pretty much had it all put together. I made a number of trips to Bloomington, I was executive producer, so it was my budget and one of the things I was concerned about was

"how much is this going to cost me?" In those days, announcers made six figures but pretty much low six figures. I asked Bobby what he was looking for and he said, "I'll tell you the truth; I don't know how much money I make. I signed a new contract after we won the championship in '76 and it goes up about ten thousand dollars a year. I'm probably on my contract making about $105,000–$110.000. I have a couple of very big clinics that bring in money for me. I have a camp at IU that brings in money. I do some speaking engagements. I'll have to talk to my accountant and see what I'm making." He said, "If you can match what I'm making, because obviously I won't be able to do camps anymore, then I'll do this." We talked about a three-year deal—the number we actually arrived at was $250,000 a year which was a rough approximation of what the accountant, from New Albany, Indiana, gave.

We were sitting at a pizza parlor in Bloomington having a couple of beers and a pizza. We were pretty much done. Knight had given me the number and I knew that we would go for that number to have him as part of our team. I said to him, "Let me ask you something, why do you really want to do this?" He said, "What do you mean?" I said, "I want to make sure you're completely committed because I know you love coaching and I know that you could stay in this racket for a long time and be maybe the all-time winningest head coach. I know you're aware of those things." I was aware of Bobby's affection for Clair Bee over the years and his tremendous advocacy of the roles of the older coaches in creating the game that we know. "It's just hard for me to believe that you want to throw all that out and get in the television business." He thought about that for a minute and said, "Where'd you grow up?" I said, "I grew up in Massachusetts." He said, "Well you must have seen Ted Williams play." I said, "Yes, I did. We didn't live in Boston, but seven or eight times a year we would get down to Fenway and see him play and obviously I saw him on television every now and again." He said, "Well, I didn't see him. I grew up in Ohio and there was no way we were gonna see Ted Williams on television, especially since the Red Sox were never in the World Series or anything. People tell me that Ted Williams is the greatest hitter who ever lived. I said, "Yeah I think that's probably true. There's probably only one other name you could mention in that context and I would agree with those who would say, as a pure hitter, that Ted was the best that ever lived." He said, "Well Ted Williams is a buddy of mine; we go fishing all the time. Ted Williams is the best fly fisherman in the world. Nobody would believe that because he's Ted Williams, the greatest hitter who ever lived, but Ted Williams is the best fly fisherman in the world. Can you believe being the best at two things?" In my mind, what Knight was saying is that he'd already awarded

himself "greatest coach in history" and he was on his way to saying "Well, you know people talk about Al McGuire and Billy Packer. I'd be so much better than them it's not even funny." That's the way he thinks. I was stunned. I said, "I know what you're getting at." He said, 'You read all this stuff in the paper about how smart Al McGuire is and all that. He said, "I'd be really good at this." He said, "I'm ready to do it and Pete and Nancy think it's the smart thing for me to do. I want to do it and I'm willing to make a commitment that for three years, I'll do this." I think in his own mind he may have been thinking, "Maybe I'll go away for three or four years and come back somewhere else."

I don't think he could imagine himself totally out of coaching forever, anymore than I could. What ended up happening after that, we put together a contract. Bobby actually made a visit to New York and met some of our senior management people. He had lunch with the chairman of our broadcast group. He met my boss who was head of sports, a man named Van Gordon Sauter. The deal was done.

Then the terrible automobile accident to Landon Turner occurred. Bobby called a couple of days later and said, "I can't do this; I can't. Landon's badly hurt, and I can't do this to the rest of the kids. It's really going to affect Indiana's fortunes, and I have to be here." It was a completely emotional response to a highly charged, really tragic situation. I have to believe to some degree that it also might have been a pretext for Bobby because when he finally agreed to come to work for us, and obviously we had not made any announcement; he had not made any announcement. I think he might have had second thoughts big time. Just imagine him leaving coaching—a man of his age who's just won his second national championship—almost unheard of. Enormously loyal to his kids; it always struck me with all this stuff that has come down periodically with Bob, particularly what's happened in the last year, I'm not sure how much Indiana University ever tugged on his heart strings or any of the other adults at the school but I always had a feeling that he had a tremendous feeling for the kids in his program. I really think that it was gonna be very hard for him ultimately to say, "okay this is the day when

Al McGuire is the only man to have a brother and son play in the NBA. . . . but former Miss America, Colleen Kay Hutchins has McGuire beat. Her brother Mel, her husband Dr. Ernie Vandeweghe and her son Kiki all played in the NBA . . . and her daughter won an Olympic medal.

I do it; this is the day that I separate myself from this." There was never any leak about this, even though this was such a hot item. I think one of the reasons was that Bobby did all of this himself, the only person who even knew he was considering this was his accountant. And, he never even told me if he told the accountant the reason he wanted this information but there was no agent involved. Nancy and Pete Newell knew what was going on. I talked with them. I remember being on vacation on Cape Cod myself that summer and talking to Pete Newell at two o'clock in the morning, which would be eleven o'clock his time from a phone booth on the Cape, in terms of Bobby even making the final decision to actually do this. I talked to Nancy a number of times. She called me because Bob wouldn't tell her what was going on. "Is he gonna do it? We think this is really important for him to do." They were very concerned about him but they never spelled it out in clinical terms but I think they just thought that winning championships wasn't gonna make him a happy man.

I saw him a number of times after that after that because he was on the executive board of the National Association of Basketball Coaches, and we used to meet with them in the summer, together with the NCAA tournament committee. And, obviously, Indiana was a big program and I was executive producer of college sports and we'd be doing Indiana games and I'd see him every once in a while. I think he respected me for the fact that I never did leak this information at that time. He's a fascinating man. You meet very few people who have that kind of command of themselves—the whole thing with George Patton, his adoration of certain military figures, his self image as being that kind of completely disciplined individual. It's obviously, in some ways, antithetical to some of his public behavior, but I think Bob used to terrorize the people at IU a little bit. He existed sort of separately from the University, in his own way. He did what he wanted. Nobody would dare to do any scheduling of games without consulting him a hundred per cent of the time. Nobody could change the time of a game from one o'clock to one thirty without consulting him. But I tell you, I saw this elsewhere—I saw it with Bear Bryant, I saw it with Joe Paterno, Lou Holtz, you know guys who had that kind of control and that kind of image and they're different sorts of personalities.

When Lou Holtz coached at Arkansas, his personal attorney was Bill Clinton. When Joe Paterno takes off his glasses, does his nose come off, too?

Bobby had more the personality of a football coach. One of the things I got to know over the years was a large group of football coaches and a large group of basketball coaches, and I used to play in their golf tournaments. I used to joke to my friends that the football coaches, even if you were playing at 8:00 in the morning, the football coaches would all show up an hour early and hit balls and stretch and be ready to hit the first tee shot at eight o'clock. The basketball coaches would all show up at ten of eight and have a Bloody Mary and go out and hit one cold off the first tee. But Bobby couldn't be any further from a P. J. Carlissimo or a Tommy Penders or some of those guys. During the summer, we got to know people like Dean Smith and Jack Hartmann and Eddie Sutton, Dave Gavitt who was himself at one time a great coach. They were a little more loosey-goosey but in their own way pretty disciplined people. Bobby always struck me as having a personality much more akin to a football coach and when you consider the regimentation involved in a football program, I think he might have been happy being a football coach except for the fact that his love of basketball was really almost a dominant factor of his life.

His Ted Williams question obviously took me back, but as I did get to know him, I realized he was a very big fan of baseball, and particularly some people in the game. He would follow particular players and managers and be aware of what they had done and that sort of thing. I never saw much of a concrete example, but he has popped up in a couple of dugouts as friends of managers, particularly, Tony LaRussa.

"Why couldn't your brother Bill have been like my cousin Tom?" "I don't know Coach, I've never met your cousin Tom." "That's 'cause he was stillborn."

Dave Benner

David Benner is the Media Relations Director for the Indiana Pacers. His brother Bill, a columnist for The Indianapolis Star News *has had a long and contentious relationship with Bob Knight. At one time David was a reporter for* The Indianapolis Star *where he covered IU basketball.*

Dave Benner

I only covered IU basketball one season. It was an interesting year. I was with the Star and I never really got a chance to talk to Knight one-on-one until late January. I would ask every week and finally got the okay. I was going to get to interview him after practice so I got to watch practice. It was extremely interesting from a basketball and tactical standpoint. Having covered Notre Dame football and that included Lou Holtz. When you got to watch a practice there, it was amazing to watch Lou Holtz. He would watch a play then be able to tell, basically, where each of the twenty two players were on the field at any particular moment and dissect what each player did. Holtz was great at it. Then I go to Indiana's practice and even though Knight has only about fourteen guys out there, it was pretty much the same thing. He would stand off to the side and stop practice and go back five minutes prior and know where everybody had been and what they had done in those five minutes. To me that's still one of the most fascinating things I've ever seen in coaches—that they could do that. I think that is not something most coaches could do—I think these were two unusual coaches. I'm sure if you went back and looked at the film, he was probably right. Like, "Todd Lindeman you were supposed to be here instead you were over there." This is like two or three minutes after the

fact—instead of stopping after every play, he would let it go, then correct the mistakes. But the fact that he recalled it all was amazing.

Afterwards I go down to what's called "The Cave." We go in and I sit down and I have two tape recorders with me. This was my first one-on-one with him and I don't want to lose anything. He's sitting on the couch watching the Phoenix Open 'cause Fuzzy Zoeller was playing in it, and he and Fuzzy are friends. I asked eight or nine "soft" ball questions and he never looked at me once. But he answered the questions and then finally I had to ask the hard question. That was in the year that he supposedly kicked his son on the bench during the Notre Dame game that December. Now mind you he had not done any post-game press conferences where you could ask him anything about this. I had talked to players and Norm Ellenberger or whatever so I finally said, "You know Coach, you may have talked about this"—I was very nervous at this point—"and you may have answered it, but if you have, I haven't seen it or heard it anywhere. What happened in the incident where you kicked your son during the Notre Dame game? I never heard your side of the story." So he goes into explaining in a pretty matter-of-fact way—he's still watching the golf tournament—he didn't believe that he did kick him. Bob Costas had come down and brought a tape, which showed that he didn't kick him. . . . So he had answered my question. I proceeded to ask a follow-up question on the same incident. For the first time in the whole interview, he turns and looks at me, and he goes, "What the hell are we talking about this for—I believe this happened in December." I said, "I know but this is the first chance I've had to ask you about it." He goes, "Go ahead." And from then on he was fine. He stuck by what he had said previously—a lot of the TV stations' videos showed he did kick him whether it was off the chair or whatever. He had this tape from Costas, which showed he didn't, but others had tapes that showed it sure looked like he did.

From then on, I didn't have any trouble with him. My brother, Bill, columnist for the Indianapolis Star News, and he have not had a great relationship so I don't know if I was "good cop" and Bill was "bad cop" but I just know that when Knight would come into press conferences and he would answer the questions and was good about it. I was there when they got beat by Minnesota by fifty points at Minnesota. I thought for sure he was going to

Fuzzy Zoeller, a close friend of Coach Knight's, is from New Albany, Indiana. Fuzzy got his nickname because of his initials: Frank Urban Zoeller.

come in 'in a fit,' but as it turned out he came in, was there for about ten minutes, and answered all the questions. I really thought he was going to be upset

I never really saw the infamous "temper," as it were. At press conferences he would have a couple of smart aleck answers for the media but, by and large, it was a pretty uneventful year. Another thing that was really strange, IU was getting ready to play in the first round of the NCAA, at Landover, Maryland. I'd been trying to get hold of Knight and I'm getting ready to go to the airport to fly to Landover. It was one of those things where I was all packed up, and was getting ready to go out the door. I get a call, and it was from Knight's secretary. She said, "Coach would like to speak to you." The first thing that goes through your mind is, "Okay, what did I write recently that might have caught his attention?" He comes on the phone and says, "David, Bob Knight, I just wondered if I could answer any questions for you about the NCAA tournament." Keep in mind, I am not really prepared because I thought there was no way I was going to get to talk to him. I was pulling my computer out of the bag and trying to get it hooked it up. Because I was so shocked, I think I asked every stupid, inane question that he probably abhors, but he answered them all in a good manner so I was surprised

One thing about him, is you see a little bit of everything—some good, and some bad. You never really knew when you were going to a game, what was going to happen. That was the year they had a really good team, a pretty decent team—I would say the last decent shot to make the Final Four but Sherron Wilkerson broke his arm against Temple.

The biggest misconception I saw regarding Knight was I never saw ranting and raving. Usually in the practices I saw, when he would single out the players or whatever, it was usually something I found humorous. "Boy he really got on that guy, but he got on him in a pretty clever and humorous way." I was sitting there trying to cover my mouth to keep from laughing even though he was addressing a fairly serious flaw in whatever was going on in practice. Again, I saw a little bit of everything.

The thing I guess maybe I was disappointed in, he did a couple of post-game press conferences where he was very entertaining and gave really good interesting answers and I thought that's a side that everybody should see after every game. Yes, we all ask stupid questions on occasion , but a teacher once told "If you have to ask a question to find out an answer, then it's not a bad question." Maybe his relationship with the media could have been a little bit better had it been a little more amicable from the first day. I was disappointed after that. He could be extremely funny, and there were times when he was very bland—very unquotable. There were other times when he would

expound on some things, and you would sit there and say, "Boy that's great stuff."

I was playing golf with a friend of mine at the Legends Golf Club in Franklin, Indiana, where he used to tape his golfing show. He was on the 18th fairway and we're coming up to ten. Ten and eighteen are side by side. He's on the 18th fairway and he's with the pro, Ted Bishop, or whoever he's doing the show with. It might have been with Sam Carmichael. They were doing a lesson on how to get out of fairway bunkers and unfortunately they were filming this while people were playing through. It was a real nice day. And some guy on the 18th fairway is just completely oblivious and hits his ball, and, I swear, it basically sailed right over Knight's head—real, real close. The guy didn't yell "fore." And needless to say Coach was a *little* upset with that. This guy comes driving up in the golf cart and says, "Oh my god, I'm so sorry Coach, I'm your biggest fan. I love Indiana basketball." Coach turns around to him and says, "Well if you're such a big fan, how come you're trying to kill the goddamn Coach?" The guy laughed. So he handled that in good humor.

I hadn't seen Coach in a long time until last year's IU Christmas tourney. I saw him in the hallways of Market Square Arena before they played their tournament there. I just said, "Hi Coach." And he said, "Hi." I don't think he remembered who I was.

Jerry Buss, owner of the Los Angeles Lakers, once owned Market Square Arena.

"Willis?" "He's innocent. He had nothing to do with the murder. Ya can trust me on that one." "How can you be so sure?" "Because I fished with him."

Ned Beatty's character in the 1999 movie, Cookie's Fortune

Glen Banks

Glen Banks of Elkhart, Indiana is retired from the lumber business but still a well-respected businessman in northwest Indiana. He and Coach Knight have been hunting and fishing buddies for years.

Glen Banks

I've known Bob Knight since 1978. He came up to raise money in Elkhart. We hit it off pretty well. I said, "Bob, you know what? If you don't ask for any damn fool questions about the lumber business, I won't bother you about basketball. I was in the lumber business at the time."

I honored that promise with him for about twelve years. Finally, a friend of mine from up in Michigan came into my office and said, "Glen, you've got to call Bob. There's a kid up in Hastings, Michigan, a little town that Bob won't know about. You've got to call him because everybody's after this kid, and Bob probably doesn't know anything about him." I said, "Harry, I made a promise that I would never do that with Bob unless he brought up basketball first." "No," he said, "You gotta call him." I said, "All right, Harry." So I got Bob on the phone right away and I proceed to tell him about this Brown kid who lives in Hastings, Michigan that was 6'1", 190 pounds, 29.2-point average—gave him all the statistics. There was a long pause, and I said, "Bob, are you still there?" He said, "Yeah, I'm here. You mean Joe Brown. He's 190 pounds. He's got a 2.9 grade average. His aunt raised him from childhood." I said, "Well, it must be the same kid; it's a small town." He said, "We cannot win the Big Ten with little guards. Why don't you stick to the fuckin' lumber business and let me run the basketball team," and hung up on me.

Knight Missed His Friends 'Til His Aim Got Better

The classic Bob Knight story is that Hilda Van Arsdale, Dick and Tom's mom, came to all the basketball games—never missed a one. Bob wanted her there because she was good luck. When they were going to Denver to play in the regionals one year, Hilda wasn't gonna go. Coach Knight called her and said, "Hilda, somebody told me you weren't coming out to watch us." She said, "Well that's right Bob. I'm eighty-three years old, and I don't feel very good, so I'm not going. I'm gonna watch it on television."

"No, by God, you're gonna go, Hilda."

"No, I'm not."

Their mother's got a lot of balls, I'm telling you. So they argued about it, and finally Bob said, "Well, tell you what Hilda, I want you to be there so we're gonna find you a place on the team plane."

So Hilda very reluctantly agreed to go, and he said, "Hilda, there's just one catch."

She said, "What's that?"

He said, "You've got to fuck the pilot."

Hilda just doesn't know what some of these words mean, thank God.

Hilda's nephew Mike Thomas whom Tom Van Arsdale was with last week in Elkhart told me that story on the golf course the day after it happened 'cause Hilda called and told him. You've got to promise me now to check it out before you use it. I went with Bob the first time he ever saw Shawn Kemp. He flew up and I took him out to Concord High School here in Elkhart and introduced him to the basketball coach and we sat and watched him for a while. Finally, I said, "Is this kid any good?" He said, "Oh my God, yes." He couldn't talk to the kid because he never breaks rules. But he spoke to the team because the basketball coach asked him to. But anyway, Shawn Kemp's counselor and I go to church together. She said, "Glen, you're wasting your time; he's a slow learner. He'll never pass the college entrance exam." Well, Bob wouldn't take that for an answer because the kid had so much talent, but Kentucky got on him, you know. He had me checking on Kemp, and somebody (Mills' father) from California showed up with $1500.00. The same day or the next day, Shawn Kemp's mother had $1500.00 that she put down on a used car. My Chevrolet dealer friend called and told me about it. So there was some coincidence there. But anyway I went out and

Bob Knight's first year at IU was Adolph Rupp's last year at Kentucky. In December 1971, they matched up for the first time with Knight's team winning by one point in double overtime.

checked the back of Shawn Kemp's car on Monday morning after he'd been to Kentucky and it was full of Kentucky clothes; he had a gold watch that he told some kid he had to quit wearing because people kept asking him where he had gotten it. So it was thought that it had come from Kentucky.

Bob told this Concord basketball coach, "Well, I don't chase women, and I don't drink, but I do use a little bad language now and then."

As far as Bob is concerned, we had another fishing trip one time where we were going through the woods with this backpacker. One of the mules got loose and there were a set of fly rods on this mule's back, and it ran between two trees and busted the rods right in half. Course we didn't know whose they were until we got back to Missoula. and, of course, they were Knights'. So we all had to loan him a rod, but he was pissed off about that. There are a lot of things I could tell you, but I don't know if they're funny. It's just that I've had so many great experiences with him. He doesn't drink, and I've never seen Bob look at another woman when we've traveled together.

It was inevitable his firing was going to happen. I'm on the Foundation Board at Indiana University. I know the President, and I know all the people. The mistake was made that they should have made some rules for him years ago, but they didn't.

He was trying to teach that kid a lesson, but he picked the wrong time to do it, and he probably used profanity whether he said he didn't or not but he probably did because he uses it so freely it's like you and I saying 'darn.'

But, God bless him. I love him, I wrote him a two-page letter right after he was fired and I just feel so bad about it. Karen's doing this stuff for the cancer drive so I called five of Bob's friends and in about ten minutes I raised about eight thousand dollars we're sending down there. And he wants to coach someplace else, he's very sincere about that, he told us that in Russia but he wants to go somewhere where there's talent and he thinks he needs to go to the east coast or maybe to California.

One time we were up in Crane Lake, Minnesota, and the guide flew four of us into this lake. We cooked our own meals, so the food was terrible. But anyway we caught a lot of fish, but when they came to pick us up, they brought four guys in from Chicago and we were standing on the dock waiting for the plane. We were packed and ready to get right on the plane and go back into town and drive home. These four guys stepped off the plane, and they looked like they had just stepped out of the Orvis catalog. Nothing on them was ever used—all brand new. Bob was standing on the dock with his hands in his pockets and this one guy got out. I don't think he recognized Bob, and he said, "Did you fellows do any good?" Bob said, "Well we caught

a lot of fish with upside down Crawford jellyfish." Well, there's so such thing as an upside down Crawford jellyfish but he just came up with it just like that. This guy looked at his three friends, and said, "You got any of those?" The guys said, "No, we don't have any of those." Bob said, "Well, you're not gonna do very well then if you don't have those." He was teasing these guys because they were really something. I don't think they had ever wet a line. They wanted to fly back into town to see if they could find that, but, of course, there wouldn't be any there. Anyway we left those poor bastards on the dock worrying about not having that bait which was a shitty thing for him to do but it was funny. He never cracked a smile. I said, "Jesus, Bob, those poor bastards are really gonna have a problem all week because they don't have that bait 'cause I doubt if they know how to fish." But it was funny.

He's a delightful guy. He's interesting. He's got an IQ of about 165, I would guess. He's got a keen mind. He's sharp. He knows a lot of funny stories. He can entertain you just talking about baseball. He's an expert on baseball, but he'll get going on basketball and it's just fun to listen to his mind work when he talks to you about it.

That's the other thing. You can't be Bob's friend if you let him intimidate you. You gotta give him stuff back. I've called him a son-of-a-bitch more than once, and you just can't let him do that to you.

Before going to Indiana from Army, he almost became head coach at Wisconsin—probably would have except it leaked out before Bob was ready to have it announced, and it made him mad, and he didn't go there, but he also said Notre Dame would have been a good job because you'd only have to recruit four or five kids a year who didn't like football. They've got such a great name that it would have been a good job for him.

I've played a whole lot of golf with him. In fact, Bob and I played Digger and George Thomas, our pro, whom I hired when he came to our country club, and we beat them, and they never forgot that. We enjoyed that. I didn't play as well as Bob did. Digger really likes Bob. I think they've got a pretty good friendship. But Notre Dame got tired of Digger, too.

There's nothing I wouldn't do for Bob Knight. He did so many nice things for me. I was allowed to go to practice anytime I wanted to. Whenever

The first time Bob Knight coached against Digger Phelps when they were at their new schools—Indiana and Notre Dame, Indiana University won 94–29. The game was not as close as the score indicated.

I needed tickets, I could always get them. I didn't abuse the privilege, but he and I had a lot of good times together. I've been fishing with him in Alaska and in Russia twice and British Columbia four or five times, and Montana.

He's a very serious golfer. He takes his golf seriously. I can't think of anything funny, but I enjoy playing with him. He loves to play. He doesn't like to hit a bad shot, though, that pisses him off.

He adores his wife. She's a nice gal. I was in the boat with her for two days in Russia, and I knew her before that but she's a lovely person and great for Bob. He couldn't have picked a better girl.

We've got two rivers up here in Elkhart, Indiana that are the best small-mouth rivers around. Small-mouth bass is a fighting bass, a very good fish, and people in the Midwest always prize it as one of the prize catches in our rivers and lakes. If you go out and catch six or eight of them, you're doing well. Well these guys that are friends of mine are fabulous guides, and I've had Bob up here two or three times. And, as I say, you catch eight or ten fish, you're doing well. Bob, and Pat and a good friend of his, Jack Brannan, came up last year, and we caught 400 bass in two days—400 bass and released them.

He liked these two guides, John Howard and Don Malcom. Bob said, "You know what, I think I can help you fellows. I'm gonna get Jerry McGinnis to do a show for ESPN on the river." I think Jerry McGinnis' program on ESPN is called *The Fishing Hole.* So Bob very graciously got Jerry to come to Elkhart. I wasn't in the movie but I was in a boat behind them when they were doing it. The fishing that day wasn't particularly good but they caught fish. From that show, these local guides now have all the business they can handle. He just did it to be nice to them. John's a good citizen in Elkhart. He and his wife are involved with abused children here; they lost some of their federal spending, and so John called me one day and asked if I thought Bob could come up and have a fund raiser. I said, "Well, I've never asked him, but I will. That's the kind of thing he usually does." So I called him and without hesitation, he said, "Sure, let's just pick a date when I can get up there. We'll go fishing, too." We did, and we caught a lot of bass that day.

Our theater holds 1700 people, and we didn't have a seat left, and I introduced him, and we raised $70,000 that night for these kids. The night before he'd been in Ft. Wayne doing the same thing to raise money for the Boys and Girls Club. They raised $150,000.00. And I'll tell you, I would be willing to bet that over the years that he was at Indiana, he raised at least ten million dollars for the kids in Indiana just doing things like that where he did not charge. He's very, very generous that way.

The first time I fished on the Blue River with him, I didn't have any hip boots, I had waders. He said, "No, you've got to have hip boots." So I called L. L. Bean and got these hip boots and opened the box and they sent me two left-handed boots. He never let me forget that.

There was a guy down there in southern Indiana, Dick Frederick, who was living in an old, old mobile home with some kids. It wasn't much, I'll tell you. Dick was always nice to Bob; we used his canoes. In fact Bob took him to British Columbia and paid his way—and he was the fourth guy who went with us to Crane Lake, and Bob paid his way—I know he did because I had to write the original check. A few years later after I had fished with Dick and Bob down on the Blue River where Bob likes to fish, I said, "How is Dick doing?" He says, "Oh, you know, Glen, I got tired of seeing him live in that damned old mobile home. I gave him a hundred thousand dollars and told him to build a house, and pay me whenever he got the money, if he could. Bob took him to British Columbia two years ago; Dick idolizes Bob.

When Connie Chung interviewed Bob a few years ago when she really screwed him, Bob said, "She used every four-letter word I've ever heard of and some I never heard of myself." But he said, "When I said that to Connie Chung, Glen, I told her not to use it, and she agreed not to." Well at the time, Tom Ehrlich was President of Indiana University. He was the last President before the guy we have now. He made the mistake of going public on the air and making some comments "that Bob shouldn't have said that" without talking with Bob first. Ehrlich admitted later it was a mistake.

Ehrlich wore a bow tie all the time. He was an Easterner and a pretty good guy really, but there were a thousand letters on his desk and 999 of them were for the Coach. Only one was for him. One of them was from a little old lady in southern Indiana, and it went something like this: "Dear President Ehrlich, You apparently don't know how much pleasure Coach Knight has brought to the fans of Indiana and how many people he's helped, and how many young men he's helped educate, and how much money he's raised for charity." And she went on and on. The last sentence in the letter was "And you can take your bow tie and stick it up your ass." Now, George Pennel, who is acting head of our foundation after Bill Armstrong died, saw the letter and told me. He said, "I saw the letter. I saw what it said."

After Bob got fired, the South Bend Tribune, after Bob was up here raising money for those kids, couldn't think of one nice thing to say about him, and all he was doing was helping a bunch of kids that had been abused. Still, the newspaper guy just railed him. And, damn it, you just don't know what these guys are gonna say when they interview you.

Then Bob Knight came to Goshen a month ago, during all this trouble that he was having with the turmoil. He had made a commitment to come up and raise money for the Boys and Girls Clubs of Goshen, Indiana. He came up, nobody asked him any questions about his problem at that point in time that he was having. He spoke, and he answered questions, and they raised $70,000.00 that night. That was just like six weeks ago.

He always has a question and answer period. Somebody said, "Coach Knight, can you tell us anything about your new recruits?" "Yes," he said, "we've got some black kids and some white kids, and they're all right handed and they all want to play defense." Someone said, "Coach, what advice would you give me? I'm from the state of Washington. I live in Elkhart now, and I've got two boys." Knight said, "Oh, that's where they carry umbrellas and eat apples, isn't it?" He said, "My best advice to you Ma'am, is to tell those boys to listen to their mother."

Then Chet said to Cosell, "Level with me Howard or I'll pull the rug right out from over you."

Chet Coppock

Chet Coppock is arguably the best sports talk radio host in America. The always-cooperative Coppock has a constant lineup of famous guests that would make Larry King envious. Coppock's variety of work can be heard and seen on Chicago's WMAQ radio, Fox Sports nationally as well as the PAX network.

Chet Coppock

Bobby Knight began our relationship in kind of a strange way. It leads up to rather interesting tidbits. In 1974 I was doing the roller derby and got a call from a sportscaster named Duane Dow and he told me about a job open at the CBS affiliate, WISH-TV, in Indianapolis. I had my agent call and they said the job was essentially filled but that they would audition me. So I wrapped up a roller derby game, took a red-eye in and drove from Chicago to Indy. I got the job and started about a week later. Indiana, about three weeks after my arrival, had its annual Basketball Tip-off Banquet. Knight, of course, was the featured speaker. I walked over to their SID and asked to speak with him afterward and was told, "No, he would not talk." At this point, believe me, I had no idea what Bob Knight was all about. I did not even know that Bob Knight had been on the Ohio State roster with Lucas and Havlicek and Siegfried, but I go on the air that night on Channel 8.

Now mind you, this guy is already the Pope, this guy is already the late Mayor Daly—this guy is larger than life. I go on the air, here I am, all of twenty five years old, and I call him a "public-relations three-year old." My general manager, mind you, is a heavy Indiana contributor, donor, an IU graduate. I am just stuck right in the middle of this massive chunk of corn-

The team that Bob Knight played on at Ohio State went 40–2 in the Big Ten. They never lost a Big Ten game until after the title was clinched.

field Hoosier hysteria. I was doing sports and one of my sidekicks, my partner on the air, was anchor Jane Pauley. I made these comments and people are looking at me like, "What the fuck are you talking about?" So anyway, Knight and I don't speak for about three and a half, maybe four years.

The station got so many calls, you wouldn't believe—I got death threats. I was told by my general manager, in no uncertain terms, that if I ever made comments like that again, I would be left in the White River. What it amounted to was, here's what was funny about it—all of a sudden, I became something Indianapolis had never had. I became a villain. This very cozy little town which had a terrible inferiority complex, which it is just now getting rid of. They finally had someone they could learn to "love to hate." That became me. And, really, for six years down there, that was how I billed myself—the man you love to hate twice a night. My relationship with Bob Knight became a big focal point in the city because Knight would not talk to me and I never backed down about Bobby.

Finally in '78, he had three ball players he tossed off the ball club for marijuana use. One of them was a kid named Roberson—as a matter of fact he made the actual confession to using marijuana on our air. I thought to myself, maybe this might be a good time to approach Bobby because he's a little bit down and the club was not playing exceptionally well. Lo and behold, I get a call, from a member of the IU Board of Trustees who had been trying to bring Knight and me together for about three years, saying that the time is finally right. "Call Bob. I think you guys can get together." Now at this point, I've recognized that it would be a lot better to have Bob Knight on my side than me feuding with Bob Knight. So I call up and we arrange to get together with no cameras. I went down. We speak for about an hour and a half. We settle up our disagreement in about 2 minutes and spend 88 minutes talking about Woody Hayes, Don Canham, Civil War history, Jimmy Carter—it was the most riveting conversation that anyone could possible hope to enjoy. We agree to get together the following week, and I'll be able to tape him. We wind up running it as a three-part series. Our relationship had been so badly strained that after we ran the first part I felt compelled to tell our anchor how Bob Knight and Chet Coppock wound up on the same page. I said let me go back in time and tell you having gotten to know the man and seeing what the man is all about I want to apologize for what I've said previously.

I became a confidant of Bobby's. For example when he had the run-in at San Juan, Puerto Rico in 1979, he called three guys. He called Bob Hammel of the Bloomington Herald Telegraph. He called Governor Otis Bowen. I know that, of course, Bowen did everything really short of threat-

ening to declare war on Puerto Rico. And he called me. What he wanted to do was get his story out with the three people he trusted. With the passage of time, my wife got to know Nancy, Bob's first wife. Anna Marie and Nancy were very, very similar to each other. Bob and I would get together periodically for dinner at a little Cantonese joint down in Bloomington. It was enjoyable. The man in his own way is every bit as charismatic as Ditka, if not more so. I think he's far more charismatic than Redford could ever hope to be.

For example, my little boy was nine years old, and I took him to a Northwestern game several years ago to watch them play Indiana. I did this for one reason. I wanted him to have the experience of seeing Bob Knight walk out of a dressing room. Because I don't think Ali—I don't think Joe Frasier—I don't think Stone Cold Steve Austin—I don't think Lombardi—I don't think anyone ever walked out of a dressing room with a greater degree of energy than Bob Knight. He's a show unto himself.

In March, 1980, I get an offer to do a boxing match on closed circuit out of Market Square Arena. It's gonna run in May which is '500' month in Indianapolis. My station manager says, "No." My agent in Chicago says, "Do it." I say, "Why?" He said, "If you do it, they'll fire you. You can take a job where you choose."—Chicago at WMAQ or another market—may have been Washington. But I didn't do it. Frankly at that point I was going through a tremendous amount of emotional withdrawal. Given the fact that in 1979, in the space of a week I was offered a job at WRC television in Washington that was eventually given to George Michaels, and the George Michaels Sports Machine. I mean that deal was done. We were out there looking for homes; we stayed in the Watergate. We shopped at Georgetown—the whole nine yards. The deal was done. Then my dream job, Channel 5 in Chicago, came available that same week. My station would not allow me to accept either offer. So I was so pissed off, I wanted out. I'm off the air. I'm not working. I'm still being paid but you know month one becomes two, and four becomes six and I'm eight months into this thing and I haven't worked. Finally, I talked to Bobby who said, "I'm not sure what I can do for you, but why don't you come down and watch practice and let's have dinner." I've never told this story to anyone. Twenty years after the fact, this is the first time I've told it. Knight and I get together at his favorite Cantonese joint in Bloomington and he said, "Really, what do you want to do?" I said, "Bobby, I want to go to Chicago. It's my home town, etc." He said, "Give me your general manager's name and phone number, and I'll call him. I'm not sure I can do anything, but let's see what transpires." Now mind you, my agent in Chicago is worked pro bono and the attorneys for WISH were working at probably four grand an hour and had been going nowhere for eight months. Knight calls up Bill Stough. It

didn't happen overnight, but in very short order, I had my release to go to Chicago. There isn't a doubt in my mind to this day that Bill Stough let me go for two reasons. One, and this is a very, very minor reason—he was sick of dealing with the situation. And, two, he did not want to go head-to-head with Bob Knight. I think he recognized that if you screw around with Bobby once and that's it. That is it.

I got my release and came to Chicago. Bob and I have remained friends for a long time. We talk periodically. When he comes to Chicago I always try to do something with him. The only thing that began to bother me was around '96, I came to realize that it's very, very challenging to have an unconditional friendship with him because it may very well be impossible. You have to agree with Bob on everything that he says and does. If you don't, you're on the outside looking in. If Bob called me right now and asked me for a favor, there isn't anything I wouldn't do for this guy—anything at all, in the world. I really don't choose to be all that close to him because I think the demagoguery factor is just too much for any individual to handle. How the hell Doc Bomba has lasted that long with Bobby Knight—I mean Good Lord. There have got to be times when he has felt like he has to be inside a Viet Cong prison camp. For a guy like Doc Bomba being in Bloomington in private practice there—If you're tied in with Bob Knight, you're tied in with God or Moses.

When Bob Knight called me from San Juan, he screamed that he was absolutely not guilty and that he was calling me because he knew I would get the truth out for him. Selfishly I didn't know whether he was telling the truth or not but I knew this: an exclusive with Bob Knight was like gold in Indianapolis. And the fact that during my last years in Indy there emerged a feeling that I was kind of "Bobby's boy" in the media. It became invaluable to me. So I'm a guy who is a complete idiot who becomes a confidant of this extremely complicated man. I've only been here an hour before I've got people wanting to run me out of town and then as I'm departing, the very guy who I was feuding with becomes the one who comes to my rescue. By the time I leave town, he's the disciple who gets me off the hook.

I feel sorry for him though. I don't think he's a happy man; I don't think he's ever been a happy man. What's tragic about that to me is he's such an engaging guy. He oozes intense degree of masculinity. He's a classic "guys guy." I remember we were playing golf one time in 1980 in Martinsville, at a beautiful golf course about half way between Indy and Bloomington. There were four of us playing. After the round was over, the wives of all of us got together to meet and we were all going to go back to Knight's house to barbecue. Knight begins giving directives, "You'll ride with this guy. You ride with that guy. Coppock, you'll ride with me." We go back to Assembly Hall

and we start talking—and talking—and the next thing you know, we're looking at game tape and we're talking about the chalkboard, and we're talking philosophy, and he's talking about Buckner, and he's talking about Scott May and he's talking about Landon Turner, etc. We don't get back to his house until 9:30. Nobody, but nobody, had gone near a morsel of food. I kid you not. He has this Svengali-like effect on people—he really does. One guy who emerges as a hero in this to me is Bill Benner of the Indianapolis Star. I know for a fact that Benner has gone to hell and back with this over the years by daring to take on Bob Knight. Benner gave me the greatest line I've ever heard about the "bad" Bobby because, mind you there is a wonderful Bobby and there is an unconscionable Bobby. Bill, because he dared to write that Knight was embarrassing Indiana, the State, the University, the whole nine yards—this guy's life in many respects was turned into hell. His wife Sherry who is as sweet as she can be had to endure a lot of flak and a lot of crap from people. Benner told me about a year ago that he thought Knight's ideal scenario for leaving college basketball would have been to have won a National Championship, and then leave the court with his middle finger extended and the cords draped off his finger. That would have been his ideal way to depart college basketball. I think to myself: calling him Bobby would be like calling FDR Frankie. I mean it would have made no sense.

In 1980 at the Final Four I'm doing my live show out of a downtown Indianapolis restaurant, a one-hour preview, and I invite Abe Lemons to come on, and Ray Meyer and Bob Ryan from the Boston Globe and Bill Jauss from the Tribune. We just have a hell of a show. Who is the star of the show? Bobby Knight. He arrives at the restaurant; the crowd starts chanting "Bob-by, Bob-by." We're in the balcony on the second level. The first thing Knight does is walk up and physically begin to grab me as if he's going to throw me over the rail and the crowd absolutely ate it up. He hops on the air. He couldn't be more charming. He couldn't be more delightful. That's why, as I look at Bobby right now, I find myself saying, "Why? Why?" As tough as he is, and as much self esteem as he seems to have, maybe therein lies the problem—why hasn't Bob ever sought some type of counseling or some type of care to undo what I think are just demonic childhood problems? He probably equates psychiatry or psychology with voodoo, for God's sake. I really can't visualize Bob ever hopping on a couch or even sitting in face-to-face therapy and really talking about what's bothering him. You know what's funny is the one time I played with him in Martinsville, he barely talks for eighteen holes. He was a bundle of laughs until we teed off and then you would have thought it was World War II. He's a remarkably competitive man. I remem-

ber back in 1975—this would have been about my tenth month in Indy—my feud with Bob Knight is already at its apex and I go off with a cameraman at the request of Indiana University to shoot their annual fund raising golf tournament. The two headliners are Lee Corso and Bob Knight. Lee hops on board and does his routine with me. I think the world of Lee and I hosted his TV show for two years. I tell my camera guy, "Get a shot of Bob Knight teeing off." Knight sees the camera and looks over and says, "Shut that damn thing off." If you were to have seen the look in his eyes, you would have thought he had just said "if you don't turn that camera off I have a switchblade that's gonna go right across your lungs." I mean, I have seen the toughest of journalists absolutely melt in front of this guy.

I remember one day in 1980 after Indiana had beaten Ohio State to win the Big Ten title. They came from a bundle down to winning it down the stretch. It was vintage Knight basketball where they stay with their game and went back to Bobby's old theory that you don't play a team, you play the game. Afterwards, Curry Kirkpatrick, with Sports Illustrated, who at that time was arguably the most recognized basketball writer in America was inside the press conference. Knight sees Kirkpatrick, who had written something negative about Bobby maybe a year earlier, looks at him and says, "Kirkpatrick, get the fuck out of here, or I don't talk to anybody." Now at that point, an honest, decent, strong media would have walked up and said, "If you don't talk to Curry, you don't talk to us, we're out of here." Nobody moved. Nobody moved as Kirkpatrick just picked up his belongings and like a poor little beaten up school child just walked out.

I wasn't even gonna go to that ball game. I was scheduled to have dinner with William Armstrong, the President of the IU foundation. That was the only reason I went. I'm on the court afterwards and this place is bedlam. One, they've rallied to beat Ohio State, two, they're tournament bound, and three, it's Senior Day so Knight is going to address the crowd and talk about Mike Woodson and Butch Carter. I walk up and say something innocuous like "Hell of a job." He went, "Ah, never in doubt," and just kinda winked at me. This sounds kind of butch, but I was melted by it. That's the kind of man he is. There isn't a doubt in mind that he's gonna coach again. Northwestern lost a hell of an opportunity. If Kevin O'Neill would have resigned one week later, Bob Knight and Northwestern would have been a marriage made in heaven. In retrospect, he should have left IU about five or six years ago.

Probably 1998, Evan Eschmeyer is Northwestern's big cup of coffee. You're going into the game thinking Northwestern's gonna do something I think it's only done two previous times during the Knight era—actually beat

Bobby. Fifty of Bob Knight's career wins have come against Northwestern. Northwestern and Bob Knight have been like Stengel's Yankees to the St. Louis Browns. That was the night that Knight got mad at the crowd for chanting, "Who's your daddy?" Here again it's the Orrville, Ohio old-fashioned factor. Bob didn't realize that the phraseology, the lexicon, of "Who's your daddy?" has been part of the urban playground way of life for years. Bobby thought it was pure racism so he's jawing at O'Neill that it's bullshit and all that and they almost wind up duking it out. Afterwards my little boy Tyler, I took him back to meet Bobby. And even though Tyler's only eleven years old, Bob is talking the way Bob talks—fuck this, fuck that and the whole bit. My little boy just thinks the world of him; he just loves him. Here he is swearing in front of my kid, but you just tend to overlook it with Bob because that's just the way he is, and you're not gonna change him.

The reason a lot of people are Purdue fans? Because they can't afford Final Four tickets

Tom Swanson

Tom Swanson made his fortune in the new car business in Minot, North Dakota and has retired to doing volunteer work at Minot State University. He has hunted throughout the world with Bob Knight.

I met Bobby Knight, probably through a name you certainly will recognize, Sid Hartman in Minneapolis, a 25+ year friend of mine. I had a car dealership here in Minot and met Sid in a roundabout way, through my college roommate at St. Cloud State, a gentleman named Todd Roe who is a golf editor, and has been for over thirty years, for the Star Tribune in Minneapolis. I met Sid through him and you talk about an absolute character. He's 81 now and works every day of the year and doesn't understand people who don't, so that gives you a little perspective on his thought processes. But he just said, "Hey, Knight loves to hunt. (I'm a hunter and a fisherman.) Would you do me a favor and write him a letter?" So I did.

I knew who he was and knew he was one of Sid's favorites. I had heard Sid say that "Everybody he knows at all is a close personal friend." So I wrote

to Bob and stated that I was, like himself, a close personal friend of Sid, and he asked me to write you. I told him fishing and hunting were a passion, and, that I was born and raised in Minneapolis but now lived in the Dakotas and found that there were very few things as satisfying as time spent out away from civilization with dogs and guys who love dogs and love to hunt birds and shoot birds. Some people don't like the word "kill" but they love to shoot birds. He called the day or day after he received the letter.

Then we had some interesting things happen. I was a car dealer and my wife and I went to a Honda convention in Las Vegas, never thinking about Bob Knight or anything else. I walked into the morning meeting and there stood Bob Knight. He was one of four guests, along with John Havlicek, a friend of Bob's, and the Olympic star, Jackie Joyner-Kersee, and I'm not sure who the other one was. They were there to do some speaking and to work with the dealers who were there and have breakfast and sign autographs and take pictures and get on the road. So after we went through the formal part of the program, I went up and introduced myself. I'm sure, at that point in time, he looked at me as not only someone he had written to but as an opportunity to use me to get the hell out of there when he wanted to get out of there.

Knight had received my letter within the last month, so the minute I said who I was, he put his arm around me like we had known each other for years. There were a couple of hundred people in line waiting for pictures and autographs, and he did everyone of them. "I've got to be to the airport at a certain time," he announced to the people, and quickly got me back by his side to get him out of there. That's the first time I met him person-to-person. Since then it's been a long and mostly glorious ride. He's one of a kind.

He's around Minot here a lot so it isn't a matter of my friends believing if I know him. They see him and he's very visible. People in Montana and North Dakota really don't dwell a lot on those things. Even though he's definitely a celebrity here, the last thing anybody would think of doing here would be to come to our table if we were having dinner or if he's at my house or at any point in time. It's probably the thing he enjoys as much or more about the area we hunt in. He's certainly Bob Knight, the basketball coach, but basically he's just Bob Knight, the guy. He's left alone.

We hunt primarily in the western edge of North Dakota a lot, sometimes into Montana, but there's a town of 200 people, Alexander. They've got a little motel there called "The Ragged Butte" which he calls the "Ragged Butt." Bob's been there since 1992 at least forty or fifty nights. Never once at the motel or any restaurant in the town has anyone ever come up and ask him for

an autograph—ever. That's pretty amazing but an absolute fact—it just doesn't happen.

We primarily hunt pheasants, grouse and partridge.

As things changed, and we become friendlier and all, he's spending more time in North Dakota now and certainly still some time in Montana, and I usually meet him there for three or four days. He's been a fixture out here for most of the last eight years.

I don't think Bob was treated fairly on the famous ESPN interview after he was fired. He's always liked Dick Schaap because he's been honest with him, straightforward. I think Schaap played a great part in the fact that his son Jeremy did the interview. Bob got criticized heavily for the Phelps-Firestone ESPN interview in May—that it was a 'homer' deal, that these guys wouldn't get tough with him, would let him dominate the conversation.

If he wants to dominate, it's pretty difficult not to have it happen. So he did definitely take advantage of that situation back in the spring and the truth be known, he did definitely determine that those were the guys he wanted on that stage. So ESPN was not gonna let that happen again. So Dick Schaap played a role in getting Jeremy in. Schaap was highly offended by Knight's remark to the effect that "You're never gonna be what your Dad was." Then he came on and demanded an apology. It was not well done. I have a little bit of sympathy for Jeremy Schaap because he was sitting there doing what he was told to do by ESPN, and that was try to keep Knight on track, try to keep Knight within the boundary of the question. And he's gonna answer your question in doing it, but he's a master at that. That's one of his absolute great strengths is to captivate people and not gonna say 'not answer questions,' but certainly put everything in its best light. He's brilliant at that.

Jeremy is immature with little experience. And he was put there for those reasons. He was told, "Listen, young man, you want to make a name for yourself. Go in there and grind this out." And he did. That's why he was there. Certainly Bob was there of his own volition. He is who he is. Jeremy Schaap is not going to change that course of destiny in an hour interview. That was basically what Bob told him, "Young man, you've got a long way to go to be what your dad is." I know that Dick is kinda wishy-washy and doesn't have a lot of respect and friends, but Bob's one of them. I know that. I've been around Bob many times when he has taken calls from his office to Schaap and returned them, I mean now. And that is something that is not in his repertoire. He's not good at returning calls. He certainly isn't perfect.

I've heard him say, "I'm Bob, or I'm coach. I'm never Knight." I've heard that long before this kid on campus. And I can tell you first hand that Bob

Knight feels terrible about that kid and about what happened to that kid. But that kid was put there, the kid only did what his dad made him do. I firmly do think that. I talked to Bob over an hour, and he feels terrible about that aspect of the thing and he'd like it to go away and he genuinely loves kids. I've got a daughter and a son, and particularly my son has spent a lot of time with him. The guy loves kids. But he genuinely feels there should be a better way to go about that.

Bob Knight is the champion, I'm not gonna say of the underdog, but of the less than privileged and in fact he has a thing about that. The cast of characters who have endeared themselves to Bob in and around Bloomington, you would not believe. The list of names is long, and they are true characters from every walk of life.

One of my favorites is a gentlemen whose last name I won't use, but will refer to as Ducky. He has MS and lives about 30 miles north of Bloomington. He's a true outdoorsman; loves to be outdoors, but the MS is well along. He has real problems with his coordination, with walking, etc. On one of our trips, 1997 or '98, Ducky was invited up with Bob, accompanying Bob, to Williston, North Dakota, to hunt in western North Dakota, on a Lear jet, as his Christmas present. Ducky, when he got off the plane (Bob had told me privately, "Now Ducky's got MS, but you're gonna love the guy. Ducky's gonna fall down some. Whatever you do, just ignore him and don't make any attempts to get him back up on his feet. He's got a lot of pride and he'll get back up and it'll be fine. Now he is going to have a gun so don't necessarily be in front of him."—which is good advice for anybody—not just with Ducky!) We had quite a lot of snow that particular winter and Ducky was out there, and it was snowing and cold. The more miserable it gets, as far as Bob is concerned, the happier he is, because it presents a new challenge. It's just like a new ball game; it's a new challenge, "Where are the birds? How do you find them?" And the harder you have to work to get to them, the happier he is. So that's the situation. And Ducky is doing poorly and falling quite a lot. My guess at Ducky's age is mid to late forties. We hunted hard for two days, and the last time out of the car Ducky was there. You can see the respect in Ducky's eyes for Bob and their relationship. But believe me, you can see the respect in Bob's eyes for this guy and his intentions and desire to be there. So I think that maybe this guy with MS—with pretty severe limitations, maybe gives me more insight into Bob Knight than any of the situations I've seen around athletes, etc. It's just one dimension, but in terms of relationship with older people, people less than privileged, the guy has a special place for those kinds of people. The guys I've met with him, like the fellow who flew the Lear

jet is in one category and is a big IU supporter and a heck of a guy. But there are many, many more of the Ducky's and characters from southern Indiana, and people of Amish descent, etc., than there are of the bluebloods. Ducky deserves special mention; he's a special guy.

In a similar vein, we spent some time out in Montana, in a place called the "Hy-line," highway number two that runs up across the northern section of Montana. One of the first multiple-use power lines ran along it and that's where it got its name. One of the towns along there is called Chester. This is another, I think, human-interest story, and again shows a side of Bob Knight that is there and not very far below the surface. There's a Hutterite colony up just north of Chester along the Canadian border, but they are of German descent and there are different colonies around the country. On one occasion, Bob was introduced to some of the elders or leaders of the Hutterite village up there and made some acquaintances and was, in fact, invited to hunt on some of their farm land, and he struck up a particular relationship with a couple of younger Hutterites, Jake and Boomer. These guys became, once again, Bob Knight favorites. At first they didn't know who he was. They can't have papers or radios or TV's; they don't believe in anything worldly. They wear the black hats, black suits and work in a colonized situation—everybody there is on the farm, or on the property, in the colony. He befriended Jake and Boomer, and they became very good friends and this went on for a number of years. Always a highlight of the October hunting trip was a trip up to the Hutterite Colony to see Jake and Boomer. These guys have never been out of this small geographical area around Chester, Montana. Bob somehow, through unknown means, was getting them newspapers and clippings and Jake and Boomer were cheating a little bit on the rest of the elders and had captured a radio and found ways to get Indiana games or results of their games. Pretty soon, Jake and Boomer were big IU fans. Consequently at one of the Final Four's, I believe 1987, they are sitting courtside, next to the Indiana bench, in their Hutterite garb. This was completely at Bob's expense—flying out of Great Falls were Jake and Boomer. I don't know how these guys got out of there, but Bob is not one to take the fact that it can't be done very lightly—so my explanation, pure and simple, would be, "He found a way to get Jake and Boomer out of there." And there they were at the Final Four, Jake and Boomer, at courtside.

Due to their seclusion, they love the guy, but they probably don't know a lot about Bob, but whenever we went there, we were blessed with homemade sausage and bread and fresh garden vegetables and apples, and they were really delighted to see Bob.

Some years later, this is where the softness of the guy enters in. One of the two, Jake or Boomer, I think Jake, but one of the two got married and had a youngster. They were probably in their mid thirties by this time and their youngster, now remember they're not much into medical advice, had some problems and by this time they were conversing. Bob became aware of some of the problems the youngster was having. They were mostly related to stomach problems and they (primarily Karen and a friend) determined that part of the problem was in the stomach and could be cured by a form of milk. So they found a way to get some shipped into the town and got it to them, and sure enough it worked. This was in late summer, so that fall Karen went with Bob, driving enough supply of that special milk to get that child through the colicky stages and give them some sleeping time at night.

The important consideration is that he takes a lot of time to help people who have a problem. This is a very, very ordinary family obviously. Those are a couple of the things that make me take particular pride in a relationship with Bob Knight is that for every—And I should say at the beginning, I'm not a wild and crazy Indiana fan. I watched Bob Knight win a few games and I watched him win the '87 Championship with a lot of interest and I saw them in 1992 in Minneapolis and lose to Duke. But other than to know who he was I didn't know him. So our relationship has primarily involved anywhere from ten days to three weeks a year hunting and fishing and probably only two basketball games a year.

Don't get me wrong; I've been made into a tremendous Indiana fan. I don't know how I'll handle this. Since his departure, I don't know how that'll go. I'll have to see what my feelings are for the program—how they go.

Certainly, born and raised in Minnesota, the Gophers have always been more interesting to my heart until the time I did meet Coach Knight and his Hoosiers and have had the privilege of being around the team, as I said, a couple of times a year—usually one road game and one home game.

The things I know about Bob Knight are not the things that the basketball public knows. That's my angle on who he is, and that's how I got started with the hunting association. From there on, we've done this fall event and a couple of times, summer fishing occasions, yearly for eight years now.

I know that Bob recruited with appearance in mind—with the idea of the kids representing Indiana University. He recruited with the idea that those kids had to be part of the campus—that they had to be not only leaders on the basketball floor, but they had to be part of the leadership on campus. They had to attend classes; they had to graduate. When they left Indiana, or when they played at home, they had to look—old school thinking—the way

he wanted them to look. All you needed to do was ask him that, and he would quickly tell you, "God damn right they do. This is my basketball team."

One of the first trip into the Dakotas, Bob and a friend of his from Indiana and myself were in the western part of the state hunting on my rancher friend's land. Over the years he has become a good friend of Bob's and the people who come with him. It was in December so the pond was frozen, and I saw some pheasants fly into the cattails there and was sending Bob and his partner out, and the last thing I told Bob when he left the truck was, "Whatever you do don't get on that ice. It looks safe, but it isn't. There are springs in there so it isn't safe. Don't do it." But Bob thought a better way to surround those pheasants was to do so by going across the ice, and about two thirds of the way, down he goes. He isn't in any depth of the pond that puts him in any immediate danger of drowning, but it's twenty degrees or less outside and he's fortunate to keep his gun above the top of the ice and is able, by the time I get there, to have himself back up on the ice and creep along and get to shore. By the time he gets to shore, the temperature is such that his clothes are beginning to stiffen up pretty quickly. So we get him into the car and head back into town, only about a ten-minute drive. We get into town and keep lamenting about his bad luck. I'm a little bit reluctant at the time to tell him, "Bob I told you so." We get into the hotel, and he gets the manager of the hotel to fetch his wet frozen clothes and get them into the dryer. We get him warmed up and into some dry clothes, and we take off and go back to hunting.

The next morning, we're in the local cafe and the rancher, whose land this was on, has heard the story about Coach taking a dunk in his stock tank. So as we're leaving the restaurant after breakfast, he comes in carrying a life jacket. He presents it to Bob and says, "Coach, I know that there are a lot of people who feel that you can walk on water, but you proved them wrong yesterday. Under the circumstances, I brought this along for you to wear on your hunting trip today." Course he did it in great humor, and that was exactly the way it was accepted.

Jim Jacobson, that rancher from that area, and his family, are very gracious to allow us to hunt on his land because many of the ranchers don't allow that. The Jacobsons have driven to Minot, flown to Indianapolis, been greeted at the airport, and taken down to Bloomington as Bob's guests at a game and flown back home to North Dakota. Maybe the only cost they incurred would be a meal or two. Even then he has taken the time after ballgames or before ballgames to sit down with these people and have lunch or late-night dinner. Now, no doubt about it, these late-night dinners are better when he wins. The

time they were down there, Indiana did win. These people were just amazed at the attention paid, and this is not an Indiana athletic endeavor, this was Bob Knight doing this personally for these people, for no other reason than the fact that when he was in their country, that was the way they treated him. Also he had the capability to do something a little bit more special, at least in their eyes. In Montana and North Dakota, Bob Knight has an equal to, or higher, number of supporters and friends than he does in Indiana. When he's here, he is gracious. He addressed the Alexander, a little bitty town where we house out of, Lions Club in 1997, giving them their Christmas keynote address. Bob said to the 'Head Lion,' "Well, who was your speaker last year?" The guy did not bat an eye, just said, "Nobody." So Bob followed 'nobody' in and did a wonderful job. This gives insight not only in what Bob thinks about the world but how he reacts to people. And this was during a particularly tough farming situation and there were questions and answers.

One thing I want you to know, and if it's in print, all the better,—I don't pretend to be a close friend of Bob Knight, the basketball coach. I am a close friend and am very proud to say so good friend of Bob Knight the human being. I think that he is really quite a guy—a great deal of fun. Hunting is a big part of my life. I enjoy people who like to hunt. I can tell you this straight out. I don't spend a second day in the field with someone that I don't respect and enjoy because those days are precious and they are few and far between. I would welcome a day in the field with Bob Knight any time he is available.

Bob came in and as a story in the paper states, I did not write this story, he was taking a break from his coaching job. This was December 11, and he was serving a one-game suspension in early December for the kicking incident with his son, Patrick. He came on the spur of the moment. The story, as it is written, he's an avid outdoorsman; he got away from it all by making a trip to North Dakota with an older son Tim. He hooked up with a couple of acquaintances from Minot and set out for pheasant hunting. We went into a restaurant in Watford City, which is a town of 2,000 right out near the Montana border, and there was a group of Chamber of Commerce people in that restaurant. They are sitting there, looking across the room and there's four of us sitting there having supper (Bob Knight doesn't have dinner; Bob Knight has supper.) and he's sitting there and there's a number of people looking and thinking they recognize him so one of the men sends his wife over—a charming lady, wife of the local bank president. In towns out here, the bank president runs the town—they're the man. So she comes over to the table and says, "My husband and his friend sent me over to ask you if you are Bob Knight." Knight, without batting an eye, looks up and says, "No, I often get

confused for Knight, but actually I'm a scout for the Chicago Blackhawks. My name is Goalie Jones and I'm going through Watford City on my way back from Canada. That's what I'm doing here." This gal, Gretchen, a blonde mother, "Oooh, a hockey scout, my boys play hockey." She goes back to the table and tells the story, "No that's not Bob Knight, that's a hockey scout, Goalie Jones, a scout from the Blackhawks and really isn't Bob Knight." This is one of the very first times that Bob is with me out in this country. So as we finish supper, they're still there partying with their group. Bob comes over to me and says, "Tom, was what I did to those people, was that improper? Do you want me to go over and talk to them?" I said, "Well, Bob, that's your call, but I don't think there's anybody there who's going to be upset with you. It would be awfully nice if we would walk over, 'cause I do know a few of those people, and I could introduce you." He said, "Oh sure." So we walk over and one of the guys there was this writer for the newspaper. Bob said, "Well, I played myself off as Goalie Jones," and Bob gave them a little dissertation about the fact that he was there to do some hunting and enjoying the country, etc. and then as kind of a parting shot—this is beautiful—he says to Neil Shipman, "Neil, I do have one criticism. Why in the world would you guys send a woman over to do a man's job and find out about who I was or who I wasn't?" So that's the end of the story.

So when we left, Bob went over and paid the bill with his credit card. And these guys went over and looked at the credit card receipt and found out sure enough he was who he said he was—not that they really doubted him.

This is the story as this Shipman wrote it in their little Watford paper. He wrote a nice little story that gave no hard feelings whatsoever. So somehow, through the wire services or whatever, the editor of the Fargo paper picks it up and instead of saying they had some fun with Bob Knight in Watford City, writes an editorial and chastises Knight for belittling this woman and closes the editorial by saying, "I guess it doesn't matter whether Knight's in Indiana or in North Dakota, he's a jerk anyway." His spin on the deal was this is the way he belittled this woman from Watford City, North Dakota. Where does that kind of thing come from?

The media, for some reason when it pertains to Bob Knight, has an agenda with this guy, and this goes back seven or eight years. This is one of Bob's favorite stories. He got letters from State Senators out in that part of the country telling him how happy they were to have him there and that they saw nothing wrong with the exchange and they knew it was all done in fun, etc. But the one guy over in the eastern part of the state in the big city, he challenged the behavior.

Over an insignificant incident hunting, I saw the temper, and I didn't like it. I was asked by Bob Knight and the other individual to see if I could help get an understanding between the two of them so they could get on with what had been a long-time relationship. It was just a burst of anger, and it was over a very trivial situation, feelings were hurt, but again I saw Bob Knight get the thing put back together in a short period of time. The people who say that he's above looking for forgiveness are just wrong.

I don't think he wants to revisit those problems. I really think one of the things he's searching for is change. I think he's is not interested at all in revisiting those situation but rather having a different start. Everybody knows he's been the whipping boy of the media. What happened in Sports Illustrated in April and May prior to the zero tolerance announcement was the worst vendetta the media has ever launched against anyone to tear Knight apart. Every week, their writers took turns for six solid weeks, disparaging Knight and what he was and just ripping him apart. If that's journalism, and if that's fairness, it isn't the way I was taught to be fair.

Coaching rage isn't new—video cameras are

Frank Kush

If anyone knows what Bob Knight is going through, it has to be Frank Kush. The native Pennsylvanian was an undersized All-American football guard at Michigan State University and became a coaching legend at Arizona State. His teams were always ranked in the top twenty in the country and he built the program so high that Arizona State was invited to join the PAC-8 Conference in 1978. In the middle of the 1979 season, Kush was fired after allegations that he grabbed a player by the helmet and jerked his head. His firing and the subsequent uproar have caused so much damage to the ASU program that it has not completely recovered to this day. In retrospect, in his heyday, Frank Kush would be regarded as the Bobby Knight of the college gridiron, in terms of his competitive spirit and his hatred of losing. Twenty years after the ruckus Kush is back working in the ASU Athletic Department and the playing field at Sun Devil Stadium has been named Frank Kush Field.

I do not know Coach Knight that well. It would almost be unfair for me to talk about him, on one side of the coin or whatever. You feel sorry for those people when things happen. And the unfortunate thing about it is

that's our society. That's why I would refrain from making any comment about him because as I said, I don't know the guy, never watched him practice so it would be difficult for me to analyze him.

When I say our society has changed so dramatically, it's because of the revenue factor. I think that's one of the factors, you know awards are given to just about anybody at anytime—so what are they worth? It starts at a lower level, and I think the unfortunate thing about it is do the people really earn it in terms of this generation, or the previous generation, or the next generation? I look at it from my generation. If you got an award, it was really meaningful. When you get a little older, everybody's getting awards. Usually, in my case, it was a pair of ribbons. Some people don't get old, that's why I'm glad I continue to get old. "It means I'm still alive and kicking around."

I just feel sorry for Bob Knight. I know he's a dedicated individual. He was so concerned about the athletes and their success, socially, academically, and athletically. Coaches like that are so meaningful to programs. Then you look at it, some people are saying well it's such a minor segment in our society, athletics, which in a way it is. But by the same token, that the trouble with our society is failure of people to take care of their own responsibilities—whether it's their children or whatever it may be and that's why I feel just from what I've read, the guy, in my opinion, was great for young people.

Into the Valley of Pranks I rode

Eddie White

Eddie White is the Vice President of Logo Athletic—formerly Logo 7 in Indianapolis. The Wilkes Barre, Pennsylvania native graduated from Wilkes College and earned his masters at the University of Notre Dame. Upon graduation, he went to work in the Notre Dame athletic department.

Eddie White

It was my first year at Notre Dame as Assistant Director of Sports Information. It would have been the 1982–83 basketball season, my first year on the job. That first basketball season, we had 'seven days of hell,' as we called it. It was three games, all at home within seven days, Kentucky, UCLA, and Indiana. The Indiana game came—remember the year before I was just a Sports Information Director at 'little" Wilkes college in Wilkes Barre, Pennsylvania and now I'm at Notre Dame: Notre Dame basketball, Digger Phelps, the 'Fighting Irish,' sold out arena, national television—the whole nine yards.

My post game responsibility was to go to the visitors' locker room, take the visiting coach to our football auditorium for the post game press conference. This was a bit of a change from what they used to do in the past but that was the main reason for me escorting the coach so he doesn't go the wrong way.

So Indiana wins. I go to the locker room, knock on the door, and the student manager opens the door. I say, "I'm Eddie White, Notre Dame Sports Information. I'm here to get Coach Knight and take him to the press conference." Again, Indiana won, which is the key deal here.

The student Manager says, "I'll be right back." He shuts the door. About two minutes later, the door opens. Now, I'm short, 5/9", there's this gigantic figure in the doorway. He says, "What the #$&*# do you want?" I say, I'm Eddie White. . . . He says, "I don't give a #$&*#." I go, "but, but, but. . . ." He's goes, "Come on, let's go." And he is just giving me crap all the way to the football auditorium. Walk into the auditorium, I'm shaking. I thought, "Oh my God, I've pissed off Bobby Knight, the legendary coach the first time I've ever met the guy." I'm getting killed here by him.

He walks into the auditorium and, of course, the media are there waiting for him. But also there waiting was Roger Valdiserri, the Notre Dame Sports Information Director—Roger winked at him and Knight winked back at Roger. Roger had set it up with Knight to give me a hard time. "Here's the rookie; let's shake him up a bit." I was like—Holy Cow! He was putting me on the whole way. After he winked at Roger, and Roger winked at him, he looked over at me and winked. I'm like "Oh, wow." Kind of like that one wink from him was worth all that nervous energy he had put me through.

Another time the local NBC affiliate, WNDU, had sent its reporter Jack Nolan down to Bloomington to do a pre-season piece on the Hoosiers. He's getting ready to tape the interview with Knight. Of course, they look at the cameraman—"Are you ready?" OK. "Coach, what do you think of the Hoosiers this year? What do you anticipate in the season?" Knight says, "Well, Jack, before I address that question and tell you about the Hoosiers, I just would appreciate it if you could do a favor for me and deliver a message back to a real good friend of mine back in South Bend, at Notre Dame, Roger Valdiserri." He looks into the camera, and says, "Roger F— you." It was all done in jest. It just took Nolan by surprise, but then they sent it to Roger as a joke and he got it and loved it and showed everybody. It was funny but you should have seen the expression on Jack Nolan's face—like where the heck is he going with this?" That's Knight. He has that side of him.

We've heard the stories here about him just driving for hours to give somebody who's sick an autographed basketball and didn't want anyone to know about it. Digger used to do that all the time. We wanted to try to do something to help him with his reputation. But Digger said, "If you tell anybody that I'm spending three hours refereeing basketball games for special education kids, I'll kill you. I don't do it for people to know." It's admirable. There are a lot of stories like that around here about Knight and the good things he has done for people that he doesn't want people to know. Some people would think, "Well, the only reason you're doing this is to get good publicity."

Digger was also polished—always the carnation, say the right things, political aspirations to be president, and here's Knight who was probably everything but polished but trying to be political, but in a way they were very, very similar.

Let's win one for the Gipper; on second thought, let's just win one

Rev. Edmund P. Joyce, C.S.C.

Executive Vice President Emeritus, University of Notre Dame.

Father Joyce retired in 1987 after thirty-five years as Chairman of the Faculty Board in Control of Athletics and the University Building Committee.

Father Joyce was born in Honduras, raised in South Carolina, and graduated from ND in 1937. Ned, as he prefers to be called, was the first Notre Dame student from South Carolina. He was an accountant in Spartanburg until he became a priest twelve years after his graduation. For many years, Father Joyce was an influential voice in the national NCAA, particularly in matters dealing with educational integrity of intercollegiate athletic programs. Because Father Joyce's close friend, retired Notre Dame President Theodore Hesburgh has traveled so extensively, Father Joyce has logged more hours under the Golden Dome than any other person in history.

Father Joyce, for whom Notre Dame's Joyce Athletic and Convocation Center is named, was the sports honcho at Notre Dame for many decades. On Tuesday, December 13, 1977, the undefeated and then number two-ranked Irish were scheduled to fly a charter plane to Bloomington to play the Hoosiers the following night. Because of harsher than usual winter weather conditions, Father Joyce cancelled the flight and had Digger Phelps bus his team to Assembly Hall. The University of Evansville had doubled booked the plane later that evening to fly to Cookeville, Tennessee. The weather in Evansville was as bad as South Bend's. Shortly after take-off, the plane crashed, killing all 29 passengers. No one cared when IU won 67–66.

Courtesy of University of Notre Dame

Rev. Edmund P. Joyce, C.S.C.

Near the end of the 1970–71 season, word had spread that Notre Dame Head Basketball Coach, Johnny Dee, was retiring. Army's Bobby Knight wanted the Notre Dame job.

My memory gets worse as I get older, and I'm pretty old right now. I do remember Bobby Knight calling me in 1971 expressing his interest in becoming the Notre Dame coach. I think he was still at Army at the

time. But we had already decided on Digger Phelps. When Knight contacted me, I didn't know who he was, certainly didn't know he was going to become a great coach. I'd had no contact with him prior to that. I have met him since and he always has seemed interested in Notre Dame—our program. I've been to several banquets when he's been there. In fact, Father Hesburgh and I received an award from what they call "Youth Links" in Indianapolis. That's a big deal; we got $35,000, which I gave to charity but Bobby Knight was the one who presented the award. He's always been complimentary about Notre Dame. But at the time I don't think I knew anything but that he was the coach at Army. It was a little bit unusual to get letters so I would remember it. Of course, as he became so successful I did remember it from time to time. He is the most astute guy in the world and always has been when I've been with him—always very cordial and interested in Notre Dame and athletes. And I think he stands for good things in athletics. I don't know how he gets himself in the scrapes he gets into with his players.

Digger had contacted us earlier than Knight, and I didn't have much to do with his hiring except to approve it. I didn't have any interviews with Digger or anything else but on the face of it he looked like a wonderful thing. He was very eager to come to Notre Dame and, of course, he had been successful at Fordham and had beaten us that year when he shouldn't have and that caught my attention. So I saw no reason not to go along with it. In his first four or five years, he looked like he was going to be a winner here and then he declined. If we had hired Bobby Knight, he probably would not have been able to get away with that language or with any of the other antics. Either we would have converted him or I don't think he would have lasted. But I think maybe in this atmosphere, he might have restrained himself more, too. He may have been very good for us. He's obviously a wonderful coach, and is certainly interested in his players which we always want a coach to be, and is interested in their education. He has a lot of qualities that would have been perfect at Notre Dame if he could control his temper better than he did at Indiana. Until now, I never discussed that we might have hired him; I was afraid I would be crucified by our alumni if it came out in public.

My personal relationship with Mr. Knight has always been warm and nice.

Father Hesburgh is the most decorated civilian in American history, eclipsing Bob Hope.

It's easier to get a lawyer into the kingdom of heaven than catch a #^@*$# fish in Russia. . . . but fishin' is a great way to hide a drinking problem

Mike Gallagher

Michael Gallagher left southern California in the early '60s to play baseball at Arizona State for Bobby Winkles. A few years later he became the youngest scout in the history of the New York Mets while going to law school. Today Gallagher heads up the firm of Gallagher and Kennedy in Phoenix, one of the biggest law firms on the west coast. An avid Arizona State fan, Gallagher has served on the boards of many Phoenix area businesses and charities and sports teams. Gallagher was not above getting in some good-natured pokes at his good friends, Dick and Tom Van Arsdale, who were also present.

Mike Gallagher

I really had a good time meeting him. We spent twelve days together fishing in Russia. I had never met Knight. My first thought about "I'm gonna go meet Bobby Knight," was, from everything I'd ever read about him, "This guy probably ought to stop drinking." Then I find out all he drinks is Tang. That's how much I knew about him going in.

Even though Tom and Dick didn't play for him, I'd never seen such respect for a guy. In fact, it got silly. I'd want to go sneak off and have a cigar and it would be eight hundred degrees below zero in the god damn tundra and we're standing behind some little fuckin' shack sneaking a cigar because nobody wants Knight to see anybody smoking. That was a tip off.

Then I made one mistake. I didn't realize what a baseball nut Knight was. We got to talking about it, and I later found out how it was with his friend, Roger Maris, how he thought he ought to be in the Hall of Fame and how screwed up that was. I don't think much about it; I don't have much of an opinion one way or the other, but I say something like "Well, I don't know,

does one good season put a guy in the Hall of Fame?" Oh fuck! I mean, it's kinda like—"I thought you were . . . you're just another dumb fuckin' lawyer," and he starts spouting off about Maris. I mean I got nothing to fight him with. He's got every statistic on Maris, and he's building this case about how Maris ought to be in the Hall of Fame; I mean, Christ, he should have been the first guy inducted. I couldn't defend myself. He just brutalized me with facts. It's like it was a religion to him. By the end of this conversation, I'm just going "yeah." I mean, I don't understand what he's talking about—Hall of Fame shit. He knew about my baseball background, and that's why we were talking about it. But my conversation about Maris and whether he deserved to be in the Hall of Fame immediately convinced him that though I might have played a little bit, I was obviously a fuckin' idiot. Oh god, he had every statistic. He could tell you what Maris hit in high school, I think. It was incredible. He was loaded for bear. He had had that conversation someplace before.

My impression of him was very favorable. I was real pleased to spend time with him. He made you feel comfortable. Whether or not it was—we were traipsing through the Hermitage Museum where Van Arsdale and I had to stand in the middle of a room with eight thousand Rubens and do a real quick 360 and say let's move to the next room. Knight actually knew what he was doing. He knows art. That's all I can say.

One time after the fishing trip, I wrote him a letter. The press was all over him so I just dropped him a note. I just said something like. "Dear Bob, Fuck 'em; let's go fishing." Or something like that. I don't hear from him for a couple of months. I thought maybe he and I didn't bond quite as well as I thought we had. Maybe he has no idea who I am or what I'm talking about. Finally a couple of months later, I get a letter back from him. "Sorry it took so long to get back to you. As you know, I've been kinda busy. Thank you for your insightful, well-written note." Something like that. "Rarely do I receive messages that are as well written."

I had read the book the guy wrote that ripped him, *Season on the Brink*. I didn't think it ripped him that bad, but I guess he thought it did. He's the kind of guy that I think if you could play, I would like to have played for him. He's old school. We had Frank Kush out here at Arizona State. I grew up with

Roger Maris was Roger Maras until 1955. He didn't like for fans to call him "Mar-ass." Maris still holds the national high school record for most kickoff returns for a touchdown in one game with five.

coaches yelling at guys and all that kind of stuff. I was never offended by anything. And I thought he was a winner. Knight was the kind of guy if I'd had a kid, I'd be happy to have my kid play for him, assuming my kid was the type who would give one hundred percent and could stand the heat.

Knight and his buddies had this trip planned, and kind of at the eleventh hour, they had a spot open up someplace so Tom or Dick Van Arsdale called me and said, "You want to go to Russia with Bobby Knight?" They were actually just looking to fill a hole I think, and Tom or Dick had told them they had a friend who might be able to go. In fact, I had a check in my desk to go on a caribou hunt in Alaska and was just getting ready to send that check off to the guide there when they called. I couldn't do both so I said, "Well the caribou will probably wait." And I bought a ticket to Russia.

So Van Arsdale told you I pissed on a cat, did he? It was really self-defense. I didn't realize it was a cat. I thought it was some kind of wild tiger of the tundra. I had forgotten about that and that sucker Van Arsdale reminded you about it. I don't even remember why I did it. Knight didn't see that because we were hiding out behind the goddamn cabin so we could smoke our cigar without him seeing us. I got the impression that he had an aversion to smoking; the Van Arsdales acted like twelve year olds if you want to know the truth. The only time they would sneak an extra drink is if Knight wasn't in the room; they'd have to go outside and hide to smoke a cigar. I was very impressed by Knight, and I thought the two Van Arsdales were absolutely candy-assed pussies.

It was incredible. First of all the Russian guys wouldn't talk to us for three or four days because they thought we were just a bunch of asshole Americans. Finally after three or four days, they might have still thought we were asshole Americans, but they decided we were okay. They started talking and all. It was a typical deal that I guess you get on all fishing trips: "Why weren't you here last week?" The fact of the matter is, we're out there on this river for eight days, twelve hours a day, serious stuff. It was a big river, couple of hundred yards wide; I think it was called the Karluftka.

Knight caught four fish on the trip, I caught one, one of the Van Arsdales caught one and one of them caught none. Now I'm talking about twelve hours a day, for eight days. You gotta understand this isn't like catching trout in Montana where you expect to catch a fish every other cast or so. A good day would have four or five fish, okay? I didn't know that before going over there. That would have been a terrific day; everyone would have been happy. You'd say you were a world-class salmon fisherman, or fly fisherman. One fish in eight days doesn't make it by any standard. Four or five for the week

doesn't get it. I tell you one thing I never heard of: competitive fishing. Knight's the first guy on the river and the last one off every day. And he knows how many fish everybody has caught. He's keeping score, and he'd been over there a year or so before with Ted Williams and he could tell you how many fish Williams caught on any given day and how many he caught on any given day, and he had more than Williams.

Who knows if we really got there a week late for the best fishing, but that was the story. I'm told that historically, when you've had bad fishing, the fishing guides will tell you "you should have been here last week" or "you ought to be here next week."

I think I can remember who went on the trip: a buddy of his from North or South Dakota, a Cadillac dealer, that he bird hunts with, Tom Swanson. The team doctor, Rink. A buddy of his from Smuckers country there where he grew up in Orrville, Ohio, an old-time school buddy of his. A dentist from Bozeman whose name I think was Steve Smith, but I'm not sure. He's a guy that Knight has gone trout fishing with up in Montana. Both his boys, Pat and Tim Knight, were there. It was fun, a great goddamn trip. I'd love to go fishing with them again sometime, not necessarily to Russia. But I had a great time. I just enjoyed being with him; I was the only guy Knight didn't know. These other guys were more than passing acquaintances—they were more like long-term friends. By the time you're there half a week, and you spent pretty good money getting there, and the fishing's like horse shit, everybody got on the rag a little bit—just about the fishing. It wasn't like everybody came in from a great day of fishing and everybody had a couple of shooters and everybody gets on one another. It was more like "Well that was a long fuckin' twelve hours, and we've got do that again tomorrow." But no, nobody really gave Knight too much shit, and if I'd known the Roger Maris story, I wouldn't have given him any shit.

As far as that choking incident in practice, I can draw an analogy from that. I don't see that grabbing a kid by the facemask or grabbing a kid physically and shaking him—I don't see any of that as the end of the world.

The Last Chapter

The last chapter has yet to be written!

It would have been written Saturday but the author watched football.

—The Middle—

CAPTIONS

Page 161. A salmon fishing expedition to Russia. (Back row left to right) Dick Van Arsdale, Pat Knight, Steve Smith, Tim Knight, Tom Swanson; (middle row) Mike Gallagher, Bob Knight, Larry Rink, Tom Van Arsdale; (in front) Dick Rhoads.

Page 162. Larry Hawkins displays his Bob Knight and IU memorabilia at his quaint Nashville, Indiana, restaurant.

Page 163. Mark McGwire, Bob Knight and Jim Edmonds exchanging power hitting tips at Bush Stadium, St. Louis.

Page 164. The Hoosiers huddle up.

Page 165. Bob Knight with his "all-time favorite Indiana player," his son Patrick on Senior Day in 1995. Knight started Senior Day in 1973.

Page 166. Bob Knight and Steve Alford of Iowa give last-second instructions to their teams before tip-off at Assembly Hall.

Page 167. Old friends Bob Knight and Rick Pitino of Kentucky exchange greetings before another IU–UK classic.

Page 168 & 169. The Generals office. The General is AWOL.

CAPTIONS

Page 113. Coach Knight with the spoils of victory.

Page 114. The mentor, Bob Knight, and the student, Steve Alford.

Page 115. In response to a reporter's question about Indiana "putting on their game faces," Knight said he didn't know what that phrase meant. He then proceeded to demonstrate what he thought it meant—prior to a 1992 NCAA tournament game.

Page 116. Coach Knight caught flak from Purdue students after he accidentally shot a hunting friend.

Page 117. Calbert Cheaney strikes back after Coach Knight's famous bull-whip episode.

Page 118. The last hurrah . . . Bob Knight's final seconds as the head basketball coach of Indiana University . . . A loss to Pepperdine in Buffalo, N.Y. on St. Patrick's Day 2000.

Page 119. Coach Bob Knight and wife Karen during farewell to IU students.

© Brian Spurlock

© Scott Rovak

Courtesy of Larry Hawkins

© Brian Spurlock

© Brian Spurlock

© Rich Clarkson

© Brian Spurlock

The BUCK STOPS here
NCAA
1987 FINAL FOUR
INDIANA
STATE
POLICE
HOGAN
HOGAN
ALL STAR